Cinematic Journeys

Cinematic Journeys

To Lindsay, Ruby and Emil

Cinematic Journeys

Film and Movement

Dimitris Eleftheriotis

Edinburgh University Press

© Dimitris Eleftheriotis, 2010, 2012

Edinburgh University Press Ltd
22 George Square, Edinburgh EH8 9LF

First published in hardback by Edinburgh University Press 2010

www.euppublishing.com

Typeset in Monotype Ehrhardt
by Servis Filmsetting Ltd, Stockport, Cheshire, and
printed and bound in Great Britain by
Printondemand-worldwide.com

A CIP record for this book is available from the British Library

ISBN 978 0 7486 3312 8 (hardback)
ISBN 978 0 7486 4938 9 (paperback)

The right of Dimitris Eleftheriotis
to be identified as author of this work
has been asserted in accordance with
the Copyright, Designs and Patents Act 1988.

This book is supported by

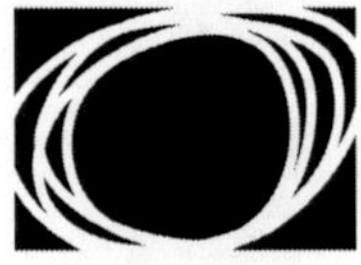

Arts & Humanities
Research Council

Contents

Acknowledgements

Many people have contributed to the completion of this project. I wish to thank all my colleagues at the University of Glasgow for their help and support throughout the project: Davie Archibald, Karen Boyle, John Caughie, Ian Craven, Ian Garwood, Christine Geraghty, Ian Goode, Karen Lury. Tim Bergfelder, Dina Iordanova and Julianne Pidduck for supporting the project in its early stages. Special thanks for suggestions and discussions to Melis Behlil, Maria Chalkou, Ahmet Gürata, David Martin-Jones, Gary Needham, Murray Pratt, Çetin Sarikartal, Philip Schlesinger, Yannis Tzioumakis. Many thanks to Lindsay Pratt for all the help that made this book possible. Many thanks to Sarah Edwards and Esmé Watson for their encouragement; Máiréad McElligott for helping with the cover design; special thanks to Peter Andrews for the meticulous copy-editing.

An early version of Chapter 7 appeared in *South Asian Popular Culture*, 4.2 (2006).

The project was supported by the AHRC.

Introduction

Cinematic Journeys was borne out of mundane everyday observations. A couple of years ago my daughter got a DVD camera as a Christmas present. Months later I discover on the computer's hard drive a series of mini-movies. One of them is a long shaky moving shot obviously taken from the back window of our car. I recognise the journey as one of our holiday trips. I become fascinated by the continuous tracking shot of the cloudy and moody (it was a Scottish holiday . . .) landscape, it reminds me of the journey yet it is different, familiar but also alien. There is sound in the movie, a CD must have been playing in the car. It can be mistaken for a sequence from a road movie but it doesn't feel like it; the music and the movement are amateurish versions of generic clichés but there is no story to give it shape, no detached pleasure in the views, just a nostalgic rekindling of memories. We visit friends and they show us their holiday video. Shots of villages, towns, beaches, sunsets, the view from their veranda, the sea . . . I get so bored that I begin to notice a pattern, a stylistic consistency. They are all long panning shots that eventually zoom into a feature in the landscape; or the exact opposite: zooming out from a detail a panning shot unfolds.

There is a thematic similarity in these two instances of travel films, the same fascination with a type of movement that provides a continuous exploration and revelation of space. Paradoxically, the same frame mobility surfaces in 'proper' travel films: tracking, panning and zooming, views on the road and of the landscape, constitute the trade stock of the genre. *Cinematic Journeys* sets out to understand and investigate the reasons that this particular set of movements of the frame becomes such an attractive and pervasive aesthetic in cinema in general and in travel films in particular. What is the genealogy of these incremental, gradual and linear explorations of space that have such a strong hold on the creative imagination of amateur and professional film-makers?

But as the boredom (for anybody else other than the family or the holidaymakers) of watching holiday videos or family movies suggests, the aesthetic attraction of such movements is not in itself enough. An overarching trajectory, provided by a narrative structure, is needed to organise the views into entertaining experiences for the general public. Thus, these types of movement become meaningful and pleasurable within the broader frame of travelling narratives. How do the pleasures of frame mobility and those of the narrative interact? How do different cinematic journeys construct distinctive affective relationships with their spectators?

As both personal examples demonstrate there is an essential displacement involved in these movies: these are other people's journeys that we watch, journeys brought home from a distant place or time. There is another form of travelling involved here that points towards the mobility of film itself, not simply in the difference between a recording and a projecting apparatus but also in the movement from one context to another. A final anecdote, from a later stage of the *Cinematic Journeys* project, gives to this point a critical dimension. In an undergraduate seminar students are invited to comment on the possibility of approaching Samira Makhmalbaf's *Blackboards* as a 'road movie'. There is deafening silence and nobody really sees the film like that at all. The discussion disintegrates into comments about the 'suffering of these poor people' or the 'universal humanist values' demonstrated even in such harsh conditions of existence. The 'road movie' with its very specific set of pleasures is not seen as an appropriate generic framework for a film that is about continuous movement on roads and on paths. How culturally specific are the pleasures of cinematic mobility? What are the effects of the crossing of cultural borders of films? What are the changes in the films themselves and what can they offer to their 'foreign' spectators?

These are some of the questions that *Cinematic Journeys* attempts to answer. The book is organised around three areas of enquiry. Part I ('Mobile Vision') situates the genealogy of movements of exploration, discovery and revelation in the articulations of subjectivity, vision and movement of nineteenth-century technologies of vision. It suggests that certain types of mobile vision prefigure the cinematic use of frame mobility and identifies two particular types of (virtual or actual) movement as particularly significant: a steady, smooth and continuous motion with linear direction and a circular movement around specific objects of interest. They are both heavily informed by specifically modern and Western epistemological, philosophical and aesthetic discourses and emotive registers. The place of movement in film theory is also investigated in order to demonstrate and deconstruct the hegemonic role that narrative plays in that discourse. Part I concludes with the proposal of two particular axes (activity↔passivity and certainty↔uncertainty) as analytical tools in the examination of the affective dimensions of movements of exploration, discovery and revelation.

Part II ('Cinematic Journeys') considers specific kinds of contemporary or recent non-American 'road movies'. It focuses on films with a historical and geographical referential setting defined by the prefix post-: postmodern, postcolonial, postcommunist. The three chapters are organised around three different ways in which the 'post' can be conceptualised. 'Quests' considers films that unfold in chronotopes situated in a 'post' era and traverse spaces that are either geo-politically reconfigured or under reconfiguration (South America, Russia). 'Intercepted trajectories' focuses on films that articulate the 'post' as a historical relationship, as a tension between colonialism and its legacy and the present. In 'Beyond the axes' the 'post' is approached as a historical, geopolitical and cultural terminus that points towards the necessity to consider and analyse films from beyond the culturally and historically specific boundaries of our analytical axes. The argument is presented through detailed analysis of a small number of shots or scenes from a limited number of films. The intention is to propose specific (and by no means exhaustive) textual articulations of frame mobility in different types of road movies and not to broadly define, describe or categorise a field.

Part III ('Travelling Films') considers the mobility of films as cultural products involved in processes of international circulation. With reference to the popularity of Indian films in Greece in the 1950s and 1960s I consider the process of textual and cultural transformation through translation and appropriation of the films themselves and the (often xenophobic) violence involved in the critical enunciation of national cinemas and identities disturbed by the importation of foreign films. In the final chapter I propose that subtitles, as a marker of difference, as material evidence that a film has travelled, can offer an insightful and optimistic way of conceptualising the 'foreign spectator' as a speculative theoretical category.

On the most obvious level the connecting thread of the three parts is the relationship between film and movement. There is, however, another theme that runs across the book which revolves around the enduring nature of nineteenth-century values regarding mobile vision. A fantasy of completeness (in knowledge, perception, experience, understanding, evaluation) permeates otherwise antagonistic cinematic practices and critical discourses: essentialist approaches to national cinema and identity converge with 'difference-sensitive' cross-cultural criticism; structuralist and poststructuralist film theory happily meets cognitivism; Godard's self-reflexive films show revealing similarities with romantic quests for self-transformation. *Cinematic Journeys* aspires to identify and criticise these fantasies and to put forward an argument that turns incomplete and imperfect but passionate and self-aware analysis into a limited but valuable understanding of the specificities of film and movement.

PART I

Mobile Vision

CHAPTER 1

Movement, vision and subjectivity in the nineteenth century

Based on the extensive and ever expanding scholarship on nineteenth century Western cultural practices and discourses, this chapter will investigate specific articulations of movement, vision and subjectivity. I shall first consider how a linear, incremental and forward movement becomes a metaphor within scientific discourses and political practices of the period before examining specific 'technologies of vision' (as evidenced in the railway journey, in the experience of the museum, in *flânerie* or in the Parisian arcades, for example) and the types of mobile vision that they enable.

Evaluations of such experiences will also be scrutinised and some of the prominent binaries (such as activity/passivity, order/disorder, certainty/ uncertainty) that inform critical approaches will be identified and analysed. The objective of this opening chapter is to investigate the genealogical ground of articulations of movement, vision and subjectivity in order to examine their reconfiguration in cinema from the late nineteenth century onwards.

The present work appears within a well-established, highly productive and rigorous line of enquiry in film studies, but one that in its approach often tends to overlook questions of movement of/in the frame. Such limitations will be briefly considered in the concluding section of the chapter and will be revisited at several points in subsequent chapters.

I.I EPISTEMIC OBJECTS IN FLUX AND MOBILE OBSERVERS

In *The Order of Things* Foucault presents a ground-breaking account of the epistemological, empirical and philosophical transformations that have come to define the very essence of Western modernity.[1] The profound shifts in the understanding of ourselves and the world occur in two successive phases, with 'outer limits the years 1775 and 1825',[2] and are exemplified by the specific ways in which the great empirical sciences of the classical era, that is natural history, general grammar and the analysis of wealth, mutate into the modern disciplines of biology, philology and political economy, respectively. The new sciences reorganise the field of knowledge around three uniquely modern empirical entities that become the epicentre of scientific enquiry: life, labour, language. The study of these three empiricities, to use Foucault's term, not only dominates the epistemological field of modernity but also provides the discursive ground on which modern subjectivity is constituted and analysed.

Importantly for the concerns of this book, what distinguishes biology, philology and political economy from their classical counterparts is the emphasis that they all place on process, change, transformation, evolution, adaptation and development in the specific and distinct ways that they each conceptualise their objects of study. In their discourses life, language and labour are understood as being in constant and perpetual flux, as mobile empiricities undergoing continuous transformation—the study of such transformations constitutes the epistemological modus operandi of modernity.

As the all-pervasive stasis of taxonomy and the obsession with classification tables are abandoned for the study of the perpetual movement of transformation, historicity emerges as the defining quality of all things, living beings and modes of thought and existence. Such historicity, Foucault points out, is peculiar to modern episteme and clearly distinct from previous forms such as mythology, collective memory or theological speculation about the past and the future. What is distinctive about such conceptualisation is that it designates specific histories allocated to distinct objects of study:

> It was discovered that there existed a historicity proper to nature; forms of adaptation to the environment were defined for each broad type of living being, which would make possible a subsequent definition of its evolutionary outline; moreover, it became possible to show that activities as peculiarly human as labour or language contained within themselves a historicity that could not be placed within the great narrative common to things and to men . . . [3]

While in the nineteenth century philosophical activity operated 'in the gap between history and History'[4] (exploring the relationship between individuals and totalities, the everyday and the universal) and was obsessed with the possibilities and limitations of thought and perception, the great scientists of the time pursued knowledge around the world, travelling in space but also in time in their effort to unravel the hidden histories of modern empiricities. The nineteenth was a century in which machines of mobility (bicycles, motorcycles, trains and automobiles) fascinated inventors but also when scientific thought became fundamentally mobile. Expeditions became crucial epistemo-logical tools as scientists travelled to all corners of the world collecting data and formulating historical hypotheses to account for change and transformation.

The clearest example of mobile science pursuing an object in flux is the formulation of evolutionary theory, with a number of scientists (von Humbolt, Brown, Dana, Gray, Hooker, Spruce, Wallace and many others) undertaking lengthy and adventurous journeys of exploration. In his 'scientific travelogue', *The Voyage of the Beagle*, on 8 October 1835 and from the Galapagos Archipelago, Darwin crystallises the overdetermination of mobility in nineteenth-century science:

> Seeing every height crowned with its crater, and the boundaries of most of the lava–streams still distinct, we are led to believe that within a period geologically recent the unbroken ocean was here spread out. Hence, both in space and time, we seem to be brought somewhat near to the great fact – the mystery of mysteries – the first appearance of new beings on this earth.[5]

Here the journey of the evolutionist, a mobile observer par excellence, leads to the cartography of a virtual historical journey to our remotest past and a somewhat programmatic identification of destination for an ever increasing scientific knowledge as it gets closer to the ultimate revelation, 'the mystery of mysteries'. In the conclusion to his journal ('Retrospect'), Darwin declares his alignment with the 'civilizing' imperialist projects of the time[6] and urges fellow scientists to travel: 'In conclusion it appears to me that nothing can be more improving to a young naturalist than a journey in distant countries.'[7]

What is also evident in Darwin's work, and in modern episteme in general, is the double role afforded to human beings in the scientific field. They are at one and the same time observers of the world, gatherers of facts and producers of knowledge, but also objects of the very same process, simultaneously collectors and sources of data. As Foucault famously proposed, in the discourse of modern episteme 'Man [*sic*] appears . . . as an object of knowledge and as a subject that knows.'[8]

This peculiarly modern double positioning of human beings as subject/object of knowledge becomes the point of departure in Jonathan Crary's study of vision in the nineteenth century.[9] In his *Techniques of the Observer* Crary explores the specific ways in which the shifts that Foucault identified in relation to modern science are accompanied by changes in the role and function of vision in the nineteenth century. As he suggests:

> The break with classical models of vision in the early nineteenth century was far more than simply a shift in the appearance of images and art

works, or in systems of representational conventions. Instead it was inseparable from a massive reorganization of knowledge and social practices that modified in myriad ways the productive, cognitive, and desiring capacities of the human subject.[10]

Coming from a history of art perspective, Crary's intervention is particularly significant in its contention that art and science, representation and discourse, operate within a continuum rather than from mutually exclusive and combative positions. The term 'observer' in the title of his book is carefully chosen as a description of the subject, the bearer of modern vision, because of its ability to overcome the passivity attributed to 'spectator', but also as a term that describes equally aptly the artist, the scientist and the general public of the nineteenth century. In opposition to historical orthodoxy, Crary also proposes that impressionism (commonly situated as modernism's moment of origin) represents no 'rupture' in the field of vision but shares the same genealogy with empiricist and positivist practices.

In his refusal to recognise a great oppositional role in modernism, Crary echoes Foucault's iconoclastic assertion that Marxism is a part rather than a negation of modernity and modernisation.[11] The rejection of oppositional visions (in the literal and metaphorical sense) will be further discussed in later sections of this chapter and will be re-examined at various points in this book. It is simply noted here in order to emphasise the continuities between a number of diverse practices and ideas that emerge in the nineteenth century.

More importantly for the present argument, Crary identifies mobility as a key factor in the emergence in the nineteenth century of not only the technological, scientific and socio-political processes of modernisation but also of specific visual practices. Contrasting the static and stable vision of the camera obscura to the mobile modern visual experience, Crary links the latter to the kinetic processes (circulation, communication, production, consumption, for instance) that 'shaped a new kind of observer-consumer'.[12] In fact mobility becomes the precondition of a modern subjectivity that engulfs a broad spectrum of social, political and cultural practices. In his detailed study of perception Crary signals out the crucial role played by an active and restless body in enabling and shaping vision. Maine de Biran's early nineteenth-century philosophical study of the senses offers a clear example of the conceptualisation of vision as firmly rooted in the active body. As Crary points out, in de Biran's work, 'visual perception, for example, is inseparable from the muscular movements of the eye and the physical effort involved in focusing on an object or in simply holding one's eyelids open'.[13] This visceral approach locates vision in the body and introduces time as a factor. As a temporal dimension is implied in the eye's process of capturing the image a new peculiarly modern relationship between subject and object is established:

But as observation is increasingly tied to the body in the early nineteenth century, temporality and vision become inseparable. The shifting processes of one's own subjectivity experienced in time became synonymous with the act of seeing, dissolving the Cartesian ideal of an observer completely focused on an object.[14]

Of particular significance for nineteenth-century scientists became phenomena of visual perception such as the persistence of vision and the exploration of the 'afterimage', a particularly intriguing object of analysis for both physiologists and philosophers. As Crary notes:

> Other writers of the time also delineated perception as a continuous process, a flux of temporally dispersed contents. The physicist André-Marie Ampère in his epistemological writings used the term *concrétion* to describe how any perception always blends with a preceding or remembered perception. The words *mélange* and *fusion* occur frequently in his attack on classical notions of 'pure' isolated sensations. Perception, as he wrote to his friend Maine de Biran, was fundamentally, '*une suite de différences successives.*'[15]

In this evocative commentary on nineteenth-century thinking on vision there are suggestive references to the fundamentals of the very existence of cinema as a technology of vision but, even more importantly, in the figure of perception as *une suite de différences successives* we discern a clear anticipation of key aspects of the film form such as camera movement, editing and narrative progression. In such a model vision exists in motion and is quintessentially mobile.

But Crary's analysis also demonstrates a striking similarity to Foucault's analysis of modern episteme. In the obsession of philosophers, physicists and physiologists with issues of perception, the eye of the scientist turns its vision into itself: the act of observation becomes in itself observed, the scientist a subject and object of knowledge. Interestingly, the studies of persistence of vision, which were primarily studies of movement, led to 'the often accidental observation of new forms of movement'.[16] In the scientific explorations of the period movement and vision are directly and inextricably linked.

While Foucault sees modernity as marked by the shattering of the stasis of the classifying table by the movement of History, Crary identifies the modern observer as one who possesses a kinetic, mobile vision that replaces the stability and fixity of the camera obscura. In both accounts the nineteenth century is defined by the configuration of a knowing, perceiving mobile subject observing the peculiar movements of life in its multifaceted scientific, social and cultural dimensions. Vision, movement and knowledge are bound together in a peculiar dialectic that defines modern subjectivity. Their articulation informs some of the most pervasive conceptual metaphors and historical narratives of modernity. As witnessed in relation to Darwin's scientific expeditions, not only travelling enables knowledge but also the process of knowledge itself is perceived as a journey, as a gradual progression of a subject towards ever increasing knowledge.

Furthermore, such ideas are at the core of Jean-François Lyotard's critical investigation of the grand narratives of modernity, the big stories used in the legitimisation of knowledge in society.[17] The first variant (the narrative of emancipation usually associated with Marx) tells the story of a knowing subject that moves forward in a trajectory of increasing knowledge that is beneficial for all aspects of social life. The second (the Hegelian narrative of the life of the spirit) tells the story of ceaseless intellectual enquiry that leads to the ultimate destination which is the full realisation of the spiritual potential of humanity. Both are essentially stories about the heroes of modernity, the individualised but also collective subjects of knowledge, in their gradual, progressive and meaningful journeys of scientific exploration and discovery. In the grand narratives the process of knowledge is powerfully and evocatively perceived in terms of points of departure, landmarks reached and surpassed, trajectories of development and change, ultimate destinations and new departures.

The linearity of such narratives inevitably corresponds to a specific linear sense of time that, as Christoph Asendorf suggests, informs the ways in which a series of modern practices and conceptual processes is perceived:

The newly created 'homogeneous and empty time' (in Walter Benjamin's term) finds its expression not only in the factories and the means of transportation but also in novel theorems in the philosophy of history. Homogeneous time runs linearly. This linearity is the precondition of a continual forward movement, that is, of progress . . . The social democratic idea of progress is indebted to the idea of 'infinite perfectibility', as if there were a straight road – following the image of the railway.[18]

Thus a linear, incremental and forward movement of a progressing subjectivity travelling towards ever-increasing knowledge becomes an all-pervasive conceptual metaphor within scientific discourses and political practices. It has a profound impact on the way Western societies perceive of themselves and of their histories and offers a powerful visual metaphor that is repeatedly deployed in the expression of such imaginings. It is time now, however, to turn our attention to a different but related conceptualisation of movement that emerges in the circulation of commodities, the financial motor of modernisation.

1.2 CIRCULATIONS: COMMODITIES, ARCADES, *FLÂNEURS* AND REGULATION

The epistemic and perceptual shifts of modernity go hand in hand with profound changes in the production and consumption of goods. Following the imperatives of capitalist development and made possible by technologies of production and transportation, goods flood the markets of Western urban centres. Commodification as the process of transformation of things and objects into commodities has far-reaching implications in the restructuring of modern life, an impact noted by countless commentators and historians of the period. Our present concerns, however, lie with changes in lived experience and culture.

Commodification offers the conceptual lynchpin in Asendorf's fascinating exploration of changes in perception in the nineteenth century. With the entry of objects into the market a dramatic ontological transformation takes place as they become abstract entities appreciated mainly for their exchange value and stripped of their materiality. One of the key effects of the circulation of objects as commodities is the weakening of their sensual, material dimensions and the destruction of links with specific contexts and processes of production and with the natural environment that they once occupied. It is this abstraction that lies at the heart of the changes in the perception of objects and more generally of the natural and social world in modernity. A similar abstraction is in operation in the collection of natural and other objects that accompanies the observations of the great scientific expeditions as objects 'uprooted' from their original context are presented as 'research data' and displayed in museums, botanical gardens or the Great Exhibitions.

The abstracting and uprooting effects of mobility are signalled out by both Marx and Hegel, who not only represent influential philosophical currents of the nineteenth century but are also the inspiration between the two competing grand narratives. From diametrically opposite political and philosophical positions they both pay close attention to the transformative potential of movement. Marx in 'The Chapter on Capital' in *Grundrisse*, while analysing the dynamics of the process of exchange, identifies the crucial role that mobility plays in the very constitution of objects as commodities:

> This locational movement – the bringing of the product to the market, which is a necessary condition of its circulation, except when the point of production is itself the market – could more precisely be regarded as the transformation of the product *into a commodity*. Only on the market is it a *commodity*.[19]

In contrast, Hegel praises movement for its ability to liberate, in line with a well established metaphor that links mobility and freedom: 'Exchange is movement, the spirit, the center, that which is liberated from use and needs, as well as laboring and immediacy.'[20] While Marx's materialism places him miles apart from the idealism of Hegel, it does not stop him from embracing the liberating potential of movement – in popular movements as an instrument of revolution and agent of historical change but also in his faith in the emancipatory potential of the forward movement of scientific progress.

The movement of commodities into the public arena of the market and their participation in highly competitive processes of circulation and exchange lead to the development of new regimes of vision. As the traditional sensuality of objects weakens, their packaging, promotion and overall display gain greater significance as components of a new sensuality, that of the commodity. The importance of the visual appeal of merchandise coincides with a new organisation of space, movement and display, crystallised in the emergence of arcades and department stores, these emblematically modern 'institutions'. Thus, the circulation of commodities is matched by the circulation of a new mass of citizen-consumers and becomes an integral part of the generalised mobility that forms the fabric of modern urban life. This gives rise to a new and powerful biological metaphor in which circulation becomes a vital force not only for the economy but also for social and cultural life:

> [when] the nineteenth century sees the health and vitality of social institutions and processes as dependent on a functioning circulatory system, it bases this view on a biophysiological notion of society and economy; yet the concept itself is merely a reflection of the actual traffic conditions. This complex meaning of the circulation concept in the nineteenth century becomes quite explicit in French, where *circulation* refers to the actual movement of traffic as well as to the circulation of the blood and the circulation of goods.[21]

Walter Benjamin found a similar ability to condense multiple overlaying aspects of modernity in the Parisian arcades.[22] His *Arcades Project*, work whose scope and ambition meant that from the outset it was destined to be incomplete, offers a fascinating if fragmented kaleidoscopic view of the complex relations between capitalism, technology and culture in the nineteenth century. The arcades were incredibly dynamic forms of spatial organisation where the displays of capitalist goods attracted the gaze of a mobile public, constituting a dense field of intersecting discourses, practices, desires and visions. It is worth noting the static meaning that the term 'arcade' conveys that misses out the connotations of dynamism and movement involved in the French *passage* – 'arcade' can be mistaken for a destination, *passage* is a passageway, space that you traverse in motion rather than a port of arrival. Often used as shortcuts, arcades were integral to a mobile, dynamic perception of the urban experience.

Benjamin provides several descriptions of some of the most popular arcades (such as the Passage de Panoramas and the Passage de l'Opéra,[23] for instance) which offer clear indications of how a certain type of mobile vision permeates the whole experience. Architecturally, arcades consisted of long interconnected galleries lined up with shops with eye-catching displays, covered by glass roofs that sheltered from the rain and the cold and provided a uniform, diffused and soft light.[24] Benjamin considers at some length what distinguishes arcades from streets on the one hand and department stores on the other, and discovers differences in terms of the ways they articulate distinctive orchestrations of movement and vision. The arcade offers a refuge from the chaotic traffic of the street and enables a more leisurely pace of movement (which also became possible in the boulevards later in the century) and a smooth, uninterrupted engagement with the window displays.[25] The department store creates a different regime of vision by offering what Benjamin describes as a command of space 'at a glance': 'Principle of the department store: "the floors form a single space. They can be taken in, so to speak, at a glance"'.[26] By contrast the space of the arcade is revealed gradually and incrementally, through an exploring, strolling gaze that moves along the long corridors discovering the commodities on offer. This type of movement demands that body and vision are perfectly coordinated to absorb the commercial and sensual offerings fully: 'But foot and eye are arrested in a nobler and more charming fashion by the paintings displayed before many storefronts.'[27] Furthermore, the gratification attached to the embodied mobile vision is complemented by the more intellectual pleasures of exploration and discovery:

> Through the doors of the shops, one spied dusky alcoves where sometimes a piece of mahogany furniture, the classic furniture of the period, would manage to catch a ray of light. Further on, a small bar hazy with the smoke of tobacco pipes; a shop selling products from the colonies and emitting a curious fragrance of exotic plants, spices, and fruits.[28]

Significantly, in the stroll along the galleries the mobile observer encounters commodities that are brought home from remote lands encouraging, thus, fantasies of and desires for further journeys and explorations.

While concentrating mainly on the railway journey, Wolfgang Schivelbusch uses the umbrella term 'panoramic perception' in order to describe the mobile vision that is engendered in a variety of nineteenth-century visual experiences:

> Panoramic perception is one which finds the objects attractive in their state of dispersal. That attraction is generated by the motion that creates this perception of the objects in the observing subject . . . We called this

perception panoramic, by contrast with the traditional one that involves a static, intensive relationship with the objects observed . . . [29]

Schivelbusch in his 'panoramic perception'[30] and Benjamin in his arcades work describe a visual experience made possible through a specific type of mobility: that of a steady flow organised in more-or-less linear fashion (the galleries of the arcade or the track of the railway) along which a series of views unravel. While this mobile visual experience is articulated in relationship to a generalised circulation of commodities it is also linked to a type of subjectivity that combines cognitive and spectacular pleasures in a process of consumption that becomes also an act of discovery for the knowing gaze of the consumer-observer. Asendorf ironically describes the displays of the arcades as an 'encyclopaedic offering' that is comparable to that of museums.[31] The different window displays invite close study of the products and comparison between types, models and prices – making your way around the arcade is not just a question of physical mobility but also of discovering where the bargains are and knowing where quality resides.

The irony inherent in the 'encyclopaedic' designation of the arcade experience is twofold: it suggests an inferior cognitive process[32] and alludes to an unfavourable comparison of the consumer with an active learner. Such activity (and superior knowledge) is usually preserved for a different mobile observer, the *flâneur*, famously celebrated by Baudelaire as a model of modern(ist) artistic subjectivity who represents a paradigmatic opposite to the mobile consumer. Endowed with the exceptional ability to capture the eternal in the ephemeral, the *flâneur*'s mobility becomes a crucial aid to his[33] superior sensitivity:

> The lover of universal life enters into the crowd as though it were an immense reservoir of electrical energy. Or we might liken him to a mirror as vast as the crowd itself; or to a kaleidoscope gifted with consciousness, responding to each one of its movements and reproducing the multiplicity of life and the flickering grace of all the elements of life.[34]

In his wandering of the streets the *flâneur* attempts to defy alienation and commodification by remaining in constant mental and sensual alert and by constantly registering fragments of life and time that constitute the ephemeral, transient, fleeting essence of modernity. Like the consumer, the *flâneur* is in constant motion but unlike the former he is an active observer studying rather than consuming the movements of modern life; as Baudelaire suggests in relation to Constantin Guys: ' in an instant Monsieur G. will already have seen, examined and analysed'.[35] Thus, the *flâneur*'s stroll is less smooth and steady as it is accompanied by ceaseless perceptual agility: he follows a myriad fleeting sensations that appear and disappear in seconds and is attracted by actions and events that demand constant alteration of direction, purpose and speed of movement. However, the near superhuman abilities of the Baudelairean romantic artist/*flâneur* attracted Benjamin's criticism:

> When Victor Hugo was celebrating the crowd as the hero in a modern epic, Baudelaire was looking for a refuge for the hero among the masses of the big city. Hugo placed himself in the crowd as a *citoyen*; Baudelaire sundered himself from it as a hero.[36]

Beyond the unbridled individualism and explicit elitism inherent in the Baudelairean *flâneur*, the figure of the romantic artist as a hero of modernity diverts attention from some of the essential complexities that underpin the figure of the *flâneur*. An essential component of the mobile subjectivity and the creative potential that it releases is the ability to 'surrender' to modernity, to become one with the crowd and to fully expose oneself to the urban experience, in other words, the ability to give oneself up completely. The active pursuit of the modern is only made possible through a fundamental passivity, and in such formulation activity and passivity are captured in a dialectic of mutual dependence rather than exclusion.

Furthermore, as numerous critics from Benjamin ('the *flâneur* . . . is no buyer. He is merchandise'[37]) to Crary ('a mobile consumer of a ceaseless succession of illusory commodity-images'[38]) point out, the *flâneur* is not a glorious outsider who opposes and antagonises capitalism and the power of the market but he is part of it. As Asendorf observes:

> Baudelaire's artist as *flâneur* is therefore to be seen precisely within this tension: on the one hand, open to the point of abandon to all possible constellations, tied to no boundaries; on the other, a fleeting money soul.[39]

The *flâneur*'s somewhat chaotic (active and critical while also passive and submissive) mobile vision pursues its journeys within an environment that itself mutates and an urban experience that is under constant transformation. The clearest demonstration of this process is the continuous change that Paris undergoes in the process of 'Haussmanisation', in the formation of a rational and functional cityscape through modern urban planning practices archetypically associated with Charles Eugène Haussman. In his construction projects the creation and celebration of new types of movement go hand-in-hand with a clear political will to regulate and control mobility. While he described himself (in rather heroic terms reminiscent of Baudelaire) as *artiste demolisseur*,[40] he was also clear that an associated objective of his project was to facilitate the violent if necessary suppression by the police or the army of any revolutionary movements and/or popular protests unfolding in the streets of Paris. In the increasingly mobile environment of modern cities the emergence of new forms of knowledge and experience is matched by the deployment of new forms of control.

Photography is particularly interesting in that respect. In the experiments of Muybridge and Marey the use of photographic technology became the most effective instrument in the analysis of human and animal motion – precisely the type of movements that became the focus of scientific enquiry within modern episteme.[41] In the use of chronophotography we see a fascination with and celebration of movement that is, nevertheless, channelled towards increasing our knowledge of human and animal motion. Movement becomes the object of analysis with a clear intention to fix it, to frame it and ultimately to control it – both literally, as movement is translated into a succession of still images, and conceptually, as motion is explained rationally, objectively, scientifically.[42]

Tom Gunning extends this double-sided aspect of photography to general processes of social mobility[43] as he suggests that photography (and later cinema) were instrumental in addressing key policing and governance anxieties caused by the mass circulation of people in cities. Following Benjamin's evaluation of detective fiction,[44] he proposes that nineteenth-century practices of police detection attempted 'to reestablish the traces of individual identity beneath the obscurity of a new mobility'.[45] Photography and later cinema offered particularly effective technologies of vision in which bodies were 'arrested and analyzed, available for comparison and identification',[46] something since recognised by countless regulatory institutions and practices ranging from CCTV to reality television.

The circulation of commodities and bodies in the arcades and the boulevards, in *flânerie* and photography, activates mobile visions peculiar to Western modernity that place the subject in positions that embrace both the consumer and the poet, fluctuate subtly between activity and passivity and complement the dynamism of an unprecedented mobility with a relentless drive for control and regulation. A fine balance between the encouragement and celebration of movements of exploration and discovery and the imperative of social order characterise the circulation of people in the commodified milieu of the nineteenth century.

1.3 POPULAR TECHNOLOGIES OF VISION: MUSEUMS, EXHIBITIONS AND PANORAMAS

Questions of control and regulation inevitably point towards Foucault's work and methodology and more specifically in the understanding of power as a 'technology' that is coupled with specific 'forms of visibility'. Through detailed studies of institutions such as the prison and the hospital that have a rather unambiguous disciplinary or regulatory function, Foucault demonstrated that institutional power is deployed through technologies of vision[47] (or 'forms of luminosity'[48] as Deleuze calls them) which produce orderly distributions of bodies and objects in space and time. The controlling gaze inscribed in panoptical structures is, according to Foucault, the ultimate regulatory mechanism, and constitutes a model of the way that power operates within modern societies. Neither oppressive nor top down, power is diffused, omnipresent and deployed through the very structure of specific technologies of vision.

Along the great institutions of regulation and control, a number of less obviously disciplinarian technologies of vision proliferated in the nineteenth century in the form of museums, botanical and zoological gardens, the Great Exhibitions and the various 'o-ramas', practices that were all geared primarily towards visual gratification more than anything else. Such 'benign' and spectacular technologies of vision constitute specific articulations of movement, vision, knowledge (and thus power) and pleasure, articulations that we shall now consider in some detail. The intensity of the visual pleasures offered by 'arcades, winter gardens, panoramas, factories, wax museums, casinos, railroad stations' was not lost in such an astute observer of modernity as Benjamin, who described them as 'dream houses of the collective'.[49] More, specifically, in relation to museums he notes:

> Museums unquestionably belong to the dream houses of the collective. In considering them, one would want to emphasize the dialectic by which they come into contact, on the one hand, with scientific research and on the other hand, with 'the dreamy tide of bad taste.'[50]

Such dialectic is clearly at the heart of the organisation of the visual experience of museums where carefully structured processes of historical narrativisation combine the scientific with the spectacular in a delicate if precarious balance. Tony Bennett in his work on the 'birth of the museum'[51] describes the visual experience in key 'exhibitionary' institutions (museums, international exhibitions and fairs) as a form of 'organized walking':

> [I]n their recognition of the fact that their visitors' experiences are realized via their physical movement through an exhibitionary space, all three institutions have shared a concern to regulate the performative aspects of their visitors' conduct. Overcoming mind/body dualities in treating their visitors as, essentially, 'minds on legs', each, in its different way, is a place for 'organized walking' in which an intended message is communicated in the form of a (more or less) directed itinerary.[52]

Leaving aside for a moment the regulatory dimension of the structured itinerary, the experience of the museum is clearly defined here as depending on a mobile vision overwritten by scientific or historical discourse. This is of great interest to many scholars who analyse nineteenth-century 'technologies of vision'. In her work on the use of 'life groups' ('the arrangement of costumed mannequins in dramatic tableaux') in natural history museums, Alison Griffiths proposes that the movement of visitors as they encounter a succession of exhibits, organised in various forms of historical or narrative order, represents a peculiar precursor to cinema, what she calls 'promenade cinema'.[53] Griffiths suggests that there are two types of mobility that operate in complementary fashion in museums: the actual movement of the visitor in space is accompanied by a virtual one activated by the narrative frames within which the experience is temporised. A composite physical and virtual mobile vision is thus perfectly materialised through the careful orchestration of spatial organisation, display and narrativisation.

As we shall discuss later the emphasis on virtual movement is crucial for Griffiths in establishing the link between the mobile vision of the museum with that of the spectatorial experience of cinema. But it is important to be attentive to the fact that the virtual can only be actualised through the physical, as it is only the collaboration of the two that delivers the full experience. This is lucidly demonstrated by Vanessa Schwartz in her detailed study of the Musée Grévin (The Parisian wax works museum that opened in 1882) as she describes the choreography of movement and vision involved in the encounter with a specific tableau representing three men and a woman watching a Comédie Française dress rehearsal:

> The tableau's structure played on its own three-dimensionality and the visitor's mobility. It was assumed that the spectator would approach the tableau from the left, where the figures in the box appeared to be watching something. As the spectator walked to the right, he or she could then see the inset of the dress rehearsal as it would appear through the eyes of those seated in the box and, because of its angle, as the museum visitor could glimpse only when aligned herself with the visual perspective of wax figures. Through her own motion, the spectator thus enabled the unfolding of the scene's narrative.[54]

The above description highlights the coordination of movement and vision and the construction of privileged viewpoints that establish specific indivualised perspectives on the represented event. While the similarities with the cinematic experience are obvious, Schwartz also compares the experience of the wax museum to the reading of a newspaper in that they both present the observer/reader with contemporary scenes of everyday life. The comparison with reading also surfaces in Bennet's dissection of the 'organized walking' of the museum:

> Each museum type, then, is like a chapter within a longer story, pressing towards an end point which is simultaneously the point at which the next chapter commences. Like the reader in a detective novel, it is towards this end point that the visitor's activity is directed.[55]

In both instances the mobility of vision is motivated and guided by a quest for information and knowledge. The mobile vision of the museum is organised around specific tracks of physical movement and progresses along carefully laid out historical and/or narrative trajectories, entertained by a sense of exploration and discovery and working towards a final destination, a conclusion that neatly reveals the ultimate meaning of the experience.

A unique combination of the museological experience with *flânerie* constitutes the most memorable type of spectacular entertainment and popular education, the Great Exhibitions which were organised in major Western cities throughout the nineteenth century. Statements of state power, celebrations of empire, shameless advertisements of technological and scientific progress and events of unparalleled visual splendour, the Great Exhibitions encapsulated Western modernity. Architecturally indebted to the arcade they provided spectacular experiences combined with clear ideological and political functions in bringing together notions of history and progress with glorifications of the achievements of capitalism, industrialism and imperialism. It is not surprising, then, that Tom Gunning finds in the Great Exhibitions the same semantic density and ability to crystallise an era as Benjamin does in the arcades.[56] In his discussion of the 1904 St Louis World's Fair, Gunning describes what is by now a familiar orchestration of vision, movement and historical knowledge:

> [This] effort in planning and arrangement marked the cultural pretension of the Expositions which sought not simply to gather the marvels of the world but to sort them into a schema which would demonstrate man's technological progress and the world wide dimensions of modern production.[57]

The organisation of the space of the Exhibition often structures the experience around a progressive evolutionary trajectory that de facto brings together the two grand narratives of modernity (technological progress and the life of the spirit) as the itinerary of teleological history results in a progressively increasing knowledge. This in turn encourages megalomaniac fantasies of complete knowledge – as George Brown Goode (responsible for the arrangement of several world expositions) stated, an Exposition should be 'an illustrated Encyclopaedia of Civilization'.[58]

Within such totalising context the exhibition experience turns the world into an 'object lesson', a displayed, attainable object of knowledge, while at the same time the spectator is treated into a virtual trip around the world. Virtual travelling was taken to an extreme in the Pike (the St. Louis World Fair's amusement area) where, as Gunning details, 'railway journeys' structured around historical trajectories or simulating actual itineraries (such as the Trans-Siberian railway), mechanically moved the visitors around landscapes or events.[59] Once again the orchestration of movement and vision is overwritten by historical narratives, articulating, thus, two superimposed layers of subjectivity as the mobile observer retraces the tracks of the subject of history.

Perhaps an even clearer demonstration of such articulation is provided by the various o-ramas, often posited by many film historians as cinema's closest ancestors in the way that they visually transported the viewers in space and time.[60] There are two main types of these often gigantic representations of landscapes, historical events and foreign lands, still and moving panoramas (the latter also known as dioramas):

The general term 'panorama' embraces two significantly different types, the moving and the still panorama. The first consists of a continuous picture, or series of scenes, painted on a large roll of canvas which is unrolled from one spool or drum onto another behind a frame. It would frequently depict a voyage or journey to foreign parts, in effect a painted travelogue: a steamboat trip down the Mississippi was a favorite. It could also serve as a newsreel depicting current events. Moving panoramas were also used in theaters as backdrops, particularly in melodramas, to create the illusion of motion. By contrast, the still panorama was a 360-degree painting covering the entire inner wall of a specially constructed cylindrical building equipped with a central viewing platform.[61]

Whereas moving panoramas most clearly display the ways in which the spectator becomes a component of a moving machine[62] it is important to recognise that the static panorama also involves a mobilisation of vision. Whereas in the former it is the mechanical movement of pictures around the spectator that provides mobility in vision, in the latter the spectator's vision is invited to move in order to complete the 360-degrees expanse of the representation. As in the case of museums and exhibitions, a fantasy of completeness (of knowledge and/or history), in this instance expressed through the construction of a vision mobilised around a full circle, a complete revolution,[63] permeates the experience.

The differences between the moving and still panoramas are sometimes overplayed by film scholars interested in establishing a realist genealogy of cinema and its prehistory.[64] While this issue is clearly beyond the scope of the present work, some of the assumptions informing certain theoretical appropriations of nineteenth-century technologies of vision will be considered in the conclusion of this chapter. For our present concerns it is important to note that both static and moving panoramas often organised their representations in chronological order offering to the spectator a succession of historical events:

> The image of a mechanically controlled narrative with a definable beginning, middle, and end encouraged a view of history as a series of unfolding scenes fluidly connected with one another, giving the audiences the illusion of mastery over random, distant, or otherwise incomprehensible events.[65]

A particularly popular technique was the construction of moving panoramas around the concept of travelling. As in the case of the Pike, various types of journey (in a river, by boat ('pleoramas'), or by train) offered travelling narratives as overarching frames of spectacle. Angela Miller provides several fascinating examples of such panoramas:

> The development of the round into the moving panorama satisfied the optical (and geographical) hunger of American audiences by artificially compressing space in a manner anticipating mechanized travel, unrolling the American landscape before the eyes of audiences in such works as the 'Moving Mirror of the Overland Trail', 'Trip to the Tropics and California', 'Fremonst's Overland Route to California', 'Texas and California', 'California on Canvas', 'Illustration of Central America', 'Panorama of the Mammoth Cave [in Kentucky]', and 'Diorama of Canada and the United States'. Other panoramic subjects included 'Lake Superior', 'Mirror of Crystal Palace and World's Fair' of 1851 in London, 'Panorama of New York', 'Perry's Expedition to Japan', 'The Holy Land', and 'Across the Atlantic in Two Hours.'[66]

While the visual experiences of the museum, the Great Exhibitions and the o-ramas orchestrate vision and movement along narrative and historical virtual trajectories, the development of the railways in the nineteenth century articulates similar relationships between time, space and vision in real journeys. The work of Wolfgang Schivelbusch[67] on the railway journey has become a standard reference in establishing that experience as yet another precursor of cinema. The conceptualisation of the train as an apparatus that offers a vision of the world in motion, with the glass window separating the seated (immobile yet travelling) viewers from the framed object of their gaze, quite clearly holds a strong analogy with cinema.[68] However, it is the relationship between vision, movement and subjectivity as structured in the railway journey that we need to address now. As we have seen earlier Schivelbusch theorises the experience of the railway journey as part of a number of technologies of mobile vision that are characteristic of the nineteenth century's 'panoramic perception'. Perhaps surprisingly, such viewing experience is described in rather negative terms. Contrasting the view of the driver with that of the passenger, for example, Schivelbusch quotes a number of nineteenth-century luminaries who express their profound dissatisfaction with the visual experience:

> Unlike the driver, the travellers have only a very limited chance to look *ahead*: thus all they can see is an evanescent landscape. All early descriptions of railroad travel testify to the difficulty of recognizing any but the broadest outlines of the traversed landscape. Victor Hugo describes the view from a train window in a letter dated August 22, 1837: 'The flowers by the side of the road are no longer flowers but flecks, or rather streaks, of red or white; there are no longer any points, everything becomes a streak; the grainfields are great shocks of yellow hair; fields of alfalfa, long green tresses; the towns, the steeples, and the trees perform a crazy mingling dance on the horizon; from time to time, a shadow, a shape, a spectre appears with lightning speed behind the window: it's a railway guard.[69]

While one can see how an impressionist might treasure such an experience, it condemns the 'normal' traveller to intense boredom and ultimately leads to the complete rejection of the visual experience for the compensatory activities of reading or sleeping.[70] In fact, a profound passivity permeates the whole being of the traveller:

> The train is experienced as a projectile, and travelling on it, as being shot through the landscape – thus losing control of one's senses . . . The traveller who sits inside that projectile ceases to be a traveller and becomes, as noted in a popular metaphor of the century, a mere parcel.[71]

The process does not leave the psychological state of the traveller unaffected – as Asendorf notes, 'the "clatter", that is, the vibrations of continuous motion, produce a calm, happily abandoned state of mind'.[72] Furthermore, railway journeys are seen as annihilators of 'real' space, reducing the world to a succession of fragmented and blurry landscape scenes, consuming and destroying in the process all the spaces inbetween destinations. While this can be seen as contributing to the acquisition of a somewhat encyclopaedic knowledge of distances between major landmarks, the overall lie of the land or the nature of the landscape, it is fundamentally perceived as an experience that strips the world of its materiality and authenticity and is part of the overall commodification of social life in modernity.[73]

The railway journey, thus, is typical not only of the way mobile vision operates in the nineteenth century but also of the all-pervasive critical suspicion against the experiences offered by popular technologies of vision. The accusation of passivity (often accompanied by laments for the loss of the real and the authentic) is levelled against a number of practices and by a number of critics: not only by Schivelbusch in relation to the railway journey, as we have just seen, but also, for example, by Fourier (as cited by Benjamin) vis-à-vis the arcades (they would 'make our cities . . . seem detestable')[74] and by Miller's interpretation of the viewing experience of the moving panoramas as essentially passive.[75]

What is particularly interesting in relation to both Schivelbusch and Miller is that they both perceive physical immobility as inextricably linked to passivity both in the railway journey and in panoramas. Such a formulation is expressed by Miller in unambiguous terms:

> The perceptual changes heralded by the moving panorama were already prepared by the experience of steam travel. Mechanized travel was a growing presence in the everyday lives of nineteenth-century Europeans and Americans, overcoming the barriers and obstacles of pre-steam overland travel, and introducing a more passive experience of space. The passive nature of mechanized movement through space afforded by both steamboat and train travel applied as well to the experience of the moving panorama, in which the static observer retained a fixed place, watching the mechanically activated canvas roll past.[76]

Within such discourse what repeatedly emerges as an antidote to immobile passivity (and the implied conformity with an alienated and commodified existence) is the adventures and sensibilities of *flânerie* as a way of inspiring and mobilising an interrogation of modernity through artistic practices.

1.4 IMPRESSIONISM: A DIFFERENT VISION?

As we have already discussed, Baudelaire quite clearly (and influentially) perceived *flânerie* as an activity that underlies the work of the painter of modern life who is dedicated to a relentless pursuit of the ephemeral and the transient. The *flâneur*'s sensibility and vision is best exemplified by impressionist art commonly seen as the first all-out form of modernism. While I have no intention to engage with the critical debates around the politics of modernism it is important to note the privileged and oppositional nature attributed to impressionism both within orthodox versions of the history of art[77] and within critical theory. In both cases impressionism (and subsequently modernism) represents a 'rupture in the field of vision' and/or an aesthetic critique of the rationale of modernisation. Leaving the latter aside for a moment, I shall now briefly consider impressionism's relationship with the technologies of mobile vision that have been the focus of this chapter so far. Is impressionist art a critique and negation of the dominant popular regimes of nineteenth-century vision? Or is it rather, as Crary suggests, their twin figure, the other side of the same coin? What is at stake in answering these questions is the way we conceptualise and evaluate modern configurations of movement, vision and subjectivity – either as structured around binary opposites of conformist/oppositional, active/passive practices or as a complex continuum of complementary (albeit often contradictory) articulations.

Movement is fundamental to impressionist perception. Asendorf comments on Degas's use of urban forms of mobility (notably the bus) as a key aid in the observation and painting of everyday scenes.[78] Furthermore, movement itself is what Degas paints: 'Whether the woman in the bus, the horse, the ballerinas, everything is for him only a "pretext . . . for reproducing movements"'.[79] Impressionist sensibility revolves around the mobile vision of the painter as *flâneur*, constantly in motion and always searching for movements of people, animals and objects. In that respect the impressionist resembles the 'mobile scientist' who studies the multifarious manifestations of the movements of natural life. Asendorf notes the 'multiple points of contact between scientific and artistic production' and he sites Adorno's view of modern romanticism:

> The excessively praised exquisite sensibility of the artist makes him in a certain sense the complement of the natural scientist; it is as though his sensory apparatus enabled him to register smaller differences than those accessible to that of the scientist.[80]

Asendorf also compares impressionist painting to railway journeys in terms of their striking similarities in the way that they operate as regimes of vision. However, the recurring complaint about the passengers' perception of landscapes and objects as blurred and 'ghostly' (as expressed in the Hugo quotation in the previous section) is dismissed in the following manner:

> As long as the eye remains fixed on things close by, like the telegraph poles, it will recognize nothing of the landscape. Only when it gains some distance, turns towards objects somewhat further away, does it perceive details. It is the same procedure a viewer of impressionist pictures has to employ: to take some distance from them so as to place the isolated spots of color into a context.[81]

Crary too sees impressionism as existing in a continuum with contemporaneous popular technologies of vision. Examining the similarities in certain works by Courbet, Manet and Seurat with the views constructed by the stereoscope (yet another popular optical gadget of the period) he concludes:

> Both the 'realism' of the stereoscope and the 'experiments' of certain painters were equally bound up in a much broader transformation of the observer that allowed the emergence of this new optically constructed space. The stereoscope and Cézanne have far more in common than one might assume. Painting, and early modernism in particular, had no special claims in the renovation of vision in the nineteenth century.[82]

Furthermore, it is in movement that the impressionist has to capture the essence of modern life, a task that is never fully accomplished as the speed of the world exceeds that of the artist in the process of creation. In impressionist art, obsessively recording objects in flux, in the transient occurrences of everyday life or in the instantaneous sensations of light and form, the world itself becomes blurred and uncertain. Asendorf discovers in the impressionist fascination with movement an 'evacuation of statuary meaning', a separation of things from their context which is reminiscent of the process of transformation of objects into commodities:

> There remains only the language of movements, which make people into speechless mobile bodies and therefore the equivalent of things . . . The body can by visualized only in movement. The eye registers the movement of persons, not the latter themselves; the objects are exchangeable like commodities in circulation.[83]

Thus, the representation of the world as an impressionist picture bears a fundamental resemblance with the turning of objects into commodities. Both involve an 'uprooting', a salient feature of the process of modernisation itself.[84]

Even for an orthodox art historian like Aaron Scharf (who approaches the visual arts of the nineteenth and twentieth centuries as a struggle between art and photography), many of the compositional devices of impressionist painting (such as framing or viewpoint) are seen as having 'far more in common with photography than they do with art'.[85] Scharf's discomfort with the affinity between modernist art and photography is palpable in the following elaboration of the 'revelation' that Cézanne used photography in his work:

> It is not to denigrate the artist's inventive powers, but rather to applaud them for exploring photographic form that I draw a parallel between the peculiar tipped axes often found in buildings represented by Cézanne

and the same, not uncommon feature found in the uncompromising perspective of photographs.[86]

And again, regarding Degas:

> The deformities of his subjects, the uncouth poses and gestures, the commonplace and even ugly expressions, the apparently artless accidents of compositions, are paralleled only by the images of the instantaneous camera. They are not, as some of his critics maintained, the results of a passive submission to the photograph. Degas made these things pictorially feasible, fabricating a style from sources which had no style.[87]

It is impossible to overlook the romanticism that permeates Scharf's defence of Degas in the assertion of a superior sensitivity that wards off claims of passivity. It is the same romantic individualism, the Baudelairean cult of the artist as a modern hero, that distinguishes between a train passenger who is just a 'parcel' and the genius of Degas in creative action as he is transported on a bus, between the rumblings of the *flâneur* and those of the arcade visitor, between the journeys of exploration of Rimbaud, Byron or Darwin and those of millions of anonymous 'passive' travellers. One can argue that it is the creative genius who in fact commits the crime of commodification by transforming experiences rooted in the flow of everyday life into separate, reified abstractions (works of art) which ultimately and inevitably enter the market as valuable commodities.

Neither should we consider the visual experience of the popular technologies of vision (unlike the blurred, uncertain, critical and destabilising vision of the artist) as one that affirms a centred and controlled subjectivity constructed through unambiguous and masterful representations of the world. In an essay considering nineteenth-century images of Paris in panoramic representations varying from o-ramas to postcards and from literature to impressionist painting, Sonya Stephens, highlights the increasing tendency to encourage the observer/reader to exercise selectivity, discretion and intelligent interpretation.[88] Like Crary, Stephens sees popular panoramas and 'high-culture' representations of Paris as belonging to the same genealogy of vision:

> Panoramas and panoramic representations were invitations to participate not only in a new space of vision (a space no longer limited by a single perspective and determined by that) but also in a form of selectivity, inviting the viewer to pick out and identify components; components which act as signs in a complex play of suppression and reconstitution in detail.[89]

She traces the emphasis on selectivity (of viewing and perceiving as a process of discovery) in panoramas, in literature (Flaubert) and in impressionist painting (Manet), as they all demonstrate a clear shift away from the monumental and the universal. For Stephens, the observer of panoramas can potentially experience a loss of control and mastery over the view and, destabilised by the uncertainty of the representation, will have to engage in a perceptual and intellectual process of negotiating and/or establishing meaning:

> Where panoramas first promised totality of vision with the observer at the centre, they soon mutate into decentred, troubling enquiries into the status of the observer, that of the artist, and the ability of the panoramic view to enable meaningful connections.[90]

While Stephens describes this panoramic experience as potentially 'dizzying', Gunning identifies a similar effect on visitors to World Expositions:

> Rather than visual mastery and understanding, the spectacle could produce an excessive experience which risked leaving no impression at all other than that of the limits of perception . . . Dazzlement played an essential role in the visual attraction of the fair, even if its place was rarely explicitly theorized.[91]

Thus a viewer encountering uncertainty and loss of control is not the exclusive domain of early modernist sensitivity but surfaces in a broad spectrum of nineteenth-century technologies of vision. As following chapters will examine in detail, mobility of vision involves a dialectic of certainty and uncertainty that in many occasions utilises destabilisation as a stimulus and motor for cognitive and perceptual activities. The challenge of perceived wisdom and the relentless pursuit of new certainties underpins many intellectual journeys and perceptual itineraries. From the perspective of scholarship considered in this section, therefore, Impressionism's unique position of critical alterity is seriously challenged as the conceptualisation of processes of modernisation is expanded to include a broad spectrum of nineteenth-century articulations of movement, vision and subjectivity.

1.5 SUBJECTIVITY, VISION, MOVEMENT

The nineteenth century was a period of unprecedented obsession with both movement and vision. In a variety of discourses and practices ranging from science to mass entertainment and from impressionism to museology, endless combinations of the mobile and the visual were tried out and deployed, captivating popular imagination, dominating the epistemological field and transforming the arts. Travelling scientists pursuing objects in flux, *flâneurs* in the dizzying speed of modern cities, visitors of museums and strollers of arcades, philosopher-observers of change and photographers, were all equally engrossed by a world in motion while also exploring types of mobility that enhance vision.

The period's fascination with mobile vision has attracted systematic and wide-ranging research and has informed influential theoretical appropriations; such scholarship offers the basis for the preceding sections with the intention to map specific articulations of movement, vision and subjectivity. The ultimate objective is to utilise that mapping in order to conceptualise and analyse cinematic movement. My concerns and objectives, however, form a field of enquiry that exists on close proximity with well-established scholarship in a number of disciplines. While I will reflect on relationships with other parallel or competing paradigms in several occasions throughout this book it is crucial at this stage to highlight some initial differences.

Within the broad fields of cultural studies and critical theory two key areas are of particular interest. First, an explicit negative evaluation of popular technologies of mobile vision articulated in terms of a crisis of the real and loss of authenticity. In such models the experience of the material world and the historical process becomes reified as the real is replaced by the spectacular – panoramas, museums and railway journeys are seen as annihilators of the authentic, as illusionary substitutes for the real. Sidestepping debates around the romanticism that informs such appropriations, the present work is only interested in what technologies of mobile vision articulate and enable in terms of visual perception and pleasure and in the specific visual forms that they produce.

Second, a debate rages around the passivity induced by popular technologies of vision as opposed to the critical perspective of early modernist art. This opposition has been discussed already at some length but it is worth noting the somewhat ambiguous terms that some conceptualisations of passivity involve. In some cases (such as the railway journey or the moving panoramas) passivity is perceived as physical immobility that assumes that unless your body is self-propelled it is passive. A romantic ideology of self-willed bodily agency underlies such formulations. In other cases, nevertheless, passivity takes the form of interpellation, of submission to the mobile vision of the numerous apparatuses of modernity. In this model it is in mobility that passivity resides, in the actualisation of a predetermined itinerary and in the adoption of the constructed viewpoints; activity entails resistance, the critical interrogation of one's own position and a rejection of the apparatus. While recognising the significance of specific articulations of the active/passive polarity my analysis will proceed with an understanding of subjectivity as unfolding in a productive fashion rather than as interpellated positioning without, however, assuming that relations and structures of power are absent or insignificant.[92]

In film studies the nineteenth century is frequently revisited as the period that led to the emergence of cinema in order to establish a historical perspective that genealogically links film to other technologies of vision that precede it or are contemporaneous with it. Work produced within that paradigm often demonstrates a tendency to foreground the separation between viewer and scene, the abstracted nature of the viewed objects, the virtual nature of temporal and spatial mobility, the illusionary seduction of the spectacle and the power of the viewing apparatus over the passive viewer, in the consideration of the multiple relationships between popular nineteenth-century technologies of vision and prominent features of cinema. While such scholarship is without any doubt extremely valuable in establishing a genealogy of cinema and in the exploration of many aspects of the film form from the perspective of associated but different practices, it can also take the debate within the rather unproductive discursive context of 'apparatus theory'.

More important for the concerns of this book, nevertheless, is the fact that a recurring and dominant tendency that emerges from that type of work is to link the specificities of nineteenth-century mobile vision to the process of editing (as a way of linking abstracted, fragmented views) and/or to narrative trajectories producing a coherent totality out of a mass of disparate events. Within such genealogy (and with the significant exception of scholarship on early travel films) movement of/in the frame is rarely considered—this is a criticism clearly expressed by Tom Gunning under 'camera movement' in the *Encyclopedia of Early Cinema*: 'camera movement has generally been subordinated in filmmaking and film theory to editing as a way of changing camera viewpoint'.[93]

While this study concurs with the approach of nineteenth-century articulations of mobile vision as an inextricable part of cinema's genealogy, it aims to redress the theoretical and analytical imbalance by focusing on movement of/in the frame. In the earlier consideration of nineteenth-century discourses and practices we have traced the prominence of two broad interconnected and often combined types of mobile vision that offer evocative comparisons with specific instances of cinematic movement. More specifically:

- A steady, smooth and continuous movement of more-or-less linear direction choreographed with a process of visual exploration and often linked to the accumulation of incremental and progressive knowledge.
- A circular type of movement around specific objects of interest that involves their exploration from a number of successive, spatially contiguous points of view; this usually forms part of a succession or a series of similar movements connected through a cognitive and/or narrative trajectory.

Both types of mobile vision are structured around a balance between the actual and the virtual that varies from practice to practice. In the first case a sense of destination, purpose and direction underpins the movement. In the second type a sense of completion informs the comprehensive observation of an object or event. In either case pleasures of discovery and exploration are combined with specular pleasures and are accompanied by contextual frames that impose coherence and meaning on the experience.

We have also repeatedly noted the encyclopaedic nature of several instances of mobile vision: in an ironic but suggestive way in relation to arcades, in the condensed geography of the railway journey, in the obvious case of the museum, in the perception of exhibitions as an 'illustrated Encyclopaedia of Civilization', even in the *flâneur*'s relentless quest of fully capturing and representing the modern. In fact the 'encyclopaedic' offers an apt conceptual and metaphorical figure that captures and condenses several key characteristics of mobile vision as articulated in/through the types of movement identified above. The encyclopaedic experience involves a combination of the linear progression of knowledge from a beginning to an end, from A to Z, with the cross-referencing of specific terms or, to put it differently, it suggests a forward trajectory in tandem with explorations of specific concepts or terms from a variety of different perspectives. Underpinning the encyclopaedic enterprise is the fantasy of complete knowledge,[94] a total mapping of the (imagined as completely knowable) world and its history—a similar fantasy informs several instances of nineteenth-century mobile vision.

What also informs both types of movement is a certain model of subjectivity, embodied in the actual combination of movement and vision and overlaid by epistemological trajectories. In the circular or the linear type and in their countless combinations a mobile subject is set upon a journey of visual exploration and discovery. Such explorations and the movements that enable them are not only quests for pleasure but also for meaning, as the mobile subject often retraces tracks already laid out and finds him/herself travelling journeys that include but also exceed individuals, the journeys of the anonymous collective subjects of grand narratives.

There also exists a third type of movement that emerges either in the form of a fearful possibility of disorder that needs to be controlled (in Haussmann's urban planning strategies of controlling unruly popular movements or in the photographic control of chaotic social mobility) or, expressed in a positive manner, in the romantic fetishisation of the restless, unpredictable movement of the modern painter in the chimerical pursuit of the eternal in the transient. In the disorder that permeates it, this third type of movement stands as the diametrical opposite of the previous two, presenting us with an all-pervasive binary that still holds sway in many of the theoretical and analytical accounts of cinematic movement. In the following two chapters I shall first examine critically the specific ways in which movement has been analysed and theorised in film studies and then, by using the specific example of cinematic movements of exploration and discovery, I shall propose a methodological alternative. Both chapters are informed by the discussion of nineteenth-century articulations of movement, vision and subjectivity undertaken here.

NOTES

1. Michel Foucault, *The Order of Things* (London and New York: Routledge, 1989).
2. Ibid. p. 221.
3. Ibid. p. 367.
4. Ibid. p. 219.
5. Charles Darwin, *The Voyage of HMS Beagle* (London: John Murray, 1890), p. 403.
6. Ibid. pp. 532–8.
7. Ibid. p. 537.
8. Foucault, *Order of Things*, p. 312.
9. Jonathan Crary, *Techniques of the Observer: On Vision and Modernity in the Nineteenth Century* (Cambridge, MA, and London: MIT Press, 1991).
10. Ibid. p. 3.
11. 'At the deepest level of Western knowledge, Marxism introduced no real discontinuity; it found its place without difficulty, as a full, quiet, comfortable and, goodness knows, satisfying for a time (its own), within an epistemological field that welcomed it gladly' (Foucault, *Order of Things*, p. 261).
12. Crary, *Techniques of the Observer*, p. 14. This is a suggestion also supported by Christoph Asendorf in *Batteries of Life: On the History of Things and Their Perception in Modernity* (Berkeley, CA, and London: University of California Press, 1993): 'There are multiple points of contact between contemporary scientific and artistic productions of the time, both of which are characterized by a sensitivity to the phenomena of movement and the dissolution of the anthropocentric image of the world' (p. 95).
13. Crary, *Techniques of the Observer*, p. 72.
14. Ibid. p. 98.
15. Ibid. p. 100.
16. Ibid. pp. 110–11.
17. Jean-François Lyotard, *The Postmodern Condition: A Report on Knowledge* (Manchester: Manchester University Press, 1984).
18. Asendorf, *Batteries of Life*, p. 151.
19. Karl Marx, *Grundrisse: Foundations of the Critique of Political Economy* (London: Alan Lane, 1973), p. 534.
20. Hegel, quoted in Asendorf, *Batteries of Life*, p. 3.
21. Wolfgang Schivelbusch, *The Railway Journey: Trains and Travel in the 19th Century* (Oxford: Blackwell, 1980), p. 187.
22. Walter Benjamin, *The Arcades Project* (Cambridge, MA, and London: Harvard University Press, 2002).
23. The Passage de l' Opéra provides the setting for Louis Aragon's seminal surrealist novel *Paris Peasant* (1926).
24. See, for example, Eduard Devrient's account as recorded by Benjamin: 'Rainshowers annoy me, so I gave one the slip in an arcade. There are a great many of these

glass-covered walkways, which often cross through the blocks of buildings and make several branchings, thus affording welcome shortcuts. Here and there they are constructed with great elegance, and in bad weather or after dark, when they are lit up bright as day, they offer promenades – and very popular they are – past rows of glittering shops' (Benjamin, *Arcades Project*, p. 42). The dynamic aspect of the arcade, its function as a 'shortcut' and the mobile vision of the visitor are well illustrated in his description.

25. 'Until 1870, the carriage ruled the streets. On the narrow sidewalks the pedestrian was extremely cramped, and so strolling took place principally in the arcades, which offered protection from bad weather and from the traffic' (ibid. p. 32).

26. Ibid. p. 40.

27. Ibid. p. 60.

28. Ibid. p. 46.

29. Schivelbusch, *Railway Journey*, p. 183.

30. It is worth noting Benjamin's reluctance to cover everything under the panoramic demonstrated by the importance that he places in the differences between arcades and department stores. This is in clear opposition to Schivelbusch who sees no difference at all in the respective visual experiences.

31. Asendorf, *Batteries of Life*, p. 47.

32. There is a similar irony in the opening of Baudelaire's essay 'The Painter of Modern Life': 'The world – and even the world of artists – is full of people who can go to the Louvre, walk rapidly, without so much as a glance, past rows of very interesting, though secondary, pictures, to come to a rapturous halt in front of a Titian or a Raphael – one of those that have been most popularized by the engraver's art; they will go home happy, not a few saying to themselves, "I know my Museum;"' (Charles Baudelaire, *The Painter of Modern Life and Other Essays* [London: Phaidon, 1964], p. 1).

33. For the gendered nature of the *flâneur* see, for example, Janet Wolff, *Feminine Sentences* (Berkeley, CA, and London: University of California Press, 1990); also Anne Friedberg, *Window Shopping: Cinema and the Postmodern* (Berkeley, CA, and London: University of California Press, 1993); Vanessa R. Schwartz, *Spectacular Realities: Early Mass Culture in Fin-de-Siècle Paris* (Berkeley, CA, and London: University of California Press, 1998); Giuliana Bruno, *Atlas of Emotion: Journeys in Art, Architecture, and Film* (London and New York: Verso, 2002).

34. Baudelaire, *Painter of Modern Life*, p. 9.

35. Ibid. p. 11.

36. Walter Benjamin, *Charles Baudelaire: A Lyric Poet in the Era of High Capitalism* (London and New York: Verso, 1992), p. 66.

37. Benjamin, *Arcades Project*, p. 42.

38. Crary, *Techniques of the Observer*, p. 20.

39. Asendorf, *Batteries of Life*, p. 69.

40. Ibid. p. 69.

41. Aaron Scharf offers the following fascinating example of how chronophotography and instantaneous photography were put in the service of governance: 'To the physiological sciences instantaneous photography was of great importance and, in one interesting case, of immediate usefulness. For in their revelations of the complicated mechanism of walking, such photographs helped to solve the difficult problems in effectively designing artificial limbs for the amputees victimized by the American Civil War' (Aaron Scharf, *Art and Photography* [Harmondsworth], p. 182).

42. Another example in which the analysis of body movement is used for direct economic and

political purposes is provided by Mark Seltzer in the figure of the 'Taylorized body', in *Bodies and Machines* (New York and London: Routledge, 1992).

43. Tom Gunning, 'Tracing the individual body: photography, detectives and early cinema', in Leo Charney and Vanessa R. Schwartz (eds), *Cinema and the Invention of Modern Life* (Berkeley, CA, and London: University of California Press, 1995), pp. 15–45.

44. Benjamin, *Charles Baudelaire*.

45. Gunning, 'Tracing the individual body', p. 20.

46. Ibid. p. 41.

47. Michel Foucault, *Discipline and Punish* (London: Alan Lane, 1977); Part 3, Chapter 3, 'Panopticism', is the clearest exposition of the relationship between power and vision in prisons. Also Michel Foucault, *The Birth of the Clinic* (London: Tavistock, 1973); Chapter 7, 'Seeing and Knowing', discusses power, knowledge and vision in the context of medicine and hospitals.

48. See Gilles Deleuze, *Foucault* (London: Athlone Press, 1989), p. 58.

49. Benjamin, *Arcades Project*, p. 405.

50. Ibid. p. 406.

51. Tony Bennett, *The Birth of the Museum: History, Theory, Politics* (London and New York: Routledge, 2005).

52. Ibid. p. 6.

53. Alison Griffiths, '"Journeys for those who can not travel": promenade cinema and the museum life group', *Wide Angle*, 18.3 (1996), pp. 53–76.

54. Schwartz, *Spectacular Realities*, p. 146.

55. Bennet, *Birth of the Museum*, p. 181.

56. Tom Gunning, 'The world as object lesson: Cinema audiences, visual culture and the St. Louis world's fair, 1904', *Film History*, 6.4 (1994), pp. 422–44.

57. Ibid. pp. 424–5.

58. Quoted in Gunning, 'The world as object lesson', p. 426.

59. Gunning, 'The world as object lesson', esp. pp. 430–8.

60. See Schwartz, *Spectacular Realities*; also Freidberg, *Window Shopping*; and Bruno, *Atlas of Emotion*.

61. Christopher Kent, 'Spectacular History as an Ocular Discipline', *Wide Angle*, 18.3 (1996) pp. 1–21, p. 6.

62. Crary, *Techniques of the Observer*, p. 113.

63. The term 'cyclorama' is introduced in the 1880s to describe the experience; this is pointed out by Angela Miller in 'The Panorama, the cinema, and the emergence of the spectacular', *Wide Angle*, 18.2 (1996) pp. 34–69.

64. See, for example, Miller: 'One major drawback in perfecting the illusion of reality in the circular panorama was the absence of motion, the static quality of the panoramic image,' ('Panorama', p. 41); also Schwartz, *Spectacular Realities*, pp. 149–76.

65. Miller, 'Panorama', p. 46.

66. Ibid. p. 38. Benjamin also notes the travelling theme of panoramas in relation to *Le tour du Monde* that operated at the Paris world exhibition of 1900 (*Arcades Project*, p. 533).

67. Schivelbusch, *Railway Journey*.

68. The relationship between the railway and cinema is most explicitly developed in Lynn Kirby, *Parallel Tracks: The Railroad and Silent Cinema* (Exeter: University of Exeter Press, 1997). As she outlines in the Introduction, pp. 2–3: 'As a machine of vision and an instrument for conquering space and time, the train is the mechanical double for the cinema and for transport of the spectator into fiction, fantasy, and dream . . . the railroad was, first of all, a social, perceptual, and ideological paradigm providing early film

spectators with a familiar experience and familiar stories, with an established mode of perception that assisted in instituting the new medium and in constituting its public and its subjects.'

69. Schivelbusch, *Railway Journey*, p. 59.

70. Schivelbusch, *Railway Journey*, gives examples of the intense dislike of railway journeys expressed by Flaubert and Ruskin among others.

71. Schivelbusch, *Railway Journey*, pp. 58–9.

72. Asendorf, *Batteries of Life*, p. 108.

73. Schivelbusch, *Railway Journey*, esp. pp. 57–76.

74. Fourier, quoted in Benjamin, *Arcades Project*, p. 42.

75. Miller, 'Panorama'.

76. Ibid. p. 46.

77. Typical in that respect is the case of E. H. Gombrich who, in his canonical *The Story of Art* (London: Phaidon Press, 1955), uses the term 'Great Revolution' to describe nineteenth-century art trends. There were three 'waves' of a 'Revolution' that culminated in impressionist painting. It is worth quoting his exact words as an explicit demonstration of the kind of romanticism that informs such discourse: 'The history of nineteenth-century painting, as we usually see it today, is really the history of a handful of such sincere men whose integrity of purpose led them to defy convention, not in order to gain notoriety, but so that they might explore new possibilities undreamt of by previous generations' (p. 381).

78. Asendorf, *Batteries of Life*, pp. 80–7.

79. Ibid. p. 82.

80. Adorno, quoted in Asendorf, *Batteries of Life*, p. 95.

81. Asendorf, *Batteries of Life*, p. 92.

82. Crary, *Techniques of the Observer*, pp. 126–7.

83. Asendorf, *Batteries of Life*, pp. 86–7.

84. Crary, *Techniques of the Observer*, p. 113.

85. Scharf, *Art and Photography*, p. 176.

86. Ibid. p. 351.

87. Ibid. p. 209.

88. Sonya Stephens, 'Paris and panoramic vision: *Lieux de mémoire, lieux communs*', *Modern & Contemporary France*, 14.2 (2006), pp. 173–87.

89. Ibid. p. 175.

90. Ibid. p. 185.

91. Gunning, 'World as Object Lesson', p. 427.

92. See Foucault's theorisatision of both subjectivity and power.

93. Richard Abel (ed.), *Encyclopedia of Early Cinema* (Abingdon, Oxon, and New York: Routledge, 2005), pp. 92–5, p. 92.

94. Etymologically 'encyclopaedia' originates from the Greek εγκυκλιος παιδεια 'encyclios paedia' which literally translates as rounded ('cyclos') or complete education.

CHAPTER 2

Movement in film studies

In the opening paragraph of an essay first published in 1977, David Bordwell points out that

> Camera movement in the cinema is one of the most difficult areas for critical analysis. Seen as an alternative to montage, or as a stylistic fingerprint, or the occasion for reverie, camera movement has usually been considered too elusive to be analyzable.[1]

Frustratingly and in a manner that epitomises the way movement has been treated within film studies, the essay devotes very little time to a detailed consideration of movement. Instead it uses the opportunity to offer an exposition of Bordwell's cognitivism and for an early skirmish in the long theoretical battle against the French-inspired psychoanalytic and Althusserian paradigm. As I will demonstrate in the following pages, movement of/in the frame becomes particularly challenging for and generally overlooked in formal analysis and film theory. In the former, movement is almost exclusively discussed in relation to its narrative function; in the latter, it is often treated as a point of departure or a metaphorical figure of secondary importance that enables theorists to elaborate on cinema's relationship with history, society or politics.

This chapter will offer a brief critical survey of some of the influential theoretical traditions, including 'early' formulations (Arnheim, Balázs, Bazin and others), the 'classical paradigm' (Bordwell, Thompson, Staiger), 'suture theory' (Oudart, Dayan, Heath, Bonitzer), the concept of 'a–cinema' (Lyotard) and Deleuze's lengthy investigation of movement and time in cinema. It is a testimony to the hold that nineteenth-century values still have on contemporary sensibilities that such theorisations seem to interface seamlessly with conceptualisations and evaluations of mobile vision discussed in the previous chapter. Within the classical paradigm and suture theory, for example, the overarching narrative dictates the use of movement (reminiscent of the historical and/or narrative trajectories that overlay mobile vision in museums or exhibitions). In Lyotard's 'a–cinema' disorderly and chaotic movements resist the order and cohesion of narrative (as the ceaseless mobility of the *flâneur* resists the conformity of consumerism). In Deleuze the 'movement-image' offers a 'false' experience of time (harking back to debates around the authenticity of the experience of the railway journey or the department store). The binarism that informs these discourses limits our understanding of movement of/in the frame in its own right and in its complex relationship with narrative structures and extra-diegetic referents and fails to address questions of pleasure.

I shall address some of these issues through textual analysis of two films which share a fascination with movement but demonstrate different formal strategies and attitudes towards pleasure. Jean-Luc Godard's *Slow Motion* (*Sauve qui peut* [*La Vie*]), France/Switzerland, 1980) embarks on a comprehensive exploration of cinematic movement, deconstructing in the process the conventions and pleasures of narrative cinema. *Hukkle* (Györky Pálfi, Hungary, 2001), in contrast, relies heavily on the mobile frame in its exploration of village life and indulges lavishly in the pleasures of movement. While the film has a distinctly non-classical feel it also provides a basic narrative structure of a rather orthodox, albeit often confusing, 'who-dune-it' type. By articulating a less polarised relationship between movement, pleasure and narrative, *Hukkle* points towards the possibility of a discourse that evades the strict binarisms of theoretical models.

2.1 THE CLASSICAL PARADIGM

The term 'classical paradigm' is used here in a deliberately over-generalised way. This is in order to foreground a rather surprising consensus among many critics and theorists (from different historical moments and methodological/political perspectives) in identifying and analysing the formal conventions of a 'classical' cinema and in claiming its hegemony. The term 'classical' also points towards the limits and limitations of a body of theoretical and analytical work that has been developed in relation to a specific, bounded and limited object of study. The normative role of such a model has been repeatedly challenged within film studies in the last two decades but several aspects of its fundamental formal analysis maintain their influence. The analysis of movement has the dubious distinction of holding a prominent position among them.

In this section I shall focus primarily on the formalist approach best represented by the influential work of David Bordwell and his collaborations with other scholars such as Kristin Thompson and Janet Staiger, with sporadic references to some earlier critics. While the work of Bordwell et al. is far more systematic, thorough and rigourous than that of Arnheim or Bazin, for example, and has a distinct focus and methodology, it also seems to share some of the basic assumptions made about cinematic movement. My intention in grouping them together is to indicate the long history and longevity of such assumptions. Work produced within a psychoanalytic Althusserian tradition does not vary significantly in terms of its conceptualisation of movement but will be discussed separately in the following section as it raises a rather specific set of issues, primarily around editing and the construction of the viewer as a subject.

The basic premise of the 'classical paradigm' is that the various components of the film form work in a collaborative and self-effacing manner in order to support the overarching narrative structure. The paramount demand for narrative coherence and clarity dictates the use of lighting, framing, sets, camera movement, etc. As Bordwell explains:

> In Hollywood cinema, a specific sort of narrative causality operates as the dominant, making temporal and spatial systems vehicles for it. These systems do not always rest quietly under the sway of narrative logic, but in general the causal dominant creates a marked hierarchy of systems in the classical films.[2]

Within such a model movement is primarily analysed either as a component that completely conforms with and contributes to narrative causality or as an unorthodox convention that somehow signals deviation from the norm. According to Bordwell, a crucial function of the mobile frame since the early days of cinema has been the establishment and maintenance of a centred position for diegetically significant objects within the frame. Most common convention in this respect is reframing, the movement *of* the frame in response to a movement *in* the frame that allows a clear and centred view of the action. In reframing, camera movement is dictated by the narratively significant movement of the characters – tracking and panning are usually employed to that effect, for their ability to provide steady and smooth movement that follows and centres action.[3]

In the classical system the coordination of movement in/of the frame and narrative transitivity is essential. A convention associated with early cinema, where the characters move to more central or frontal positions for no apparent narrative reason, is seen as awkward as it foregrounds the process through which the centred composition of the frame operates.[4] An incessant regulation of movement permeates both performance and camera work. While praising great actors for their 'characteristic melody of movement', Rudolf Arnheim laments the need to tame that signature characteristic in order to meet the narrative demands of a role: 'The common narrative film cannot stress the form qualities of gesture and gait to the same extent since this would not be in keeping with a realistic style of performance.'[5] The classical system dictates a careful management of even the tiniest of movements (the turning of the back to the camera, in the following example) and recognition of its narrative significance:

> Frontality constitutes a very important cue for the viewer. When characters have their backs to us, it is usually an index of their relative unimportance at the moment. George Cukor points out a scene from *Adam's Rib* (1949) in which Katherine Hepburn was turned from the camera: 'That had a meaning: she indicated to the audience that they should look at Judy Holliday.'[6]

The mobility of the frame can also function as commentary on or interpretation of diegetic actions or narrative situations. As numerous textbooks point out, movement of the camera can create a link, a meaningful relationship between objects or characters, enabling spatially dispersed worlds to form a coherent and meaningful whole under the aegis of narrative. In its ability to explore cinematic space and in conjunction with other aspects of the film form such as the *mise-en-scène* or the soundtrack, movement of/in the frame facilitates narrative progression by providing information on a locale or a character. Even purely formal qualities of movement such as direction or speed are often analysed in terms of narrative functions as they produce patterns and motifs that act as meaningful interpretations of the diegesis.[7]

These few examples indicate the discursive tendency of the 'classical paradigm' to consider movement in analytical terms that revolve almost exclusively around its narrative function. Such analysis informs classifications and evaluations. Movement that extensively disentangles itself from the demands of the story is interpreted as a sign of 'otherness', as noted in the example of the 'awkward' use of reframing in early cinema or in the association of 'independent of narrative' movement with experimental, avant-garde or 'art' cinematic practices.[8]

Bordwell et al. do recognise that frame mobility has other dimensions but these are still addressed in terms of their ability to enhance the coherence of the narrative and the plausibility and impact of the diegetic world. Historically, movement of/in the frame has been seen as a foundational aspect of the realist nature of film as a medium.

The heralding of cinema as the most realist form upon its introduction in the late nineteenth century was based on its unique ability to produce moving pictures, in the mobility in and of the frame. But beyond this definitional role, movement of/in the frame creates the possibility to explore and reveal the three-dimensional volume of objects and space and to construct in that way what is considered to be a more realistic representation of the diegetic world. Writing in the 1920s and 1930s Béla Balázs uses the term 'panorama' to describe camera movement, a term that resonates with connotations of nineteenth-century mobile vision. Setting the tone for a key debate in film criticism, Balázs suggests:

> Panoramic shots provide changes without editing. The director does not link together the pictures of objects shot separately, but makes the camera move so that in gliding past the objects it takes pictures of them in the same order as that in which they are aligned in reality, even if this reality is only the reality of a studio set. Thus the sequence is not brought about by editing; it already exists in nature or in the studio and the rhythm and speed of change is not the work of the editor's scissors but of the camera movement which sometimes accompanies someone who is moving along and shows what the person in question sees in passing; sometimes it turns on its heel as it were and records the surrounding objects in a circular sweep. This type of changing shot is called panoramic and modern cinematography is making increasing use of it.[9]

Balázs saw in movement the ability to endow space with a reality of its own and praised the authenticity of such representational strategies. Of course, attaching critical value to the ability of camera movement to represent the world in a more direct, realistic fashion has a long pedigree. Perhaps the most celebrated example is the opposition between the use of camera movement, deep focus photography and long takes and the use of editing most explicitly formulated by André Bazin and accompanied by the belief that realism is not just the ontological essence of cinema but also its aesthetic and moral destiny.[10] Such idealisation of realism is resisted by Bordwell et al. as they discover in the mobile frame's exploration of space and perspective, not the essence of cinema but the ability to produce representations that are more 'vivid', 'solid' and 'three-dimensional' and thus more effective.

Formulating movement's realist function in that way makes it possible for the classical paradigm to embrace without insurmountable contradiction what appears to be realism's diametrical opposite – the spectacular. Movement of/ in the frame enables a thorough visual exploration of expensive and expansive spectacular sets, as in the early examples of *Cabiria* (Giovanni Pastrone, Italy, 1914) and *Intolerance* (D. W. Griffith, USA, 1916) but also by turning the technical virtuosity of movement itself into a spectacle.

Opening-up questions of spectacle and drawing attention to qualities of movement in its own right, however, destabilises the unquestioned dominance of narrative within the classical paradigm. Bordwell recognises that numerous instances of flamboyant use of movement exist throughout the history of cinema but remains anxious to interpret them as either anomalies (exceptions that prove the rule) or imperfections that classicism strives to iron out. Yet the presence of movement that makes itself noticeable beyond and above its narrative function remains problematic. It detracts attention from the narrative and can be an obstacle to clarity, coherence and causality. Bordwell offers the following comment by Robert Mamoulian as indicative of the undesirability of spectacular movement:

> [Camera movement] focuses the attention of the audience on the mechanical rather than upon the story, and confuses instead of clarifies the issue. Unjustified movement is a sign of directorial weakness, rather than strength.[11]

From a slightly different and more subtle perspective, camera movement that attracts attention to itself has the potential to hint towards (or even reveal) the presence of an enunciating apparatus and thus disturb the self-sufficiency, naturalness and transparency of the diegetic world. Overreliance on movement, which openly intervenes in the telling of the story and points towards the identification of the camera as the enunciator, represents a dangerous tightrope that puts in jeopardy the supremacy of narrative. Within the 'classical paradigm', the use of unmotivated, unconventional movement is sporadic and is either symptomatic of the occasional spectacular extravaganza or surfaces within clearly identified and isolated narrative context:

> During the 1940s, for example there was something of a competition to see how complicated and lengthy the cinematographer could make his tracking shots . . . It is probable that such casual splendors offered by the Hollywood film owe a great deal to its mixed parentage in vaudeville, melodrama, and other spectacle centred entertainments. Nevertheless, digressions and flashes of virtuosity remain for the most part motivated by narrative causality . . . or genre . . . If spectacle is not so motivated, its function as artistic motivation will be isolated and intermittent.[12]

Evident in the above is not only the emphasis on curtailing 'deviant' practices regarding movement but also the interpretation of such practices in terms of artistic intentionality and creativity.[13] Arnheim's recognition of the radical possibilities of certain types of movement, as expressed in his 1933 essay on 'The Making of a Film', is indicative of a critical tradition that values 'flashes of virtuosity' despite (or rather because of) its challenge to the classical norm. In his consideration of techniques such as backward, accelerated and slow motion, he observes:

> We shall now discuss certain artifices by means of which reality may be interpreted, but which do not result in images that are superficially

realistic. With a revolving camera the spectator may be made to feel that if he were drunk he would see the world swaying in such a manner. But if he sees a shot in which people, motor-cars, and everything move backward, all illusion of reality is lost. Since nowadays the film artist generally speaking is not allowed to carry his formative ideas beyond the point at which the average spectator might be prevented from thinking that he is watching 'real' events, these admirable camera devices, which do not conform to realism, remain neglected.[14]

What is particularly interesting about Arnheim's argument is that movement is attributed to two distinct (and as it happens conflicting) types of consciousness: that of a diegetic character (whose point of view can authorise deviant movement and is acceptable to the 'average spectator') and that of the 'film artist' (who authors a movement that can disturb the 'illusion of reality'). Within the 'classical paradigm' the adoption of a character's or the camera's point of view is seen not only as an acceptable convention but one that has particular appeal to the viewers:

> It is usually impossible not to see camera movement as a substitute for *our* movement. It is not just that objects swell or shrink; we seem to approach or retreat from them. This is not, of course, the case in a literal sense: We never forget that we are watching a film in a theater. But camera movement provides several powerful cues for a convincing substitute movement. Indeed, so powerful are these cues that filmakers often make camera movements *subjective* – motivated narratively to represent the view through the eyes of a moving character. Narratively subjective or not, the roving camera eye, the mobile framing of the shot, acts as a surrogate for our eye and our attention.[15]

The ability of the immobile spectator to participate in virtual movement (through the processes of primary and secondary identification) is seen by 'apparatus theory' as a fundamental component in the constitution of a unified and powerful subject position for the spectator; as Jean-Louis Baudry put it: 'the mobility of the camera seems to fulfil the most favourable conditions for the manifestation of the "transcendental subject"'.[16] The constitution of such subjectivity is also reminiscent of nineteenth-century practices which often overwrite mobile visual experiences with virtual narrative trajectories that often retrace an (imagined as universal) subject of history.

What informs such formulation is that a form of 'consciousness' or 'will' is inscribed in the act of movement. Movement that does not conform to the demands of narrative causality or the expression of a character's subjective mobile vision is ascribed to the creative intentions of the director. This is an all-pervasive notion that informs critical understanding and posits distinctive patterns of movement of/in the frame as one of the main 'signatures' of the great auteurs, from Ophuls to Hitchcock to Visconti. Even within (what should have been) the anti-auteurist context of Deleuzean post-structuralism, the director's creative agency is revealed through the characteristic use of movement:

> Certain great movements are like a director's signature, which characterise the whole of a film, or even the whole of an oeuvre, but resonate with the relative movement of a particular signed image, or a particular detail in the image.[17]

In contrast, V. F. Perkins brings auteurism closer to the 'classical paradigm' by proposing that the expressive qualities of movement should be used in order to enhance the meaning and the impact of a scene rather than attract attention to themselves. Self-effacement behind a perfectly constructed artifice (which, Perkins suggests, should also capture the essential reality of a situation) is the sign of the great director:

> The position or movement of the camera, however extraordinary, need not affect our belief in the film as record, unless the event itself is falsified – as it is in *The Criminal* and *The Red Desert* – simply in order to create an image. In both these cases the director's effort to point the *meaning* of an action blunts the raw impact of the action itself. The process is self-defeating since it calls attention to the director at the expense of the events *through* which he set out to convey meaning . . . [18]

Despite the fact that it implicitly accepts the hegemony of realist narrative, Perkins's formulation opens up interesting questions that point towards the limitations of the formalist approach. By addressing expressive aspects (Hitchcock's use of movement in *Rope* is praised in these terms: 'while highlighting a particular quality of gesture and movement, the motion of the camera itself takes on that quality')[19] Perkins brings to our attention qualities of movement that remain outside the scope of the 'classical paradigm'.

Within that model the analysis of cinematic movement is purely functionalist concentrating on its effect on cognitive and perceptual processes and resolutely refusing to address or even acknowledge the existence of affective or emotive dimensions. Inevitably questions of pleasure are articulated exclusively in terms of narrative progression, clarity and coherence and/or the vivid representation of the diegetic world; spectacle's importance is restricted to the showcasing of production values. But what pleasures are experienced in movement beyond a purely narrative function? What emotive registers might inform such pleasures? What values are invested in and mobilised by spectacular movement? And what pleasures do they draw upon?

The 'classical paradigm' theorists turn their back to these questions, perhaps as a reaction against approaches that valorise psychic processes in accounts of the cinematic experience or possibly because pleasures and emotions are notoriously problematic for a formalist methodology devoted to an almost scientific, systematic and objective study of cinema. The 'classical paradigm's unwillingness to address aspects of film that go beyond narrative function is clearly expressed by Bordwell in the following dismissal of 'excess':

> But in the first shot of *Rear Window*, we can choose not to construct a story world and instead savor random colors, gestures, and sounds. These 'excessive' elements are utterly unjustified, even by aesthetic motivation. Now this attitude is actually quite difficult to maintain over a long period, since it offers little perceptual and cognitive pay off. The *trouvailles* will never add up . . . whatever its suggestiveness as a critical concept, excess lies outside my concern here. The rest of the book is devoted to the process of narration.[20]

What is startling about this is the mechanistic way in which the experience of pleasure beyond narrative is perceived as a disturbing diversion, in opposition rather than symbiosis with cognitive and perceptual functions, as an additional burden that the spectator is incapable of carrying throughout the film. Bordwell's 'corrective' move, away from unwieldy psychoanalytic models, not only enables an astute, detailed and focused study of production contexts and film-making practices but also leads to a reductive and limiting account of the relationship between films and viewers.

2.2 SUTURE THEORY

A major conceptual limitation of the classical paradigm is that it undertakes an analysis that, restricted as it is to narrative function, leads to a polarised binary structured along the lines of motivated versus unmotivated, normal versus artistic use of movement, a subset of the classical/modernist opposition that dominated film theory in the 1960s, 1970s and 1980s. Of course, such binarism is not the exclusive property of the classical paradigm but also dominates the theoretical discourse of its arch-rival, the French-inspired model that in UK film studies is usually associated with *Screen*. This section focuses on a specific and influential (albeit ephemeral) discursive moment, the appropriation of the psychoanalytic concept of suture in the theorisation of processes of editing and the construction of subject positions for the film spectator. The binarism that informs this body of work leads to a conceptualisation of movement very similar to that emerging from the classical paradigm. Suture theory, however, brings sharply to attention questions in two areas that evaded previous discussion: movement between shots and the virtual mobility of the spectator, the movement of the subject across the succession of shots that make up a film.

The political and critical agenda of such a model is drastically different from that of the classical paradigm as it aims to foreground and deconstruct the formal conventions and to disrupt the pleasures of narrative cinema, instead of asserting their normative power. A prime target for such a critique is continuity editing, the process of a smooth and seamless transition from shot to shot, as a mechanism that covers up the constructed, put-together nature of film and produces an illusion of experiencing the film as an unmediated unfolding of the story (in the words of Benveniste and Metz, as *histoire* rather than *discours*).[21] In classical cinema, continuity (or 'invisible') editing operates through a specific configuration of the symbolic and the imaginary in which the former, while always constructing and controlling the latter, remains largely unnoticeable and is thus rendered transparent. A very similar relationship between the imaginary and the symbolic informs the psychoanalytic concept of suture and it is precisely the ability of the term to describe at once both the process of maintaining the illusion of the unified transparency of the film and of constituting the spectator in unity and cohesion that appealed to film theorists.

In the UK one of the earliest instances of the emergence of suture theory was the publication in *Screen* in 1977 of a special dossier that included Jacques-Alain Miller's psychoanalytic definition of suture, Jean-Pierre Oudart's extension of the concept to cinema and Stephen Heath's commentary on the previous two.[22] Addressing the articulation of shots, and based on Miller's psychoanalysis, Oudart notes the basic disparity between the position from which a film is enunciated and that inscribed in the enunciation itself. This can be best demonstrated on the level of the shot where the position of the camera as enunciator (as the invisible subject of the cinematic look) is distinct from the subjectivity of the diegetic characters depicted. Suture refers to the process whereby that difference, that splitting of the subject, is overcome through a process of stitching together that continuity editing accomplishes. The absence of the position and space that constitutes (but is excluded from) the field of vision, the absent camera that erases the signs of its presence in the pro-filmic event, is continuously denied through a form of editing that in the succession of shots anticipates and presents the excluded space.

> The suture (the abolition of the Absent One and its resurrection in someone) has a dual effect. On the one hand it is essentially retroactive on the level of the signified, since it presides over a semantic exchange between a present field and an imaginary field, representing the field now

occupied by the former – within the more or less rigid framework of the shot/reverse shot. On the other hand, it is anticipatory on the level of the signifier; for just as the present filmic segment was constituted as a signifying unit by the Absent One, that something or someone, replacing it, anticipates on the necessarily 'discrete' nature of the unit whose appearance it announces.[23]

Oudart's formulation indicates why suture became almost synonymous with shot/reverse shot structures of editing – such structures offer the clearest demonstration of how lack and its negation function as the organising principles in continuity editing. However, such generalisation is theoretically simplistic and practically unhelpful in addressing questions of movement. A number of critics, most notably William Rothman,[24] have brought attention to the fact that the shot/reverse shot structure is only one of the many ways in which editing operates. However, one can discern in Oudart's quotation (in the anticipatory rather than the prescriptive activity of the signifier) a more subtle way of accounting for the succession of shots beyond the shot/reverse shot principle, a suggestion taken on board by theorists such as Heath and Daniel Dayan who extended the application of the concept in ways that bring questions of movement back into play.

Heath points out the role played by 'incompleteness' in the process of suture: individual shots are organised around their own negation, productively using incompletion (of which the absence of a point of view that motivates the shot/reverse shot structure is only one example) to bridge the gap with the shot that follows:

The image is never complete in itself . . . and its limit is its address . . . To understand cinema as discourse, the general aim of the Oudart article, is to understand the relation of that address in the movement of the image of and between shots. The realization of cinema as discourse is the production at every moment through the film of a subject address, the specification of the play of incompleteness-completion.[25]

Movement is evoked above in two important ways. First, as produced within the shot in ways that can prefigure at least certain aspects of the shot that follows. In that respect the most obvious example is the action-match convention of continuity editing which utilises movement initiated in one shot as a link with the next which picks up and continues or completes that movement. In that model completion of movement is like an arrow that pierces and stitches a succession of shots together while also moving the narrative forward.

Second, the process of incompleteness-completion has the function to 'carry' the spectator (as a subject position) from shot to shot, scene to scene and sequence to sequence, from the beginning to the end of film. For suture theory the spectator's position motivated by lack and desire is in continuous motion, mobilised in the flow of images, participating in an involuntary and inescapable journey, the unfolding of the film. It is that incessant movement that preserves the unity of the spectator and the cinematic experience, erasing in the process any traces of the workings of the symbolic in the immediacy and transparency of the imaginary.

However, for suture theorists, the constructed nature of film remains a constant threat that needs to be pushed back to invisibility. Dayan suggests that the very presence of the frame and framing, the most obvious function of the symbolic as the arbitrary divider of space, is a constant reminder (and thus a potential denial of the illusion of transparency) of the constructed nature of the viewing experience:

> To *see* the film is *not* to perceive the frame, the camera angle and distance, etc. The space between planes or objects on the screen is perceived as real, hence the viewer may perceive himself (in relation to this space) as fluidity, expansion, elasticity. When the viewer discovers the frame – the first step in reading the film – the triumph of his former *possession* of the images fades out. The viewer discovers that the camera is hiding things, and therefore distrusts it and the frame itself, which he now understands to be arbitrary. He wonders why the frame is what it is. This radically transforms his mode of participation – the unreal space between characters and/or objects is no longer perceived as pleasurable. It is now the space that separates the camera from the characters.[26]

Of course such a threat is counteracted by a plethora of conventions and techniques deployed in classical cinema: by the creation of a self-sufficient framed dramatic space through meticulous composition, for instance, or in the dramatisation of the relationship between on- and off-screen space. It is important to note the role that movement plays in that respect, once again most clearly demonstrated in reframing. In the orchestration of the movement of and in the frame the barrier of the frame is pushed back as the diegetically motivated movement of characters reveals new space overcoming and transcending the limits that framing imposes on on-screen space. The subordination of movement of the frame to that of movement in the frame is in this case instrumental in maintaining the illusion of transparency, foregrounding the imaginary and negating the presence of the symbolic. In that way a powerful illusion is created that the limits of the frame are continuously transcended – while obviously the frame remains constant the progression of the narrative emphasises the diegetically meaningful new space that movement reveals rather than what it leaves behind. In the process, the anxiety around what the 'camera hides' is overtaken and compensated by the pleasures of what the camera reveals. The affect of travel films and road movies (the focus of several chapters of this book) can be partially attributed to the ability to push the limits of the frame further and further, in journeys which reveal a succession of new images, amplified by narratives that see the possibility of movement in itself as an act of freedom, an escape from the constraints of social conventions.

The double role ascribed to movement by suture theory can be therefore summarised as follows: movement of/in the frame is instrumental for the seamless progression of a film, which in turn produces a virtually mobile and unified spectatorial position. Both processes are fundamentally informed by a 'play of incompleteness-completion' that produces the illusion of a film as a self-sufficient totality. As in the case of many of the nineteenth-century technologies of mobile vision, completeness is a crucial value that motivates and informs the experience. For suture theory completeness is a fantasy, an unobtainable state of subjectivity that surfaces through the illusionary power of the classical film. However, the desire for ('real' as opposed to 'false') completeness, in the cinematic experience and in life seems to permeate the discourse.

As Heath comments in relation to Oudart's essay:

> Cinema as discourse, that is, is seen as implicated in loss, the loss of the totality of the image, the loss of the extreme pleasure of absorption in the image as the spectator is set as the subject of the film.[27]

The positioning of the spectator in classical cinema can only provide an illusion of totality – what is lamented by theorists like Oudart is the impossibility of 'real' completeness. It is with this political (and emotional) investment that suture theory mobilises the classical versus modernist binary that pits a cinema that foregrounds the workings of the symbolic against the carefully constructed transparency of the imaginary. The kind of cinema championed by the suture theorists is characterised by deconstructive, self-reflexive practices that not only reveal the apparatus and means of representation but also aim to destroy the dominance of narrative causality and motivation.

The pleasures of such cinema are intellectual, based on and revealing an awareness of the symbolic, a point noted by Pascal Bonitzer in a brilliant if a bit eccentric essay[28] that introduces a special issue of *Film Reader* dedicated to point of view and addressing extensively issues of suture. In Bonitzer's formulation the binary modernist/classical is reworked as 'intellectual versus physical eye' and demonstrated in a comparison between Eisenstein and Hithcock. While the latter is exploring the full 'productivity' of the shot the former is preoccupied with the signifying possibilities of a succession of shots. Significantly, it is movement that provides a clear example of the difference between the two: while Eisenstein 'was systematically unaware, in his theory and practice, of camera movements'[29] Hitchcock delved in them, utilising them to implicate the spectator in complex and powerful manipulations of point of view. For Bonitzer this epitomises the difference in the way that the two opposing cinematic modes address the spectator:

> The spectators are therefore assumed to be subjected differently to the film. The absolute 'changes in the dimension of bodies . . . ' [valued by Eisenstein] of course presuppose an all-powerful master, an absolute master, to bring about these metamorphoses in which physical reality plays no part, but also correlatively, an eye absolutely detached from the metonymy of space, a purely intellectual eye, so to speak. While in the American cinema it is primarily the 'physical' eye that is put to work by the film, that of the spirit being treated as secondary . . . , it is on the contrary this intellectual eye which Eisenstein puts to work.[30]

In the intellectual/physical eye opposition we can discover echoes of the Baudelairean praise of *flânerie* as opposed to the stroll of mobile consumers that values the ability to capture transient movements and to treat them as fragmented indices of modernity's elusive totality rather than as a source of pleasure in their immediacy. Bonitzer's terms reconfigure the classical/modernist binary, that emerges within *Screen* theory as a demand for and blueprint of an alternative cinema, pointing not only towards the romantic sensibility that informs the discourse but also to some of its fundamental paradoxes. While the invisible power of the apparatus is denounced, the all-too-visible power of the 'master's intellectual eye' is embraced – hence the persistence of auteurism within a pro-modernist discourse that otherwise demonstrates a profound distrust for any form of individualism. As in the classical paradigm, the pleasure of/in movement is again denounced, not as unnecessary, messy excess, but as a politically suspect effect of an ideological apparatus that addresses the physical eye of the interpellated spectator.

2.3 LYOTARD AND DELEUZE

A similar, but differently articulated and argued set of binaries, surfaces in the work of the French philosophers Jean-François Lyotard[31] and Gilles Deleuze.[32] Given that the latter has produced a lengthy study of cinema (that has led to the establishment of a 'Deleuzean paradigm' in film studies) while the former only addresses film in one rather short essay, it might appear inappropriate to group the two together in the present section. There are, however, striking similarities and overlaps between the two approaches, especially if one considers in addition to the 'Acinema' essay Lyotard's extensive work on aesthetics.[33] Deleuze and Lyotard both propose that a normal and normative use of movement prevails in cinema which is then contrasted to alternative practices; time occupies a privileged position within their work; they both praise aberrant, disorderly and partial movements; they both propose clear binaries (cinema/acinema and movement-image/time-image) to account for different uses of movement; and they both demonstrate a deep-rooted elitism in the choice of films about which they consider it worth writing.

In Lyotard's formulation movement is subject to a peculiar 'political economy' that distinguishes between a useful and productive kind (movements that conform to the demands of and enhance the tightness and coherence of the narrative) and those 'sterile' movements that assert their own partial independent existence. In complete agreement with the 'classical paradigm', Lyotard suggests that movements of the second type are systematically suppressed and excluded:

> the film produced by an artist working in capitalist industry (and all known industry is capitalist) springs from the effort to eliminate aberrant movements, useless expenditures, differences of pure consumption. The film is composed like a unified and propagating body, a fecund and assembled whole transmitting instead of losing what it carries. The diegesis locks together the synthesis of movements in the temporal order; perspectivist representation does so in the spatial order.[34]

The concept of the 'whole' is crucial for Lyotard as he sees in the subordination of the partial to the total and the elimination of the aberrant not only the basis of the aesthetics of classical cinema but also the modus operandi of normative power in general. Resisting the hegemony of the whole are two 'extreme' uses of movement, 'immobility' and 'excessive movement', which are the defining characteristics of 'acinema' and are evident in experimental films of the time (1970s).[35] Thus Lyotard's analysis boils down to a clear binary between cinema (in which movement is subservient to the demands of narrative causality and purposefulness) and acinema (in which movement exists on its own right beyond and against the control of any narrative conventions).

Deleuze's concepts of the movement- and time-image are ultimately informed by a strikingly similar binary but his overall theorisation is more comprehensive, is used with reference to film history and had a lasting impact on film studies. I do not intend to add to the numerous summaries of the movement- and time-image: they are concepts that have become familiar in film studies through the extensive literature that operates within the Deleuzean paradigm.[36] Instead I shall point out some of the connections between Deleuze and Lyotard, relate some of the critical assumptions informing the former's analytical method to nineteenth-century sensibilities, and conclude this section by referring to some of the problems that his model poses for film studies.

The concept of the 'whole' occupies a central (if rather unclear through deliberate semantic slippage) role in Deleuze's formulation. He sees the cinematic image as operating through changes between parts of a set (*ensemble*) – for example, the movement of a character alters the spatial relationships in and the composition of the frame. However, any change in film involves duration and thus a direct or indirect reference to a whole: 'movement is a mobile section of duration, that is, of the Whole, or of a whole'.[37] A key distinction is implied (but unfortunately never explicitly articulated) between 'whole' and 'Whole'. The translators clarify that the term 'whole' is sometimes used to translate *tout* but also, on other occasions, *ensemble*. The distinction suggested by Deleuze appears to be that 'whole' is used to suggest the totality of an assembled film (the organic sum of its sets and parts) whereas 'Whole' (*tout*) refers to the Real, the experience of 'pure' time that includes but also exceeds the film. The defining characteristic of the movement-image is that it only enables the production of an *ensemble* whereas the time-image offers a privileged experience of the Whole:

> The shot indeed has a unity. It is unity of movement and it embraces a correlative multiplicity which does not contradict it. At the very most it can be said that this unity is caught between two demands: of the whole whose change it expresses throughout the film; of the parts whose displacements within each set and from one set to another it determines. Therefore the whole must renounce its ideality, and become the synthetic whole of the film which is realised in the montage of the parts. And, conversely, the parts must be selected, coordinated, enter into connections and liaisons which, through montage, reconstitute the virtual sequence shot or the analytic whole of cinema.[38]

Like movement in Lyotard's cinema, the movement-image functions as a prime facilitator and aesthetic motor in the production of a coherent and meaningful assembly of parts whose existence is subordinate to the demands of the whole.

Furthermore, within such a model time becomes secondary, an 'indirect representation', purely the product of the synthesis of movement-images, the virtual time of the narrative that they articulate. The time-image, again remarkably similar to Lyotard's acinema, reverses the relationship between time and movement and liberates the parts from the *ensemble*, creating the possibility to experience the Whole:

In modern cinema, by contrast, the time-image is no longer empirical, nor metaphysical; it is 'transcendental' in the sense that Kant gives this word: time is out of joint and presents itself in the pure state. The time-image does not imply the absence of movement (even though it often includes its increased scarcity) but it implies the reversal of the subordination; it is no longer time which is subordinate to movement; it is movement which subordinates itself to time.[39]

Time is not a concern of the 'Acinema' essay but becomes crucial to Lyotard's influential theorisation of the postmodern in the concept of the 'sublime'. In avant-garde art, the sublime appears not in the romantic iconography of vast, inconceivable objects and/or ideas but as an openness of the work to 'happenings', as a form of 'perception "before" perception' in which 'occurrences' are experienced in themselves rather than as meaningful components of traditions or other overarching meta-narratives:

> The avant-gardist effort records the occurrence of a perceivable 'now' as something unpresentable that remains to be presented in the decline of the grand-representational painting . . . the avant-garde does not worry about what happens to the subject, but about *Is it happening?*, a raw state. In this sense it belongs to the esthetic of the sublime.[40]

The avant-garde's ability to record and perceive time as 'now', as a 'raw state', is in fact identical to the defining characteristic of the modernist cinema of the time-image. While Deleuze traces early appearances of the time-image in the unpredictability that he sees as underlying all film-making he fails to develop or consider their function within the movement-image:

> There is always a moment when the cinema meets the unforeseeable or the improvisation, the irreducibility of a present living under the present of narration, and the camera cannot even begin its work without engendering its own improvisations, both as obstacles and as indispensable means. These two themes, the open totality and the event in the course of happening, are part of the profound Bergsonianism of the cinema in general.[41]

Lyotard and Deleuze, writing at about the same time and concerned with philosophical questions regarding the nature and politics of the modern, arrive at identical formulations of movement in cinema, formulations that despite the distinctiveness of approach align movement of/in the frame to binaries similar to those of the classical paradigm and suture theory.

A clear difference, nevertheless, emerges in the historical dimension that informs Deleuze's binary. While in Lyotard cinema and acinema are seen as coexisting tendencies, movement-image and time-image represent two different and successive phases in the history of cinema. Deleuze's willingness to engage with film history (and pre-history) is commendable, but his historicism is perhaps the most serious flaw in his argument. In Deleuze's account cinema is technologically and discursively linked to modernity, as the experiments of Marey and Muybridge, the critique of certain concepts of time in Bergson and the technologies of locomotion are interpreted as indications of a new perception of image (as an analytic of movement between instants) actualised through the movement-image that cinema creates. But while practices such as art or philosophy also envisage a conceptualisation of time that corresponds to the time-image, cinema only embraces it some fifty years after its invention. Deleuze's attempt to justify this time lag is totally unconvincing, suggesting that the true potential of cinema had to 'conceal itself' as all new things have to 'when they begin'. He uses early cinema as an example of such a tendency, as a type of cinema that is not yet a movement-image (and certainly not a time-image, which leaves one wondering what it actually is): 'the view point was fixed, the shot . . . spatial and strictly immobile'.[42] – an account that has been exposed as a reductive overgeneralisation by film historians.[43] Significantly, it is travel cinema, one of the most important and popular genres of early cinema, that offers the most obvious examples of mobile camera and of continuity with other nineteenth-century forms of mobile vision rather than a break, a 'newness' that it feels obliged to conceal.

It is in many ways astonishing that Deleuze's study of the movement-image does not address travel cinema (arguably the most obvious of its manifestations) until the very end of *Cinema 1* where the centrality of the 'voyage' (a term elaborated in *Cinema 2* as *bal(l)ade*, the 'trip'/'ballad') is cited as one of the five characteristics of the emergent time-image. One suspects that overlooking the historical importance of the travel film in the fifty years of movement-image is not simply an oversight but a deliberate reading of film history that ultimately serves to explain the distinctive characteristics of time-image. According to Deleuze,

> These are the five apparent characteristics of the new image: *the dispersive situation, the deliberately weak links, the voyage form, the consciousness of clichés*, the condemnation of the plot. It is the crisis of both the action-image and the American Dream.[44]

The list of characteristics inevitably invites numerous counter-examples. But what is perhaps more important and reveals his Eurocentric elitism is that the range of films that Deleuze examines and which leads him to construct his universal analytical and historical binary is limited to European art films and Hollywood classics.

Deleuze's historical explanation for the emergence of the time-image fares no better. The 'crisis of the American Dream' (a crisis evoked by critics as background context to American films of almost every decade of the twentieth century) is suggested as the main cause of the shattering of the unity between situation (S) and action (A) that undermines the action-image and enables the emergence of the time-image. Once again the exclusive nature of the model and of the historicism that informs the movement-image/time-image binary is startling – not only the films but also the processes of history of any significance are exclusively Euro-American.

Apart from the awkwardness of the travel film to conform to Deleuze's version of film history, the genre also challenges (at least partially) the way that the movement-image is analysed. *Cinema 1* proposes two distinct forms of the action-image: a 'Large Form' (SAS'), in which situation dictates action which in turn modifies situation; and a 'Small Form' (ASA'), in which action 'discloses the situation, a fragment or an aspect of the situation, which triggers off a new action'.[45] The Small/Large binary, however, does not account for travel films whose form involves both terms of the dichotomy. As we will discuss in detail in the following chapters, in the travel film the act of travelling unfolds in parallel with a constantly changing situation/location. While the action reveals new situations it also places the traveller(s) into a receptive position subjected to the changes of situation that the journey brings. In other words a form that is simultaneously of the ASA' and the SAS' kind.

The Deleuzean scheme is informed by an active/passive binary that accounts for the two modes of the action image: in the Large Form the American Dream guides the actions of an individual, whereas in the Small Form individual actions yearn for and achieve the American Dream. In the travel film, however, activity and passivity are bound in a dialectic rather than exclusive relationship: the active traveller is simultaneously passive in his/her openness to the experience of the journey. A similar dialectic was suggested in the previous chapter in relation to the railway journey, which by articulating the experience of the journey as simultaneously active and passive overcomes the binary logic that sees the passenger of the train as a 'parcel'.

To the already long list of binaries that inform Deleuze's (but also Lyotard's) work we must add his conceptualisation of cinematic constructions of time as either 'false' or 'real': whereas the movement-image only enables the presence of the former, the time-image offers us privileged access to the latter. Underlying this binary are assumptions about the nature of spectatorship and subjectivity that are surprisingly informed by nineteenth-century romantic notions regarding authenticity and perception. The time-image first surfaces in Italian neorealism which brought about a 'pure optical situation',[46] an achievement that Deleuze compares to 'the conquering of optical space in painting, with impressionism'. Liberated from the demands of narrative causality the time–image makes possible 'a cinema of the seer and no longer of the agent'. In the latter 'what the viewer perceived . . . was a sensory-motor image in which he took greater or lesser part by identification with the characters'. In contrast, the 'seer' is treated to a dose or a glimpse of the Real: 'He records rather than reacts. He is prey to a vision, pursued by it or pursuing it, rather than engaged in an action.'[47] Within such cinema a new hero emerges:

> A new type of character for a new cinema. It is because what happens to them does not belong to them and only half concerns them, because they know how to extract from the event the part that cannot be reduced to what happens: that part of inexhaustible possibility that constitutes the unbearable, the intolerable, the visionary's part.[48]

For ever lost in *bal(l)ade*, he (for it is always a 'he' for Deleuze) bears more than a passing resemblance to the Baudelairean 'painter of modern life' and the *flâneur*.

2.4 *SLOW MOTION*

Appearing in 1980, a couple of years before the first publication of the *Cinema* books, and featuring heavily in definitions of the time–image, *Slow Motion* is a transitional film[49] situated somewhat awkwardly between the heavily political concerns of *Tout va bien* (Italy/France, 1972), *Letter to Jane* (France, 1972) and *Numéro deux* (France, 1975) and the more aesthetic concerns of *Passion* (France/Switzerland, 1982) and *Prénom Carmen* (France, 1984). It bears the marks of transition: the experimentation with form is at its most explicitly 'didactic', as Godard's 'pedagogy' (a Deleuzean term[50]) shifts from the political to the aesthetic.

Slow Motion is an exploration of the film form with movement as a main focal point. The film's main characters are defined in relation to movement: Denise (Nathalie Baye) is moving out to the country, Isabelle (Isabelle Huppert) to the city to work as a prostitute, whereas Paul Godard (Jacques Dutronc), a film director, remains undecided and thus immobile. Movement has clear narrative dimensions (it pulls apart Paul and Denise) but it is also represented as a physical or mechanical action in the numerous images of Denise cycling and Paul driving, in the human and vehicular traffic in the city and in the busyness of the hotel. Both types of movement are analysed and deconstructed by the film through a number of textual strategies.

The narrative emphasis of the film lies in movements that lead to isolation but also in isolated movements – both titles, the French *Sauve qui peut (La Vie)* and the English *Slow Motion* are equally eloquent in that sense, the former foregrounds solitary and isolated existence as the essence of (bourgeois?) life, the latter indicates a technique that demobilises and scrutinises individual images.

In the film's formal system isolation becomes the product of a thorough disassembling of movements. The relationship between Paul and Denise, the main storyline of the film, is in a state of disintegration symbolically represented by Denise's centrifugal movement rather than dramaturgically investigated in terms of narrative causality and motivation. The breaking apart of the couple is, on the level of narrative, the clearest manifestation of Godard's focus on assembled and disassembled movements. In a telephone call to Paul, Denise describes her dissatisfaction with their relationship in these words: 'They say you need someone to lean on. I wanted someone to lean *with*, see? We've never been together, never leaned on each other. We never leaned together.' In the French dialogue the word *ensemble* is used to refer to the 'leaning together' that she longed for. The decision that togetherness failed brings liberation and Denise's bid for freedom, the movement away from the city and Paul, is enabled by the 'un-coupling', the decomposition of the *ensemble* that leads to independence.

Godard's critique of 'coupled' movements is extensive. The characters are introduced at almost arbitrary points of their lives ('any-instants-whatsoever'), in full motion or *in medias res* as it were, and their present state is isolated, extracted from the continuous flow of time, hardly ever linked to past or future. The soundtrack, and in particular the music, is repeatedly disengaged from the optical track, the extra-diegetic nature of it revealed and played against its absorption by the diegesis. Continuity editing, which involves a combination, a mutual dependency of movement in/between shots, is not the way that *Slow Motion* is put together. Denise's phone call to Paul discussed above, is one of many examples of a process of 'un-stitching' that informs *Slow Motion*'s syntagmatic organisation.[51] Shots of Denise speaking on the phone, engaged in an intense dialogue but with only her words audible, are intercut first with a shot of Paul at his work continuing his activities and then, at the end of the scene, with him on the phone. In that way the editing and the soundtrack 'uncouple' the one-to-one engagement of a dialogue. Even the coherence of the narrative space that Denise occupies is pulled apart as her phone call is interrupted by a parallel conversation with an off-screen character. The scene systematically rips off layer after layer of the spatial and temporal conventions used to produce the assembled unity of classical cinema. In the short video *Scénario de 'Sauve qui peut (La Vie)'* (Jan-Luc Godard, France, 1979), made before the actual film, Godard explicitly rejects the shot/reverse-shot structure which he describes as appropriate for 'ping-pong', a 'match,' a reductive version of dialogue and interaction, and explains that he is interested in 'fading', in creating comparative overlaps between situations rather than matching shots together.

A lengthy scene, in which Isabelle participates in an erotic 'ensemble' with two men and another woman, explores and deconstructs the bringing-together of movement, actions and sounds. The ensemble is signalled as an act of power, of sexual services bought by the man who orchestrates the 'orgy', in which the participants are given specific and detailed instructions on how to move and what to say. The scene exposes the artificiality of the assembled movements and sounds and, by foregrounding the controlling power involved, drains away any pretence of naturalness and pleasure. While this can be read as a clear allusion to the concealment of the orchestration of movement and sound (as well as the shallow pleasures and the power) involved in classical cinema, Deleuze also sees it as a characteristic of the time-image in its exploration and decomposition of the multi-layered cinematic image in that it constitutes

> An 'archaeological' conception almost in Michel Foucault's sense. It is a method that Godard was to inherit, and which he would make the basis of his own pedagogy, his own didacticism: the lessons in things and the lessons in words in *Six fois deux*, up to the famous sequence in *Slow Motion*, where the lesson in things bears on the postures that the client imposes on the whore, and the lesson in words on the phonemes that she has to come out with, the two being quite separate.[52]

The archaeology of *Slow Motion* takes the form of an investigation of cinema, a thorough analytic of the image that, as the previous examples demonstrate, is also a decomposition of the 'couplings' that hold classical films together. Part of this investigation is the relationship between symbolic and imaginary (clearly informed by suture theory as demonstrated by the video of the 'scenario' of the film) which implicates movement of/in the frame. In the video Godard describes the moment of his inspiration for the film as the moment when, while working at the typewriter he noticed (imagined?) the vertical emergence of images intercepting the horizontal line of words. The emergence of an imaginary that defies the workings of the symbolic ('to write standing up, so to speak, with words that follow the image')[53] becomes the central theme of the film, translated in dramaturgic terms into two opposing movements. That of Denise, as she 'dives with her feet together in the opposite direction of meaning', to see 'what happens beyond the border', in the 'unknown', and that of Isabelle who 'will move closer to meaning, in the opposite direction to Denise's movement', coming 'out of darkness.'[54] Denise's movement to the countryside, a move towards the imaginary, and Isabelle's movement to the city, to the symbolic universe of employment, traffic, exchange, commerce and power, form a structuring binary that mobilises contrasting semantic regimes.

Godard's conceptualisation and visualisation of the imaginary in the film is motivated by the political desire (also prominent in suture theory) to escape the tyranny of the symbolic, to liberate experience from the imposition of meaning, to transcend the border and escape the hold of power. While Godard's cinema operates through the dispersal of often ambiguous connotation rather than through heavy symbolism, a cluster of images and movements of a distinctly romantic character emerges, betraying a longing for imaginary completeness. The film offers numerous shots of Denise cycling, mainly in the section marked by the inter-titles '*L'imaginaire*', but also appearing shortly before – perhaps a case of 'words following the image'.[55] The slowing-down and freezing of movement in these shots is perhaps the most memorable and recognisable feature of the film and a distinctive dimension of Godard's analytic. His interest in slow motion and freeze-frame (again explained in the video of the scenario) lies in their ability to 'show the work' in the construction of the image and to explore the image in itself, liberated from narrative function and the demands of realistic time, and enabling the imaginary to emerge out of the straightjacket of the symbolic.

This, nevertheless, points towards the essential utopianism that permeates the fantasy of escaping the rule of the symbolic. The cycling shots are overwhelmingly informed in their construction by cinematic conventions and layers of signifiers infused with symbolic meaning. For example, the second of these shots, 27″ long, opens as a long shot of Denise cycling in a rural road and consists of a panning reframing that ends in a medium shot of Denise against the fuzzy background of trees. The slow motion and freeze-frame that occur at irregular intervals during the shot not only draw attention to Denise's effort, determination and pleasure in her mobility but also place her within a changing frame composition. The final part of the shot where her body dominates the frame against an indeterminate dark green backdrop becomes the paradigmatic opposite to the opening, where the road and the traffic signs are occupying the central part of the frame. In this supposedly isolated movement that, like Denise's flight from the city, aspires to escape meaning, to suspend the symbolic and reveal the imaginary, the overarching narrative trajectory resurfaces in the movement of reframing that organises the *mise-en-scène* around a clear culture/nature binary. This points towards the fundamental paradox, the tragic utopianism, that informs *Slow Motion* as well as the romantic sensibilities of Deleuze, Lyotard and the suture theorists. In the desire to enable the completeness of an unrestricted imaginary the classical function of the symbolic is disassembled only to be reassembled at the master's hands, forming what Godard calls his 'system'. While the aesthetic values of the partial, the indeterminate and the disorderly are evoked, the power of the symbolic re-emerges in the unity and power of profoundly romantic imagery as exemplified by the credits sequence where the irregular, directionless movement of the frame explores a cloudy sky, yet another cliché reference to the sublimity of nature.

Godard is clearly aware of the perseverance of the symbolic in the imagery of his film (Denise makes a passing remark that contrasts landscape to nature) but the disassembling of movements and the deconstruction of conventions can only lead to a reconfiguration rather than a destruction of the hegemony of the symbolic.

Furthermore, *Slow Motion*'s deconstruction is also a parasitic dependency on classical conventions and thus a testimony to their inescapable power. In the closing sequence of the film Godard delivers a double blow to conventions: not only does he kill Paul in a most unconventional fashion (as he lies on the road dying he says 'rather stupidly, I started thinking, I'm not dying, my life hasn't flashed before my eyes') but also reveals, through carefully constructed movement of/in the frame, the actual orchestra that provides the music of the scene. In the video of the scenario, Godard describes that movement of revelation in apocalyptic terms: 'And then the camera pans and we see the orchestra . . . and this will introduce the descent into hell.' The death of Paul (a film director whose second name is Godard) is accompanied by that of the interpellated spectator of classical cinema, swallowed by the *mise-en-abyme* created by the directorial *coup de grâce* that reveals the presence of the symbolic and destroys its unifying, self-effacing and ultimately reassuring function that holds the subject together. Thus, the film completes its disassembling by unstitching the bond between the imaginary and the symbolic that underpins identity.

While Godard's confidence in his cinematic power to initiate 'the descent into hell' is astonishing, perhaps more astonishing is the underlying assumption that what he reveals to the spectator is the actual reality of production (as if there is an actual orchestra off-screen providing the music for every shot of the film). The film's conclusion is not in fact a revelation but itself a representation of the means of representation. Of course this might be in itself aesthetically and politically important but what it ultimately achieves is a mere translation of the symbolic into a figure of the imaginary, a set of movements and objects in the audio-visual field, brought to life through Godard's masterful control of the cinematic apparatus.

Despite its radical ambitions, *Slow Motion* remains trapped within a binary logic that employs deconstruction as a strategy that counteracts the pleasures attached to the conventions of classical cinema. This renders the film contradictory and deeply problematic as the movement of/in the frame has the double function of composition and decomposition, being at once an instrument of exploration, discovery and revelation and at the same time their object. The impossibility of overcoming such contradictions and the inevitable realisation of the inescapable power and control of the symbolic over the imaginary can account for the pessimism that emerged within radical film-making and film criticism in the post-1968 period and culminated in the 1980s. The stakes in both theory and practice became extremely high, an all-or-nothing, life-or-death game, perhaps unintentionally captured by the conclusion with the death of the main character of a film whose 'other' title is 'life' (*La Vie*).

In a famous scene in *Slow Motion*, Paul addresses a group of students (of film?) against a background dominated by the words 'Caïn et Abel, cinéma et vidéo' scribbled on a blackboard behind him. In that image death (in fact murder) emerges as a possible commentary on the feature of film (or video?) very much in line with the generalised European anxiety about the future of cinema so evident in the 1980s.[56]

In the same scene Paul reveals that he makes films 'because he is afraid of doing nothing' (a Marguerite Duras quotation which, as Godard confirms, also represents his view).[57] Comparing that to how Godard sees the inspiration of his film, the character of Denise (who willingly 'moves away from meaning')[58] points towards the deep ambiguity in the negotiation of the relationship between imaginary and symbolic. The images of nature and the sky that are often evoked by the film bear the marks of a nostalgic iconography of the sublime and are effectively signs of the impossibility of the dream of completeness. Interestingly, the way the camera moves in such shots is unsystematic, sometimes disorderly (as in the credits sequence), other times orderly (following the linear progression of tracking). This is perhaps a symptom of the film's uncertainty about movement as an instrument and object of exploration, a hesitation that leaves the film torn between a fantasy of allowing the emergence of disorderly, aimless sterile movements and a 'will to power', the application of an iron grip over the cinematic apparatus.

2.5 *HUKKLE*

The critically acclaimed debut of director György Pálfi offers a close but rather detached observation of life in the fictional Hungarian village of Kesernyés. *Hukkle* explores the movement of and interaction between plants, animals, humans and their surroundings. The process of observation is dramatised in the figure of old Uncle Cseklik (played by Ferenc Bandi, a villager like most of the film's actors) who sits on a bench in front of his house and watches the life of the village unfold while suffering from incurable and permanent hiccups which give the film its title and a natural rhythm. But this is only a fictional representation of the film's extensive observations that include macro and time-lapse photography of natural life, slow motion, X-ray animation as well as elaborate and spectacular camera movements.

The credits sequence sets up the tone and the scope of the film and offers a symbolic 'map', an early announcement of its thematic and stylistic concerns. The credits appear over a series of extreme close-up shots of parts of the body of a slithering snake with its skin brightly lit against a very dark background. The movement of the snake dominates the frame with occasional jerky movements of a reframing camera. Then follows a complex shot starting as an aerial view of the snake curling around stones. The camera first circles around the snake as it moves closer to it and when it approaches ground level it starts a forward and slightly upward movement over the stones and the grass leaving behind the snake, as it gradually reveals a moonlit view of the village from an elevated perspective. The soundtrack (typical of a film that contains no audible dialogue) is of natural sounds of the snake, birds, insects, dogs, the wind and, towards the end of the shot, the first staccato sound of Uncle Cseklik's hiccups.

The sequence encapsulates the association between the natural and human worlds that punctuate the film. The final shot also identifies a visual motif of the film in the elaborate orchestration of movement of and in the frame that links the macro and micro levels, the observation of nature and the presentation of fragments of a narrative concerning the village and its inhabitants. In the connection that the movement creates we can also detect an interpretative perspective on the events and images that will follow: something lethal lurks in the shadows.

The film explores the movements of animals (pigs, moles, bees, fish, cats) and employs a plethora of cinematic techniques (special effects, studio shots, time-lapse, macro lenses) in order to offer rich and powerful images. The villagers are also observed, but whereas the natural world is represented in clear, centred (often through reframing), close-up shots, human movements are often unclear and uncertain. The film's narrative revolves around the relationship between the villagers and more specifically a series of mysterious deaths that decimate the male population. While the plot concerns the humans, nature remains implicated as a narrative agent (lily of the valley provides the murderous poison) and by offering a constant point of reference and a wider context and possible commentary on human actions. There are several scenes of animals devouring or killing other animals, while a scene of a male pig with enormous testicles (the subject of several close-ups) forcing himself on a sow is witnessed silently by a couple, as the wife offers a glass of liqueur to the quietly satisfied husband.

The observational and narrative aspects of the film co-exist in a non-hierarchical relationship. Movements with clear narrative implications (such as the preparation and administration of the poison or the circulation of the phials) are in no way foregrounded and play a rather minor part in the film's broader system of observation and exploration. Characteristic of this tendency is a succession of scenes initiated by the pigs' mating discussed above. The initial steady close ups of the couple watching the pigs are gradually replaced by shots marked by jerky uncertain movements (probably from a handheld camera) that begin to render visible the space between and behind the man and the woman. In a series of similarly mobile shots we see through the windows of the neighbouring house the midwife (Józsefné Rácz) filling with a liquid several phials and marking them with a cross. The view is unclear, with large parts of the frame obscured by obstacles in the foreground (the fence, the window panels) and the camera's movement attempting to negotiate the restricted field of vision and to capture the elusive movements of the woman. The scene that follows takes place in a clothes factory, where many of the women of the village work, and opens with a series of close-ups of the moving mechanical parts of the sewing machines followed by close-ups of the faces of the women. The camera pans around, exploring the factory, and reveals the midwife delivering phials to one of the women. We return to another series of close ups of machinery which include shots of a bottle as it rattles from the operation of the sewing machines and then a tracking shot that follows the line of a central working bench with women sewing on either side of it. This is by far the longest and busiest shot of the scene, lasting 43″ and dominated by the hectic pace and ceaseless movement of the factory with women constantly depositing and lifting up pieces of cloth from the central bench. Twenty-seven seconds into the shot, as the camera continues its steady tracking, a small object (a phial) is passed between two of the workers. The narrative significance of that movement almost vanishes in the context of the frantic activity in the shot and by the refusal of the camera to interrupt or slow down its movement.

This is representative of the determination of the film to reject the priority of narrative structure without nevertheless banishing it from the film altogether. While the classical model is abandoned, narrative trajectories remain evident, part of the rich texture of the film. Like *Slow Motion*, *Hukkle* rejects a linear chain of causality, uncoupling in the process the orderly succession of narrative events. However, the film's disassembling is accompanied by a higher order of synthesis of movements, an extensive orchestration of what constitutes almost an eco-system of movement, a symbiosis of the activities of nature and culture, of narrative transitivity and casual observation. This is perhaps best demonstrated by the soundtrack of the film which is an amalgamation of natural and human sounds, chosen for their ability to provide a rhythm rather than for their authenticity or as subservient to narrative function. Uncle Cseklik's hiccup is particularly suggestive as a sound generated by an involuntary movement of the diaphragm, human in origin but not the product of self-willed and intentional action and in that sense natural.

In *Slow Motion* classical narrative conventions offer the raw material for a thorough exploration of movement that leads to its decomposition and their deconstruction. In *Hukkle* the exploration of movement includes narrative as another component of a world in motion. While *Slow Motion* disassembles the chains of causality and continuity, *Hukkle* creates unexpected and often surprising couplings of movement, inviting in the process imaginative ways of making sense and experiencing movement. Such an inclusive, extensive approach produces multiple connections exploring in parallel the pleasures of movement for its own sake and those of a 'whodunit' narrative structure.

An early scene where a man (János Kovács) getting water from a well encounters a shepherdess (Edit Nagy) is constructed around a series of movements that create a multitude of connections: the movement of the horse-drawn cart on the road linked to the rattling of the water containers it carries; the movement of the various components of machinery in close-up shots coupled together to give a partial account of the man's activities; the movement of the man in and out of frame as he operates the pump; the movement of two ladybirds on the shepherdess and the flight of one of them to the nose of the man who is thus revealed as spying on her; the return of the cart without the man indicating perhaps that something out of order has happened; and finally the movement away of the camera into the thickness of the forest and into the ground before re-emerging in a series of time-lapse images of the blossoming of the lilies of the valley and their subsequent harvesting by the midwife. Importantly, the connections effected through the orchestration of movement are of different orders ranging from mechanical, natural and physical to spatial, emotional and dramaturgical. While the scene on one level offers an observation of the movements of nature and people it also suggests possible (but not definite or fixed) trajectories of narrative causality and motivation. Is this a scene in which a rape is attempted? Can this possibly explain the systematic poisoning of the men of the village? Do subsequent scenes observing the laziness of men and the hard work of women or the pigs' mating belong to the same causal chain?

As the analysis of the credits sequence also demonstrated, the symbiotic relationship of narrative and observation, of the human and the natural, is to a great extent accomplished through movement of/in the frame. As Pálfi repeatedly suggests in the audio commentary provided with the DVD, the film pushed its minimal budget to the limit in the use of elaborate moving shots (crane and tracking shots are used on several occasions) or in sophisticated eye-catching shots of moving objects (notably a striking shot of a low-flying American jet in slow motion and freeze-frame). The eccentricity of the narration and the lack of narrative clarity, however, do not detract from the enjoyment of the film. Critical reception was overwhelmingly favourable and praised the film for its ability to entertain despite its lack of a clear story line: 'What on earth is it all about? I haven't got the foggiest. That didn't stop me being gripped';[59] '*Hukkle* is 75 minutes but even without a plot this bold experiment feels just about right.'[60]

Pálfi in an interview described *Hukkle* as 'an experimental movie that respects the audience'.[61] 'Respect' here might indicate the director's commitment to attempt a type of experimentation that has not as its sole objective to expose and deconstruct narrative but also aspires to explore and exploit the capabilities and the pleasures of cinematic form and technique. Crucially, pleasure in movement and in the richness of the image extends to the self-reflexive, deconstructive moments of the film. An airplane shot of the village changes, through a sharp zoom-out of the lens, into an image of the actual filmstrip on which the shot is printed, only to change again, through another fast zooming-out, into a strip of material, part of a screen partition that covers the door of the village inn that opens up as a man enters. The transformations in the shot offer an eloquent conceptual tool that reveals the film's understanding of itself. This is the only shot in which the geographical location of the village is indicated through an aerial view and bears the promise of a masterful, controlling perspective. That possibility, however, is refused as the shot reveals its construction and turns itself into yet another object in the world that the film observes. The film's ambition appears to be to become part of the observed universe rather than to maintain a detached distance, an ambition that seems to guide the way that some of the complex camera movements were set up. As Pálfi's DVD commentary indicates tracking shots in the forest, for example, had to embrace the technical difficulties that nature posed and work with them rather against them, in effect to mould the film's formal system around the shape of the world that it observes.

At the same time the aerial scene can also be read as an indulgent moment of self-reflexive film-making. This is not only plausible but very much in line with the way Pálfi talks about his film, a final year project in the Budapest Academy of Drama, Film and Television. This particular scene seems to attract negative criticism: 'although eye-catching *coups de cinéma* . . . [but] somewhat jarring when set against *Hukkle*'s generally realistic staging'.[62] It is important however to compare this act of 'showing-off' technical competence and an explicit fascination with the means of representation to *Slow Motion*'s 'showing-up' of the constructed nature of the cinematic image. While in *Hukkle* film-making is a process of pleasurable experimentation, with movements of/in the frame explored and exploited for their ability to please, in *Slow Motion* pleasure is politically suspect, the object of deconstruction and decomposition. To follow Bonitzer's formulation, Godard's approach to film-making is that of the 'intellectual eye' that constructs an overall system within which movement is positioned and analysed, whereas Pálfi's 'physical eye' recognises and embraces the productivity of movement.

This inevitably raises questions of power. It is perhaps a banality to bring up Godard's relationship to women but also unavoidable. While he represents them as being subjected to male power, he also arbitrarily and with rather feeble narrative excuses subjects them to arbitrary nudity and fetishisation (the cow shed scene, the scene where Isabelle's sister is asked to show her breasts).

Godard's awareness of the power involved in the relationship is probable. He dramatises the situation in a number of ways, most obviously through the character of Paul Godard in his crude and exploitative treatment of women, including his own teenage daughter. Despite that, Godard seems to be unable to resist exercising such power himself – his awareness might be a form of confession but is not proof of innocence. There is also the 'symbolic' objectification of both Denise and Isabelle as opposing movements, as embodiments of abstract ideas who give concrete expression to Godard's grand binaries (darkness/meaning, nature/city, etc.) Particularly indicative is the absence of a representation of Isabelle's movement to the city substituted by that of another (anonymous) prostitute suggesting that, in its representational exchange of one prostitute for another, the film reproduces the logic of 'trading' that sets out to criticise. This is an ambiguity evident in many aspects of Godard's cinema and more specifically in his attempt to liberate the imaginary from the hold of the symbolic while at the same time exercising the tightest control of the symbolic imaginable.

Hukkle seems to operate with a rather more relaxed attitude to the symbolic/imaginary relationship in which the former is valued for its ability to produce and reveal the latter. Perhaps an indication of that is Pálfi's respect for the village and the villagers that are not only the object of his film but also participants in its construction. *Hukkle* deploys its cinematic apparatus in an adoptive but ambitious manner that, as the director claims, also 'respects the spectator' in treating them to the pleasures that the interaction between film technique and wonderful setting makes possible. In contrast, *Slow Motion* pursues its desperate quest for completeness in a way that sets out to assault the cinematic apparatus, destroy its pleasures and push the spectator into the 'descent to hell'.

Godard's cinematic practice, like the theoretical discourses of the classical paradigm, suture theory, Lyotard and Deleuze, places movement within a strict and unproductive binary that perceives it either as subordinate to narrative ends or as against them. *Hukkle*, in contrast, brings to attention the intense and varied pleasures involved in movement of/in the frame, pleasures that extend beyond serving narrative transitivity or initiating ideological demystification. By focusing on these 'other' pleasures, *Hukkle*'s conciliatory, symbiotic cinematic practice suggests a methodological trajectory that the following chapters will adapt and develop in some detail. Movement will be examined not for its narrative function but parallel to it. The pleasures of movement are simultaneously re-enforcing and re-enforced, weakening and weakened, modifying and modified by narrative trajectories but also activated by and reliant upon their own peculiar emotive registers and historical sensibilities.

NOTES

1. David Bordwell, 'Camera movement and cinematic space', in Ron Burnett (ed.), *Explorations in Film Theory: Selected Essays from* Ciné-Tracts (Bloomington and Indianapolis: Indiana University Press, 1996), pp. 229–36, at p. 229, first published in *Ciné-Tracts* in 1977.
2. David Bordwell, Janet Staiger and Kristin Thompson, *The Classical Hollywood Cinema: Film Style & Mode of Production to 1960* (London: Routledge, 1994), p. 12. While addressing Hollywood cinema specifically the book claims that classicism is a universal mode established through the global hegemony of the American film industry: 'It is evident that the "ordinary film" of France, Germany, and even Japan and Russia constructed causality, time, and space in ways characteristic of the normal Hollywood film. The accessibility of Hollywood cinema to audiences of different cultures made it a transnational standard. This trend has, of course, continued to the present' (p. 378).
3. This has been extensively commented upon; for example, see Bordwell et al., *Classical Hollywood Cinema*, and also Barry Salt, *Film Style and Technology: History and Analysis* (London: Starword, 1983).
4. Bordwell et al., *Classical Hollywood Cinema*, p. 215.
5. Rudolf Arnheim, *Film as Art* (London: Faber & Faber, 1958), p. 151.
6. Bordwell et al., *Classical Hollywood Cinema*, p. 52.
7. David Bordwell and Kristin Thompson, *Film Art*, 2nd edn, (London: Addison-Wesley, 1980). This is by far the most popular textbook in film studies. There are several later editions with significant parts rewritten and new sections introduced; however, the sections on 'The Mobile Frame' remain virtually identical in the 1980 and 2001 editions.
8. Such tendency is epitomised in the concluding part of the section on 'The Mobile Frame', in Bordwell and Thompson, *Film Art*, where *Wavelength* (Michael Snow, Canada/USA, 1967) and *The Grand Illusion* (Jean Renoir, France, 1937) are used as examples of two opposing uses of the mobile frame: in the latter, 'frame mobility is motivated by larger formal concerns,' whereas in the former movement is 'the principal formal concern' (pp. 129–36).
9. Béla Balázs, *Theory of the Film: Character and Growth of a New Art* (London: Dobson, 1952), p. 139.
10. André Bazin, *What Is Cinema?* (Berkeley, Los Angeles, and London: University of California Press, 1967).
11. Bordwell et al., *Classical Hollywood Cinema*, p. 109.
12. Ibid. p. 21.
13. Interestingly Bordwell continues the argument cited here with a discussion of artistic motivation within the context of specific types of fiction, for example, in sequences that demonstrate the artificiality of other forms of art compared to cinema.
14. Arnheim, *Film as Art*, pp. 97–8.
15. Bordwell and Thompson, *Film Art*, p. 123.
16. Jean-Louis Baudry, 'Ideological effects of the basic cinematographic apparatus', in Leo Braudy and Marshall Cohen (eds), *Film Theory and Criticism: Introductory Readings* (New York & Oxford: Oxford University Press, 1999), pp. 345–55, p. 350.
17. Gilles Deleuze, *Cinema 1: The Movement-Image* (London and New York: Continuum, 2005), p. 22.
18. V. F. Perkins, *Film as Film: Understanding and Judging Movies* (Harmondsworth: Penguin, 1978), p. 86.
19. Ibid. p. 89.
20. David Bordwell, *Narration in the Fiction Film* (London: Routledge, 1990), p. 53.

21. Emile Benveniste's terms used by Christian Metz in his essay 'Story/Discourse (a note on two kinds of voyeurism)', in *Psychoanalysis and the Cinema: The Imaginary Signifier* (Bloomington: Indiana University Press, 1982), pp. 91–7.

22. Jacques-Alain Miller, 'Suture (elements of the logic of the signifier)', Jean-Pierre Oudart, 'Cinema and Suture', Stephen Heath, 'Notes on Suture', *Screen*, 18.4 (Winter 1977/78), pp. 24–34, 35–47, 48–76.

23. Oudart, 'Cinema and Suture', p. 37.

24. William Rothman, 'Against "the system of suture"', in Braudy and Cohen (eds), *Film Theory and Criticism*, pp. 130–6.

25. Stephen Heath, *Questions of Cinema* (London and Basingstoke: Macmillan, 1981), p. 94.

26. Daniel Dayan, 'The tutor-code of classical cinema', in Braudy and Cohen, *Film Theory and Criticism*, pp.118–29, pp. 126–7.

27. Heath, *Questions of Cinema*, p. 89.

28. Pascal Bonitzer, 'Here: the notion of the shot and subject in the cinema', *Film Reader 4* (Evanston, Illinois: Film Division, Northwestern University, 1979), pp.108–19.

29. Ibid. p. 113.

30. Ibid. p. 113.

31. Jean-François Lyotard, 'Acinema', *Wide Angle*, 2.3 (1978), pp. 52–9.

32. Deleuze, *Cinema 1*, and Gilles Deleuze, *Cinema 2: The Time-Image* (Minneapolis: University of Minnesota Press, 1989).

33. See for example, Jean-François Lyotard, 'Presenting the unpresentable: the sublime', *Artforum*, 20.8 (April 1984), pp. 64–9, and 'The sublime and the avant-garde', *Artforum*, 22.8 (April 1982), pp. 36–43.

34. Lyotard, 'Acinema', p. 55.

35. Lyotard does not offer any specific examples other than in-passing references to much earlier works by filmmakers such as Richter and Eggeling, but one can see the relevance of his description to the works of such directors as Warhol, Snow or Brackage.

36. See, for example, David Rodowick, *Gilles Deleuze's Time Machine* (Durham, NC, and London: Duke University Press, 1997); Laura U. Marks, *The Skin of the Film: Intercultural Cinema, Embodiment, and the Senses* (Durham, NC, and London: Duke University Press, 2000); Barbara Kennedy, *Deleuze and Cinema: The Aesthetics of Sensation* (Edinburgh: Edinburgh University Press, 2000); David Martin-Jones, *Deleuze, Cinema and National Identity: Narrative Time in National Contexts* (Edinburgh: Edinburgh University Press, 2006).

37. Deleuze, *Cinema 1*, p. 8.

38. Ibid. p. 28.

39. Deleuze, *Cinema 2*, p. 271.

40. Lyotard, 'Presenting the unpresentable', p. 41.

41. Deleuze, *Cinema 1*, p. 210.

42. Ibid. p. 3.

43. Chapter 3 refers to some of the historical work in the field.

44. Deleuze, *Cinema 1*, p. 214.

45. Ibid. p. 164.

46. It seems that the term can perfectly describe a film like Fernand Léger's *Ballet Mécanique* (France, 1924) which, however, Deleuze places firmly under movement-image (Deleuze, *Cinema 1*, pp. 44–5).

47. Deleuze, *Cinema 2*, pp. 2–3.

48. Ibid. pp. 19–20.

49. For contemporary critics it signaled a 're-appearance' of Godard after years in the film-

making wilderness. See Jill Forbes, 'Jean-Luc Godard: 2 into 3', *Sight and Sound*, 50.1 (1981), pp. 40–5.

50. Deleuze, *Cinema 2*, p. 247; a term borrowed from Serge Daney.

51. The sequence is discussed by Edward Branigan in *Narrative Comprehension and Film* (London and New York: Routledge, 1992), p. 72, as an example of 'unusual depiction of phone conversations'.

52. Ibid. p. 248.

53. *Scénario de 'Sauve qui peut (La Vie)'*.

54. Ibid.

55. Ibid.

56. I have discussed the particular significance of the 1980s and 1990s for European notions of cinéphilia in Dimitris Eleftheriotis, *Popular Cinemas of Europe: Studies of Texts, Contexts and Frameworks* (London and New York: Continuum, 2001), pp. 196–209, and in Dimitris Eleftheriotis, 'Early cinema as child: historical metaphor and European cinephilia in *Lumière & Company*, *Screen*, 46.3 (Autumn 2005), pp. 315–28.

57. 'Jean-Luc Godard . . . for himself: an interview', *Framework*, 13, (Autumn 1980), pp. 8–9, p. 9.

58. *Scénario de 'Sauve qui peut (La Vie)'*.

59. Peter Bradshaw, '*Hukkle*', *The Guardian* (26 November 2004).

60. G. Allen Johnson, '*Hukkle*', *San Francisco Chronicle* (26 March 2004).

61. <http://www.indiewire.com/people/people_031126palfi.html>, accessed on 28 January 2008.

62. Micahel Brooke, '*Hukkle*', *Sight & Sound*, 15.1 (January 2005), p. 52.

CHAPTER 3

Movements of exploration, discovery, revelation

3.1 EXPLORATION, DISCOVERY, REVELATION: CINEMATIC PRACTICES AND HISTORICAL SENSIBILITIES

This chapter will examine movements of exploration, discovery and revelation, in their foundational relationship with sensibilities engendered in nineteenth-century mobile vision and in their reconfigurations in cinematic narratives, most obviously in travel films. As an analytical aid I will propose two particular axes (activity↔passivity and certainty↔uncertainty) along which cinematic movement and corresponding regimes of modern sensibility can be mapped. The first axis refers to the relationship between the camera and the diegetic body of characters and the second to movement of/in the frame that explores, discovers or reveals. Through close textual consideration of movement in *Voyage to Italy* (Roberto Rossellini, Italy, 1954) and *Death in Venice* (Luchino Visconti, Italy/France, 1971) I will illustrate the relevance and analytical value of the two axes. The analysis will point towards the cultural and historical specificity of the emotive registers activated in/by movements of exploration, discovery and revelation.

As a way of summarising and clarifying the argument so far, let us briefly revisit the case of the movement of reframing, perhaps the most obvious demonstration of the hegemony of narrative causality over frame composition and mobility. There is no dispute that a crucial function of the convention is to provide a centred and clear view of action that places the viewer in a position of control and mastery. Nevertheless, every movement of reframing necessarily involves an exploration and discovery of new space and the revelation of new objects and settings, creating a visual experience that exceeds meaning-making processes and cognitive and perceptual functions. As pleasures attached to visual mobility have been a fundamental attraction of early cinema (and of the technologies of vision that preceded and prefigured it) any analysis of movement that focuses exclusively on narrative function and overlooks their formative role in the cinematic experience is inevitably limited and often reductive.

It is worth considering briefly a specific example of analysis of camera movement in its relation to movement in the frame. David Bordwell in *Narration in the Fiction Film* discusses at some length two celebrated shots in Murnau's *Sunrise* (USA, 1927), the movement of the Woman of the City (Margaret Livingston) towards Anses's (George O'Brien) cottage and his subsequent movement to their meeting place by the lake. Bordwell's analysis specifically addresses 'offscreen space' and the role of the 'camera' as a 'schema', the comparison of the two shots aiming to demonstrate how movement of the camera in the latter draws attention to itself and 'heightens the narration's self-consciousness'.[1] While the example serves fully Bordwell's objective and the interpretation is correct, it is also limited. The suggestion that the first shot is 'normal' (as it contains movement with a clear and transparent narrative function), overlooks both the complexity of the shot's semantics and the visual pleasures that it engenders. It is my contention that the spatial exploration and the visual discoveries on offer in the shot are of equal if not greater importance than the narrative determination of space and the creation of an illusion of depth and volume.

In this 52″ panning and tracking shot, the Woman of the City, through her evening stroll in the village, not only acts as a narrative agent (to seduce Anses and destabilise his relationship with Indre [Janet Gaynor]) but also actualises her narrative situation (a 'vacationist', 'lingering' in the village, as the intertitles preceding the scene explain). It is this second narrative dimension that Bordwell completely overlooks and crucially is the one most closely related to pleasures of visual mobility. This is a particularly surprising omission as throughout the film actions of spatial exploration and discovery form major narrative trajectories – emphatically so in its opening which offers a series of spectacular and dynamic images of moving vehicles, trains and boats as a metonymic way of representing the movement out of the city and into the countryside associated with holidays. The introduction culminates in mobile shots of the village from the point of view of an arriving boat carrying holidaymakers. These shots briefly reveal part of the location as the camera movement frustrates the desire for panoramic views by tilting down and limiting the scope to the small harbour.

In that respect the evening stroll of the Woman of the City is not only the prelude to the narratively significant liaison with Anses but also offers an insider's view of the (hitherto unexplored) holiday space, providing thus the visual information teasingly withheld by the preceding shots. The overall quality of movement in the shot (the slow and steady panning and tracking, the Woman's carefree stride and easy pace, the stillness of the other figures in the frame) creates important associations and comparisons not only with the subsequent shot of Anses' movement towards their secret meeting place but also with the hectic, chaotic and overwhelming movement of people and traffic that Anses and Indre discover in their exploration of the city. It is in that respect an integral component of the film's exploration of rural and urban space and of the evaluation of the protagonists' experiences in them.

Furthermore, visual exploration is powerfully inscribed in the shot itself. The shot opens with the static camera positioned just behind an old couple as the Woman emerges from the cottage in the distant background. Her presence is noticed and observed by the two villagers who continue their conversation while directing fleeting glances at the Woman as she moves closer and eventually passes them. The camera pans to the left abandoning the couple and following the Woman who now takes central place in the frame. The panning reframing movement reveals a side road, a man with a horse appearing around the corner and a group of three women sitting outside their house. The villagers seem to register her presence but she walks straight past oblivious to their existence. The camera completes the panning movement and begins to track behind the Woman, revealing in front of her another house. As she passes by, she turns around twice to explore the domestic activities through well-lit windows. Her movement and that of the camera stop when she arrives opposite yet another window, that of the cottage where Anses and Indre live.

In that way a relay of acts of observation is constructed with the Woman established as both the subject and the object of visual exploration. This is not merely restricted to diegetic exchanges of looks but extends to the space that the camera movement itself reveals and is presented to the spectatorial gaze as a sequence of semi-autonomous *tableaux vivant*: the old couple, the man and the horse, the three women, the occupants of the house. The assistance of lighting is enlisted to that effect as it organises the composition by highlighting configurations of bodies against the dark backdrop of the evening village streets. The evening stroll of the Woman enables the presentation of a succession of vignettes of village life with very limited (if any) narrative significance. Thus, the careful orchestration of movement of/in the frame, aided by composition and lighting, provides a comprehensive and pleasurable visual exploration of 'life in the village' that runs parallel to what Bordwell identifies as the shot's main narrative function:

> the camera movement plays down the figure and plays up our anticipation of her destination . . . Thus the shot, which begins with her leaving one cottage, points us toward the end point of her walk, creating a mild crescendo . . . [2]

Unfolding in between the starting and ending points of narrative causality and transitivity, the steady linear movement of the Woman and the camera incrementally discovers and reveals the space of the village. The textual organisation of the spatial exploration (the progressive revelation of distinct but interrelated tableaux enabled by the Woman's movement) in conjunction with the narrative situation (travelling, holidays, the carefree stroll in a new space) establishes clear connections between the pleasures activated by the shot's movement and those of nineteenth-century mobile vision. Such pleasures are informed by emotive registers with genealogies rooted in modern sensibilities, following in the footsteps of the visual explorations afforded by the window displays in Parisian arcades, the exotic vistas of moving panoramas, the organised walks around 'museum life groups'[3] and the simulated journeys around the world.

This brief analysis of an instance of reframing brings to attention the 'parallel universe' of pleasures that co-exist with those of the narrative. On a more general level, in conjunction with any other function that it might have, movement of/in the frame tends to alter the representation of space and, thus, to initiate a process of spatial exploration whose presence is felt at varying degrees depending on the type and organisation of shot and movement. It can be of small significance in cases, for example, where very little changes in the represented configuration of space or when only a limited view of the revealed new space is afforded. Alternatively, as in the mobility of the evening stroll in *Sunrise*, spatial exploration can take central stage and fully indulge in the display of eye-catching views or lead to significant revelations. The innate ability of movement of/in the frame to activate spatial exploration is always moderated by other aspects of the film form such as *mise-en-scène*, performance, framing, sound, editing and narrative, but that should not reduce its significance.

Furthermore, as the example from *Sunrise* demonstrates, the cinematic pleasures of movements of exploration, discovery and revelation connect on an archaeological level with modern sensibilities. In his ground-breaking work on entertainment and utopia in film musicals, Richard Dyer offers a strikingly similar formulation in his proposal that cinematic pleasures must be understood in their double relationship to forms of textual organisation and historically specific regimes of sensibility.[4] In his model, sensibilities operate as 'effective codes' that use both 'representational and non-representational signs' ('colour, texture, movement, rhythm, melody, camerawork').[5] The argument is motivated by his frustration with contemporary film theory and criticism that privilege 'representational' signs and overlook the significance and effects of 'non-representational' aspects of the film form:

One the one hand, the *mise en scène* approach (at least as classically developed in *Movie*) tends to treat the non-representational as a function of the representational, simply a way of bringing out, emphasising, aspects of plot, character, situation, without signification in their own right. On the other hand semiotics has been concerned with the codification of the representational.[6]

Dyer overcomes the impasse (and thus points out to methodological possibilities that extend beyond his specific considerations) by linking the textual relationship between narrative and numbers to the activation of utopian sensibilities that are inscribed in the emotive registers of film musicals. Such emotive registers, Dyer notes, are fundamentally historical as they are informed by long and complex processes of interaction between forms and practices of entertainment and social and cultural values.

The present work not only shares Dyer's frustration with the discursive subordination of the non-representational but also his central thesis. This makes possible an analysis of the pleasures that movements of exploration, discovery and revelation encode and activate that is informed by the historical sensibilities of mobile vision. This is further supported by scholarship on early travel cinema that details the multi-stranded and far-reaching connections between the emerging cinematic form and nineteenth-century technologies of vision. It is not my intention to discuss such work extensively at this point (this will take place later), but to highlight some of its key findings and their methodological implications. Early travel cinema has been signalled out here not only because it offers the most obvious connection between cinematic and pre-cinematic mobile vision but also because it is in that generic context that frame mobility most regularly emerges, establishing and developing all-pervasive conventions and techniques.[7]

Research in the field outlines a dialectic process of adoption and adaptation whereby narrative conventions, subject positions, practices and techniques of movement, and pleasures engendered in nineteenth-century technologies of mobile vision are assimilated into the formal system of early cinema.[8] Tom Gunning's work, for example, points out that the promotional material of early travel films often uses the term 'panoramic' in the description of shots that involve either panning, as a camera movement that scans the landscape, or a camera mounted on mobile vehicles that provides views of a 'moving' landscape.[9] In that way the familiarity of audiences with various panoramic spectacles is summoned, utilising movement and travel as a bridge that connects the new medium to its popular contemporaries and precursors. Other theorists and historians investigate the relationship between the nineteenth-century illustrated travel lectures and early travel films. X. Theodore Barber, in his examination of the 'shows' of celebrated lecturers such as John L. Stoddard and E. Burton Holmes, discovers 'narrative strategies subsequently adopted and developed in cinema'.[10] The transparencies and photographs used in travel lectures were organised around clear linear narrative trajectories, structured around the itinerary of the journey, and centralised the body of the lecturer/traveller as the agent of movement and the guarantor of the authenticity of the experience. The material was presented in ways overtly informed by narrative conventions such as suspense (withholding key events or images for maximum effect) or the use of climaxes to conclude dramatic 'episodes', and focused extensively on scenes and views that were deemed to be particularly spectacular.

Charles Musser, in contrast, identifies the 'viewer-as passenger' convention as a prominent feature of travel lectures:

> As travel lectures became more elaborate, they often placed the traveller/ photographer within the space constructed by a narrative. Thus spatial relations between the slides – such as cut-ins, exterior/interior, point-of-view, and shot/counter-shot – became codified within the framework of the travel genre . . . The later travel lectures of John Stoddard, who was active in the 1880s and 1890s, included shots of the traveller/lecturer in his railway car that were intercut with scenes of the countryside through which he was travelling. In some instances, the spectator saw Stoddard in his car, then saw what he had seen out the window.[11]

This not only suggests an implied virtual editing system that becomes actualised in travel cinema but also strongly suggests that the act of travelling itself becomes embodied in a textually inscribed subject position that is detachable from the actual experience. What gives the travel lecture its power to entertain is the ability to recreate the experience and thus necessarily to disembody it from its unique and unrepeatable reality. In a slightly different context, Lauren Rabinovitz points out the continuity of amusement park 'movie rides', such as *Hale's Tours*, with the rides involving virtual voyages in World Fairs and Expositions.[12] The experience of mobile views by an immobile spectator constitutes a 'complex interplay between embodied forms of subjectivity and arguments of disembodiment'[13] that defines the spectatorial experience of travel cinema.

The dialectic of embodiment/disembodiment that both Musser and Rabinovitz propose is further explored by Rick Altman in his analysis of the textual and industrial process of separation of the travel lecturer/explorer from the object of his/her explorations.[14] Altman focuses on a period when the invention of cinema enables lecturers to include moving pictures in their shows. He describes a transition from the lecturer initially functioning as the organising agent of the flow of still images to the interim introduction of short films as an integral part of the show that leads to the eventual emergence of self-standing travel films. In this process of transformation the figure of the lecturer survives for a short period, as expedition films were often introduced by the explorer himself or herself, ultimately to be assigned to history by the mid-1910s as films eventually are 'severed from the live stage, turned instead into commodities expected to stand by themselves'.[15]

Thus travel films (either fictional or 'travelogues') absorb in their textual (and indeed industrial) organisation the nineteenth-century figure of the traveller/lecturer as a subject position. In their narratives, spatial exploration is inscribed both in the actions of the mobile protagonists and in the extraordinary ability of the cinematic apparatus to reveal the world. The formal conventions and textual strategies of travel films are therefore genealogically contingent with nineteenth-century articulations of movement, vision and subjectivity. Narrative trajectories, patterns of editing, point-of-view structures, spectatorial positions and, importantly, movements of and in the frame, while uniquely employed in the specific textual strategies of the new medium of film, are also informed by 'effective codes' emerging from culturally and historically specific regimes of sensibility. We are now in a position to offer an initial mapping of such effective codes as they emerge from nineteenth-century mobile vision and in cinematic movements of exploration, discovery and revelation.

In the first chapter we noted the prevalence of two types of mobile vision, a linear movement that explores, discovers and reveals space and a circular movement that circumscribes an object or surveys a scene. These are inter-related, working with and reinforcing each other, embodied in mobile subjects and often guided by specific narrative trajectories or historical frameworks. They are assimilated in early travel cinema in movements of panning and tracking (and their countless combinations) and are an indispensable instrument in the construction of spatial explorations.[16]

Nineteenth-century technologies of mobile vision construct a specific kind of subjectivity that combines pleasure with the acquisition of knowledge, entertainment with self-improvement. Such positions (embedded within modern institutions and practices such as museums, panoramas and railway journeys) are informed by broader moral, political and cultural discourses that place value in the mobile explorations of travelling and the experiences that they offer. Travel films rework such pleasures and values through their stories, in their *repertoire* of characters and in their moral universe, in the construction of spectatorial positions and in the mobility of the frame. Travelling becomes instrumental in the construction and actualisation of this peculiarly Western modern subjectivity: as an essential tool of scientific discovery and the extension of metropolitan imperial power on a macro level, as a way to complete one's education and acquire valuable cultural capital on a personal level. Thus, mobility becomes indispensable not only in the pursuits of pleasure and knowledge but also in providing access to social and cultural power. As the celebrated traveller/lecturer E. Burton Holmes pronounced: 'to travel is to possess the world'.[17] Power, pleasure and knowledge are intertwined within cinematic journeys that place their protagonists in processes of spatial exploration and captivate the spectator with the spectacular discoveries and revelations of the mobile frame.

But while movement becomes instrumental in modern quests for knowledge, pleasure and self-accomplishment, it is also fundamental in processes of mass transportation, popular entertainment and consumerism, igniting anxieties around questions of agency. These are expressed in a peculiar dialectic between activity and passivity that permeates the experience of mobile vision and places the traveller in a position of being simultaneously an active observer and a 'parcel', both explorer and explored. Journeys not only lead to the discovery of startling new places and experiences but also propel towards self-discovery, as the travelling reveals new worlds and well-hidden emotions, memories or traumas, placing the traveller in a position of control over movement while being subjected to it.

As the movement towards increasing knowledge endlessly replaces the old with the new, further anxieties around mastery and control arise. The dizzying experiences of mobile vision challenge established and traditional certainties as they push travellers out of the stability of the home and into unknown and uncertain territories. The infinite variations of this dialectics are liberally exploited by the narratives of travel films, drawing on the extensive dramatic possibilities opened up by the incessant negotiations of the pleasures and anxieties of movement.[18]

As noted in the first chapter, fantasies of complete knowledge and/or self-exploration inform the construction and perception of movement in nineteenth-century popular technologies of vision. Travel films in their narratives of (self-)discovery and movements of exploration reverberate with such fantasies, often organising their journeys and the mobility of the frame around meaningful destinations, trajectories of ultimate revelation or processes of transformation. Mobility in that context promises not only a complete perception and understanding of the world (the 'panoramic') but also a total experience, a thorough exploration and a full revelation of the emotional, spiritual or psychological secrets of life.

3.2 ANALYTICS OF EXPLORATION, DISCOVERY, REVELATION

In cinematic journeys the mobility of the frame is substantially employed to construct and represent movements of exploration, discovery and revelation. As the previous discussion demonstrates, the emotive registers that inform the salient techniques, shape the form and the aesthetics and modulate the uses of such movements are genealogically linked to modern sensibilities. The values, desires, fantasies, anxieties and pleasures that surface in nineteenth-century mobile vision form a matrix of sensibilities (an 'effective code' in Dyer's words) that will be used to guide the analysis of the cluster of cinematic movements under consideration in the present chapter. In the following sections and chapters, movements of exploration, discovery and exploration will be addressed in terms of four interrelated textual and contextual levels:

1. Within shots we will consider the movement of and in the frame in relation to each other and to other aspects of the film form.
2. In a succession of shots, forming a segment, scene, sequence or the totality of a film, we will analyse the spatial transformations engendered through editing, the syntagmatic management of movement and the organisation of frame mobility in transitions from shot to shot.
3. We will identify the formal, moral and ideological trajectories articulated in overarching narratives that orchestrate several aspects of the previous two levels. Travel films provide the broad generic framework for the main case studies that will be discussed.
4. The analysis undertaken in all the previous levels will be contextualised with consideration of the history and geo-politics of movements of people. On this level we will identify pertinent socio-political and cultural practices and processes (such as travelling, tourism, displacement, exile and diaspora) that provide the historical referent for travel films and shape their emotive register.

On all levels, exploration, discovery and revelation form a cluster of genealogically and formally connected but not identical types of movement. Exploration (often linear and systematic) is an organised methodical process that unfolds over time and involves a series of discoveries and revelations. The evening stroll in *Sunrise* is a visual exploration of the village that leads to the discovery of several *tableaux vivant* and culminates in the revelation of the ultimate destination of the character's movement. As the example demonstrates, discovery is expressed by signalling out significant objects that become distinct milestones within a more general context of exploration and can ultimately lead to narratively significant revelations. Thus, revelation often emerges as the climactic outcome of exploration, is usually dramatically charged and can alter the direction of narrative trajectories and/or lead to further exploration and discovery.

Given the key function of knowledge acquisition in mobile vision, it is not surprising that there is a homology between representations of scientific processes and movements of exploration, discovery and revelation. Slow, steady movements that explore space, discover significant objects and lead to dramatic revelations seem to echo a popular epistemology that perceives science as a long forward progression, marked by key discoveries and inventions that gradually and incrementally unlock the mysteries of the world. Cinematic movements with even pace and clear sense of direction (most obviously tracking and panning shots) constitute assured and confident visual explorations, offering comfortable and spectacular views.

In contrast, fast and unsettling movement that reveals a key dramatic object or narrative situation is akin to inspirational moments of scientific 'revolution' when discoveries alter the course of knowledge. Movement has the potential to 'shock', constructing a dramatic revelation that destabilises certainty and revises narrative trajectories, challenging the perception of characters and/or spectatorial positions.

These two possibilities of movements of exploration and tropes of revelation seem to replicate the crucial order/disorder binary that underpins theoretical classifications such as classical/modernist, discussed in the previous chapter. It is important, however, to see them merely as formal conventions employed by a wide range of films for their ability to solicit the desired affect. The catastrophic and eye-opening shock of the new and the steady linear progression of accumulated knowledge, far from being mutually exclusive, are firmly embedded in modern epistemology and sensibility. Let us demonstrate the point with a brief discussion of examples from two apparently radically different films.

We have already noted in relation to *Slow Motion* how the concluding tracking shot of the film, which discovers an orchestra as the source of the film's musical soundtrack, is seen by Godard as initiating a 'descent into hell' in its dramatic revelation of the cinematic apparatus. A celebrated shot in *Tout va bien* (Jean-Luc Godard, France/Italy, 1972) is used to a similar effect. During industrial upheaval in a factory in post-1968 France, the two main characters, Jacques (Yves Montand) and Suzanne (Jane Fonda), are in the manager's (Vittorio Caprioli) office. Their conversation is framed in a conventional long shot with all three centred and clearly positioned. The shot is suddenly and unexpectedly interrupted and replaced by an extreme long shot that reveals them as occupying one particular 'box' in the factory which is now unmasked as a film set.

This sharply brings to attention the missing 'fourth wall' (the absent space of the 'camera') that typifies the illusionary nature of classical cinematic constructions of narrative space. Thus, an abrupt displacement of the camera's position through editing creates a 'shock' that reveals the illusionary nature of the apparatus and challenges 'passive' spectatorial positioning.

This 'pulling back' of the camera has an effect that is akin both to Brechtian distantiation (in itself a term suggestive of movement that creates distance and opens up perception) and to the Althusserian 'knowledge-effect'[19] (in which the revelation of one's positioning within an ideological apparatus can dispel interpellation and lead to 'real' knowledge). In this example, movement between shots becomes an instrument of enhanced vision that challenges the limits and expands the scope of spectatorial perception. Ironically, the 'revealing' shot continues with a parallel tracking to the right and then back to the left that offers one of the most pleasurable moments in the film in the panoramic exploration of the factory, unwittingly restoring the spectator in a position of sovereign and superior vision.

In *Far from Heaven* (Todd Haynes, USA/France, 2002) the shock-inducing effect of movement is used in a more conventional manner in the scene where Cathy (Suzanne Moore) takes the decision to surprise her (gay but in the closet) husband Frank (Dennis Quaid) by bringing dinner to his office where he is working late. The scene opens with four shots that follow Cathy's movement as she enters the building and heads for Frank's office. Traversing empty, dark corridors and rooms she eventually arrives in front of his office and the fifth shot comes from her exploring point of view, a close up of a patch of light emerging under his door. The sixth shot is the reverse shot with Cathy smiling and looking reassured and the seventh is a repetition of the fifth, but eventually her shoes appear in the frame and then the camera tilts upwards towards her face. The eighth shot provides the climax of her movement and starts with a medium shot of her entering the room before the camera performs a very fast right pan (to dramatic cords of the theme tune) to reveal Frank kissing a man. The moment of revelation is constructed as the conclusion of a spatial exploration with Cathy standing still (frozen from the shock?) and the camera mobilised in a fast and dizzying movement. Thus Cathy's agency is doubly undermined as her immobility is contrasted with the extreme agility of the apparatus which takes decisive control of the point-of-view system.

Several other uses of movement in this series of shots create a sense of increasing uncertainty that anticipates the 'shocking discovery'.[20] The panning and tracking of the camera in the first four shots is relatively detached from Cathy, rarely offering centred and smooth reframing movements. In the first shot her entrance in the frame is very fast with her body too close to the camera constructing a blurred image until the eventual pan to the left offers a clear view of her. The second shot pans left in apparent coordination with her movement but as she exits the frame the camera lingers for a while on the empty space hesitating to follow her action. The third shot starts with the camera immobile and Cathy moving further and further away towards Frank's office but suddenly begins to track behind her at a pace much faster than hers. In all instances the organisation of movement questions Cathy's agency as the camera's relative independence creates a distance from which to observe her. Thus, Cathy's movement of exploration becomes the object of the exploring camera. This is reinforced by the point-of-view structure of subsequent shots: while the seventh shot replicates the fifth (which comes from her point of view) it places her in the field of vision and the camera subjects her to a fast-searching movement. The final revealing shot is particularly interesting as the fast camera movement that starts from her face functions as a shift in point of view that creates a semantic and emotive connection between Cathy and her discovery. Throughout the segment Cathy's act of exploration is systematically undermined as frame mobility destabilises her agency, patterns of editing in conjunction with camera movement usurp the exploratory prowess of her point of view and the narrative situation leaves her subjected to an unwanted discovery and a painful revelation.

The examples from *Tout va bien* and *Far from Heaven* demonstrate different ways in which films can employ movements of exploration, discovery and revelation to challenge the status quo of perception, to expose its limitations and to replace it with new (in both cases 'shocking') forms of knowledge. They both deploy a combination of orderly and disorderly movements demonstrating the representational capabilities of that tension but crippling its classificatory potential. Nevertheless, what in both cases underpins the movements of exploration, discovery and revelation is a dynamic and dialectical relationship between processes and positions of certainty and uncertainty, activity and passivity. Cathy's discovery comes as the climax of an increasingly uncertain spatial exploration in which the frame mobility erodes her agency.

A theoretical and political discourse overwrites the terms in the case of *Tout va bien*. The perceived passivity of the spectator is challenged by the distancing editing that shatters the (false) certainty of the image as reality. In the tracking shot that follows, however, a (by now) active spectator, with a newly found and qualitatively superior certainty, is generously treated to a lavish visual exploration of the film set. The possibility that the alignment with a distancing apparatus that creates complete and masterful vision can in itself produce a passive spectator (subjected to the skills of a great auteur) is indicative of the complex dialectics of the relationship.

Oppositions such as order/disorder, slow/fast or linear/circular (employed in the examples discussed) play a key part in the way films construct and represent movement, whereas the dialectics of certainty↔uncertainty and activity↔passivity constitute broader axes that map the emotive registers that inform frame mobility. While descriptive binaries provide valuable tools in understanding the qualities of cinematic movement it is the dynamics of the two axes that will guide our analysis.

3.3 CERTAINTY↔UNCERTAINTY: *VOYAGE TO ITALY*

But the true voyagers are those who move
Simply to move – like lost balloons . . .
. . . Through the unknown we'll find the *new*.

(Charles Baudelaire, *The Voyage*).[21]

Movement of/in the frame necessarily involves transformations of the configuration of cinematic space, revising in the process viewing positions and narrative situations. Frame mobility has the potential to confirm and enhance spatial information placing viewers and/or characters in positions of control and mastery or, alternatively, it can undermine such positions by initiating unclear, contradictory, destabilising or 'catastrophic' spatial explorations, discoveries and revelations. These two possibilities define two extremities, the limits of the continuum that constitutes the axis 'certainty↔uncertainty' along which qualities, values and affects of movement of/in the frame can be plotted and analysed. Within such a continuum certainty and uncertainty are not mutually exclusive binary opposites, nor rigid classificatory labels, but poles that shape the field of a dynamic interaction.

The dialectics of the relationship between certainty and uncertainty, the known and the unknown, *cogito* and the unthought, shape the very foundation of Western epistemology and permeate the political and cultural sensibilities of modernity. The hyperbolic Cartesian doubt that discards accepted wisdom and delves into a profound uncertainty in order to establish a new basis for knowledge of the self and the world not only typifies modern attitudes to knowledge but establishes the very possibilities of its emergence.[22] Uncertainty, commonly perceived as the cause of intense anxiety, is also a valuable motivating force and a crucial cognitive instrument in the quest for new knowledge.

Within modernity certainties are always ephemeral – persistent certainties, intransigent ideas and stubborn values are often perceived as obstacles in processes of social progress and self-fulfilment. Recognising the value of uncertainty and of destabilising, belief-shattering discoveries, Benjamin suggested that 'knowledge comes only in lightning flashes',[23] that it constitutes an unpredictable, perpetually moving, constantly mutating, perceptual and epistemological field. The replacement of the old with the new, the mobility of transformation and change, becomes the motor of history and the essence of modernity, an idea that Marx and Engels famously expressed in their *Manifesto of the Communist Party*:

> Constant revolutionizing of production, uninterrupted disturbance of all social conditions, everlasting uncertainty and agitation distinguish the bourgeois epoch from all earlier ones. All fixed, fast frozen relations, with their train of ancient and venerable prejudices and opinions, are swept away, all new-formed ones become antiquated before they can ossify. All that is solid melts into air, all that is holy is profaned, and man is at last compelled to face with sober senses his real condition of life and his relations with his kind.[24]

The destabilising effect of uncertainty is not only an inevitable and integral part of modernity but also instrumental in the acquisition of 'real' knowledge

– that is a sentiment that extends beyond epistemology and political activism and engulfs every aspect of modern life and emphatically so the arts. Rimbaud's desperate and perpetual fleeing movement, in 'drunken boats', in dark and dangerous streets and remote lands, is the archetype of a modern sensibility that values rebellion against the certainties of bourgeois life. Immersion into uncertainty, the subjugation to uncontrollable experiences to the extent of self-destruction, becomes for Rimbaud a fundamental pre-condition for art and poetry that strives to reach 'the unknown by the derangement of all senses'.[25] Travelling, the movement away from the certainty of one's habitat and culture, becomes a privileged form in modern processes of self-exploration. The revelation of new and qualitatively superior forms of knowledge, the discovery of new sources of inspiration and fresh means of expression, are the rewards that the artist (and the ordinary traveller alike) can reap by surrendering to the uncertain environments and unforeseeable encounters that journeys set in motion. Cees Nooteboom, a celebrated traveller and writer of our era, standing 'at the edge of the Sahara', eloquently expresses the fascination with the unknown, the unclear, the incomprehensible:

> The same old sense of excitement. Seeing things you do not understand, signs you cannot read, a language you cannot fathom, a religion you do not have any real conception of, a landscape which rebuffs, lives you could not share . . . The shock of the wholly unknown is one of gentle sensuality . . . And that makes this type of travel a pleasant sort of void, a state of zero-gravity in which, although the self does not lose all significance, a good deal does get written off . . . [26]

This partial 'loss of self' is the effect of the destabilising movement of journeys and not all together undesirable. The abandonment of control can lead to hedonistic pleasures, to the more moderate 'gentle sensuality' that Nooteboom notes, or to an enrichment of one's life through new experiences. As the demise of Rimbaud reminds us, throwing oneself into the unknown can be dangerous, but it is nevertheless worthwhile, the adventures and challenges paying handsome dividend to travellers for whom journeys offer the opportunity 'to doubt oneself in order to be more sure of oneself'[27] – travelling as a rite of passage to a more confident, more mature, more assured mode of being. It is not surprising, then, that the dynamic dialectics of certainty and uncertainty, that form a field swarming with possibilities and productive tensions, are omnipresent in cinematic narratives of travelling and permeate the emotive registers and aesthetics of frame mobility.

Voyage to Italy was Rossellini's third film with Bergman, and like their first (*Stromboli* [Roberto Rossellini, Italy, 1950]), it resonates with intertextual references. It dramatises the journey of upper-middle-class couple Cathy (Ingrid

Bergman) and Alex (George Sanders) to the South of Italy in order to sell an inherited villa. The overall narrative revolves around the latent crisis of the couple that the voyage to Italy brings sharply to the foreground. The future of their relationship becomes increasingly uncertain and Cathy and Alex question the meaning of their lives, both as individuals and as a couple, as the new environment challenges their assumptions and routines and initiates an exploration of emotions, desires and anxieties. The tone of an early argument upon their arrival at the hotel in Naples is revealing in that respect:

> ALEX: Are you sure you know when I am happy?
> CATHY: No . . . ever since we left for this trip I'm not so sure . . .

Divorce appears to be the only option (although none of them seems to be certain about it) but they somehow realise that they love and need each other and vow to change their destructive pattern of behaviour. The happy ending arrives as Cathy becomes increasingly anxious about the possible separation, while Alex's apparent certainty is exposed as a 'stiff upper lip' facade. The rediscovery of their love comes when they find themselves in the midst of a religious parade (whose significance they do not know or understand) among a frenzied crowd that engulfs them in its irresistible, chaotic motion. As Cathy gets entangled in a mass of people that drag her further and further away, the looming possibility of losing Alex (in a literal physical sense) dispels her uncertainty and with a final effort she overcomes the flow of the crowd and falls into Alex's arms. A 'miracle' that restores mobility in a disabled pilgrim is happening at the same time, signalling a moment of transcendence that parallels the 'miracle' of the sudden removal of all doubt in Cathy and Alex that makes possible an otherwise improbable ending. Importantly it is movement, the uncontrollable movement of the crowd, that dramatically amplifies Cathy's uncertainty of direction and leads to the discovery of a new stability.

While the narrative trajectory moves the characters from an initial ('false' as the story reveals) sense of certainty through an increasing uncertainty to a new miraculously discovered certainty, the audio-visual exploration of the South of Italy (the Naples area in particular) involves its own peculiar deployment of movement along the certainty↔uncertainty axis. Against expectations kindled by the increasing international interest in the 1940s and 1950s in the culture and 'sights' of Italy, the film's use of frame mobility undermines typical masterful and exploitable 'tourist' representations. I will focus my analysis on two important instances of spatial exploration, the opening sequence with the couple's car moving through Italian countryside towards their destination and Cathy's drive through the streets of Naples that leads to her visit to the archaeological museum.

The opening sequence of *Voyage to Italy* is 5′30″ long and consists of 28 shots of the couple as they drive towards Naples, as well as views of the space that they traverse. Starting in daytime, the sequence concludes at night with their arrival at the hotel. About half of the shots are medium or close-up shots of the couple together or individually – these shots, however, take up about three times more screen time than exterior shots. In that way the sequence's editing creates a parallel but hierarchical connection between the two processes of visual exploration, that of the couple and their relationship and that of the Italian land and cityscape. Whereas the former initiates the narrative trajectory of personal crisis, the latter constructs the surrounding physical space as unpredictable, unknown and incomprehensible, placing Cathy in particular in a position of perceptual uncertainty.

The credits fade out and into a 17″ long shot of the road ahead from what appears to be a fast-moving vehicle. The Neapolitan song of the credits persists throughout this shot until it is replaced by the sounds of a train in the next. The movement is fast and linear but its rhythm and steadiness are disturbed by continuous small jerky movements that destabilise the view. The camera position is low and limits perspective. The grey sky dominates the frame and matches the dull landscape, the low contrast of the exposure blurring the horizon. Trees line up the sides of the road exaggerating the speed and irregularity of the movement. Several signs mounted on billboards are also discernible but they are unreadable in the jerky frame. The second shot is 10″ long, comes from the side of the car and shows the grey landscape traversed by a long and noisy cargo train moving in the opposite direction; the trees are now in the foreground, completely obscuring the view at times.

Thus, the parallel and forward tracking of the first two shots[28] offers no mastery over the landscape and its geography, creating no sense of location or direction and offering no identification of ownership of the point of view. This is rectified by the following medium shot of a sleeping Alex and a driving Cathy. Throughout the scene exterior views come mostly from her point of view – this is signalled by occasional sidewards glances or turns of the head. As Alex wakes up the lack of clarity of location is reinforced by the first piece of dialogue in the film:

ALEX: Where are we?
CATHY: Oh, I don't know exactly!

Uncertainty in the movement of spatial exploration is inscribed in the scene in a systematic manner that employs recurring techniques and conventions. The editing often alternates brief exterior views with considerably longer shots of the couple, restricting in that way the duration of spatial exploration. Lighting and exposure introduce further limitations. The first night shot is so dark that only minimal spots of light (in themselves blurred by the car's movement) are discernible; a later shot reduces the view of the dark streets of Naples into unclear shadowy spaces. Thus while low contrast makes geographical features hard to identify in the opening, high contrast in the night shots renders large parts of the frame invisible.

Composition of the frame in relation to its mobility further exacerbates uncertainty. In several shots views of the landscape are obstructed by objects inserted in the foreground, in others the forward movement of the car is intercepted by obstacles that block its passage (such as a donkey-drawn cart and cattle). One particular shot combines the two, as the panning that follows slow-moving cattle concludes to a view partially masked by the frame of the car's window (the shot rendering the window a hindrance rather than an aide to visual exploration).

In another shot, as the car (now driven by Alex) approaches and passes a side road, the movement of the frame (from Cathy's point of view) becomes divorced from that of the vehicle, through a hesitant panning of the camera to the right that goes against the forward progression of the vehicle. In this instance the splitting in the direction of movement is both expressive of the increasingly divergent lives of the protagonists and of the uncertainty that permeates the film's spatial exploration of Italy.

The scene of Cathy's trip to the museum follows an argument with Alex and is neatly divided into two sub-scenes, the drive through the streets of Naples and the actual visit to the Roman exhibition. The first part has an obvious symmetry in its editing structure, opening up with a close up of Cathy driving and cutting to her point-of-view shot, a pattern repeated seven times in that segment. Some of the disorientating and destabilising conventions of the opening scene are also present here as the car's path is constantly intercepted by other vehicles and pedestrians. The movement of the frame, in itself a composite of the linear progression of the car and the panning effected by Cathy's scanning looks, is complicated by movement in the frame, as side streets open up new perspectives that constantly alter and confuse composition and the movements of people and vehicles constitute multidirectional, chaotic vectors that offer dizzying and confusing views of the urban space of Naples. This is further aggravated by the fact that the views of the streets come from either side of the car, thus offering no firm direction of movement.

The use of movement to create uncertain configurations of Italian land- and cityscape is remarkable as it comes from a director whose fame and style are based on astute, clinical representations of city life.[29] Perhaps the greatest achievement of the film (and probably the reason behind its commercial failure) is the rejection of both the penetrating observations of neorealism and the comfort of a masterful 'tourist gaze'.[30] Instead an uncertain 'foreign' perspective (mediated through the vision of the protagonists) is constructed that fully serves the demands of the narrative but creates an obscure, almost alien representation of Italy.

The experience of the exhibition that follows is represented in a way that systematically questions the progressive certainty that an 'organised walking' in a museum is expected to provide. Cathy is approached by a man who guides her and provides a historical narrative that accompanies the visit. The authority of his narration is decisively undermined as editing fragments his voice and the soundtrack mixes it with eerie non-diegetic music.

Both the syntagmatic position of this segment (following the drive that is structured around Cathy's mobile vision) and its referent (Cathy's act of the spatial exploration of the museum) centralise the point of view. Once again, however, the mobility of the frame and Cathy's movement are systematically misaligned. All of the shots open up with an exploring movement around or across statues that concludes by discovering Cathy gazing at the exhibits or entering the frame. The system of looks that the previous segment introduced and that the experience of the museum anticipates is rejected, creating an intense uncertainty about the ownership and control of the point of view. Like the visual exploration of the landscape in the opening scene and of the streets of Naples in the preceding shots, Cathy's experience of Italian culture and history fails to cohere, infusing these typical processes of knowledge acquisition and space discovery with unnerving doubt and helplessness. This not only undermines Cathy's certainty but also her agency, as the guide imposes his unsolicited narration that frames the experience and, more importantly, as she submits herself to the movement of the camera that turns the act of exploration on its head by transforming her into the object rather than the subject of the process.

The composition and organisation of the frame, the use of the soundtrack, the cinematography (especially lighting levels and exposure control), the incongruous splitting of the direction of movement of and in the frame, mobility obstructed and intercepted by obstacles, a system of editing that curtails views of the land and cityscape, a syntagmatic organisation that questions the point of view and a narrative that problematises Cathy and Alex's beliefs and emotions, work collaboratively to infuse the visual exploration of Italy with uncertainty. While this uncertainty permeates the film's abundant movements of exploration, discovery and revelation with uneasiness, distance and anxiety rather than comfortable contemplation, it also becomes the motor for character transformation and enables the almost miraculous resolution of their problems. Thus, in *Voyage to Italy* certainty and uncertainty are caught up in a mutually dependent relationship that fully exploits the semantic and emotive possibilities of their productive tension: the visual exploration of Italy challenges the certainties of a consumerist all-possessing tourist gaze, while Cathy and Alex's stagnant but safe relationship is revitalised by the intense uncertainty of the experience and by the discovery of the desire to overcome it. As the museum sequence most clearly demonstrates the removal of Cathy and Alex from secure positions of control and mastery also subjects them to a thorough examination, inserting thus the axis of activity↔passivity in a parallel trajectory to that of certainty↔uncertainty.

3.4 ACTIVITY↔PASSIVITY: *DEATH IN VENICE*

> That night he had a fearful dream . . . its theatre seemed to be his own soul, and the events burst in from outside, violently overcoming the profound resistance of his spirit; passed him through and left him, left the whole cultural structure of a life-time trampled on, ravaged, and destroyed. (Thomas Mann, *Death in Venice*)[31]

Movement of/in the frame inevitably raises questions of agency. As we have seen, frame mobility tends to be attributed to conscious, meaningful and deliberate acts: dictated by the actions of characters in the classical paradigm, commending on narrative situations through purposeful tracking and/or panning shots that run the danger of revealing the agency of narration, displaying flares of virtuosity in 'unmotivated' movements attributed to the artistic intentions and skill of the film director. This is particularly evident in movements of exploration, discovery and revelation because they implicate the cinematic apparatus and the diegetic subjects in a continuous processing of the unfolding spatial information. The axis activity↔passivity will be used to map the complex relationship between the actions and mobility of characters and those of the camera, a relationship, that as we will demonstrate, is heavily informed by modern sensibilities regarding agency. The active extremity of the axis refers to spatial explorations performed by characters as masterful subjects in total control of the viewing apparatus – by contrast passivity refers to characters turned objects rather than agents of exploration.

As in the case of certainty↔uncertainty, the active and passive positions represent the outer limits of a continuous spectrum and are involved in a dialectic rather than mutually exclusive relationship. The peculiarly modern values and sensibilities that permeate the axis refer to dynamic configurations of the active/passive tension and not to fixed binary opposites. Such dialectic is ingrained in the (modernist par excellence) Marxist accounts of processes of social change and transformation. By replacing the agency of the individual with that of class and history, Marx does not simply reject bourgeois individualism but initiates an infinite series of interaction between social formations (relations of production, conditions of living, levels of political organisation) and the possibility of their transcendence. Social movements (trade unions or political parties) become the collective agents of change but they remain ultimately determined by the material reality of history. Thus, agency is conceptualised as residing in the interplay between the oppressive power of capital (that nevertheless 'pushes' the proletariat into action) and the organised political struggle of the masses, traversing the axis of activity↔passivity.

The Marxist deconstruction of a purely active, self-sufficient, self-willed and autonomous individual is of course only one among several other modern processes (elaborated and analysed in psychoanalysis and semiotics, for example) that render the human subject decentred and fragmented. Within such epistemologies human actions are perpetually suspended in the charged field formed by the forces of history, society, the unconscious and language and those of revolution, desire, expression and creativity. Foucault's work on knowledge, power and sexuality offers perhaps the most sophisticated account of how a productive rather than an oppressive deployment of discourses and practices produces a subject that hovers between pleasure and discipline, activity and passivity.[32]

The same dialectic informs artistic sensibilities. Baudelaire's desire for the unknown goes beyond a simple longing for new and undiscovered experiences and sensations and becomes descriptive of a modus operandi for the modern artist. The key characteristic of such formation is the ability to give up one's self completely to raw events and happenings and to transform them into works of art.[33] In that way passivity becomes electrified with action: abandonment to the experience, letting go of one's guard, becomes the key to enhanced perception, making receptiveness instrumental in the production of great art. Once again Rimbaud provides an example of the extreme tendency of the process by advocating the complete surrender of his inner self to the world: 'This is not my fault. It is wrong to say: I think. One ought to say: people think me.' In his extreme assertion 'I is someone else',[34] we discern both the romantic lamentation of the loss of a premodern sense of self and the self-destructive unwillingness to abide by the modern dialectics of identity.

As we have already discussed, travelling becomes a privileged practice that mobilises the activity↔passivity dialectic to its full potential and across the whole spectrum. Movements of exploration become doubled processes in which the discovery of new places, people and landscapes are of equal importance as the revelation of hidden facets of the inner self. In cinematic terms such duality is carried out through point-of-view structures and orchestration of movement of and in the frame. Of course, the power differential involved in being afforded the ability to explore rather than be explored, to control the system of 'looks' of cinematic narration rather than become the object of it, has been a fundamental political issue in film studies.[35] In the present work questions of power, privilege and exclusivity inform heavily the context that provides the referential background to narratives of movement and displacement.

Although there is no dispute that the distribution of looks and mobility within film narratives and strategies of representation is structured around lines of gender, ethnicity, class, sexuality and physical ability, the strictly binary nature of many approaches (with active/passive holding prime position) tends to restrict the scope and blunt the analysis of travel films. While every cinematic traveller is in a fundamental way active, he/she also embodies the potential of passivity, a vulnerability and openness to the experience. It is the interaction between the two, and the particular values and emotive registers that they mobilise in the articulation of their relationship, that the axis activity↔passivity maps.

Luchino Visconti's 1971 *Death in Venice* is a travel film that exemplifies this dialectic in its use of movement of/in the frame. An adaptation of Thomas Mann's formative modernist text, the film reworks the aesthetic sensibilities that obsess the novella proliferating in the process its already multilayered textuality. The character of Gustave von Aschenbach, played memorably by Dirk Bogarde, is inspired by Gustav Mahler and contains autobiographical aspects of both Mann and Visconti. The film tears apart Mann's rather lame attempt to conceal the real identity of his protagonist (disguised as a writer in the book) as here Aschenbach is a composer and the soundtrack reverberates with Mahler's music (predominately the Adagietto from Symphony No. 5).

By also introducing flashback conversations between Aschenbach and Arnold Schönberg, reconstructed from the latter's correspondence with Mahler, the film not only summons some of the major figures in European late nineteenth- early twentieth-century modernism but also some of its major themes. Crucially, the heated debates between Schönberg and Mahler, as presented in the film, revolve around the conceptualisation of the agency of the artist in the creation of great art: for the former beauty exceeds the efforts of the artist, the latter claims that it is simply a product of masterful labour made possible by the artist's domination of the senses.[36]

Aschenbach's emotional and intellectual journey (in both the novella and the film) is one between extreme activity, in the creation of great music through complete control of the means of expression, to utter passivity, in the complete abandonment of creativity and a total submission to the experiences that Venice throws at him. As the quotation that prefaces this section indicates, this gradually leads to his absolute emotional and physical annihilation, the inevitable outcome of transgression beyond an outer boundary, of taking passivity to an intensity that modern sensibility cannot accommodate. Like Rimbaud's usurped self, Aschenbach's 'trampled' identity leads to inevitable destruction.

The film's use of movement plays a key part in tracing Aschenbach's traversing of the activity↔passivity axis, offering in the process some particularly illuminating examples of a cinematic articulation of the dialectic. I will confine the analysis to two short but important segments: the film's opening and Aschenbach's first encounter with Tadzio (Björn Andrésen). The credits sequence (titles emerging against a dark, almost black, background and accompanied by Mahler's music) leads to a foggy, partially masked shot of dark blue and purple sea and sky, with a distant steamboat approaching and momentarily dominating the frame before disappearing to the left . The oval mask and the grainy fuzzy quality of the image offer a very limited, geographically indefinable, view of the seascape. There are two kinds of movement of the frame, a forward accelerated motion towards the steamboat and a gentle swaying up and down. The composite movement constructs a subjective floating vision, strongly suggesting the point of view of somebody travelling on a boat reinforced by the masking of the frame that replicates the shape of a circular lens of glasses.

The second shot is a long shot that shows Aschenbach on the deck of the steamboat sitting on a chair, wrapped in a blanket, with a book on his lap. By placing him on the steamboat the film rules out the possibility that the previous shot came from his point of view, leaving unknown the identity of the subject of the gaze.

After a long while, the initially static camera begins a very slow zoom-in, ending in a medium/close-up shot of Aschenbach with his eyes closed. What follows is an elaborate piece of acting that is executed almost exclusively with the eyes and is the defining characteristic of Bogarde's performance in the film. This primarily involves movement: rolling the eyes up, turning them to one side, directing them back to the book, averting them again, turning to one and then to the other side and finally looking upwards. The continuous but listless movement of the eyes, combined with the framing that isolates the man from his surroundings, suggest an uneasy relationship, a tension between inner and outer worlds, self and others, and a subject reluctant to assume full agency of the act of visual exploration that the journey demands. Anecdotal evidence indicates that Visconti's direction paid particular attention to Bogarde's 'looks'. Margaret Hinxman in her report from the set of the film highlights the actor's irritation with his ordeal: 'Dirk Bogarde calculated that he had reached his two hundred and forty-third "look" and the end of his tether.'[37] But Visconti was also very interested (not in a very flattering manner) in the actor's looks in a different sense:

> He [Visconti] later justified his choice of Bogarde to the baffled front office of Warner Brothers by explaining that, 'Bogarde is like a dead pheasant, which you hang from the neck and when the head falls the body is ripe. Bogarde is exactly ripe for this role.'[38]

Indeed, what Bogard looks like and how he delivers his 'looks' are absolutely crucial in the formulation of the film's aesthetic and emotive address and encapsulate the activity↔passivity dialectic.

The segment continues with parallel or forward moving shots of the gradually more recognisable Venetian sea and landscape interspersed with shots zooming in on Aschenbach or exploring his face and 'looks' in static close ups. The pattern of editing amplifies his alienation from the act of spatial exploration. The first shot, whose construction strongly implies a subjective point of view, is followed by a shot that in its exploring movement turns Aschenbach into an object of observation, thus not only playing-up his 'dead pheasant' passivity but also revealing a lack of control of the point-of-view system. In that manner the act of travelling is contextualised with a system of looks that undermines his agency and initiates the activity↔passivity dialectic. Significantly the novella's opening, drastically different as it is set in Munich and at a time prior to the Venice trip, contains an incident devoid of any narrative significance that displays a similar dialectic, as Aschenbach becomes unwillingly engaged in a 'battle of looks' with a strange man:

> Aschenbach's gaze, though unawares, had very likely been inquisitive and tactless; for he became suddenly conscious that the stranger was returning it, and indeed so directly, with such hostility, such plain intent to force the withdrawal of the other's eyes, that Aschenbach felt an unpleasant twinge, and turning his back, began to walk along the hedge, hastily, resolving to give the man no further heed.[39]

It is probably a far-fetched suggestion (but all the same a tempting and plausible one) that in the film this ferocious battle of looks takes place between character and camera, between Visconti's controlling obsession and Bogarde's irritated submission. But is the relationship with Tadzio, a relationship that is almost exclusively visual, that fully traverses the activity↔passivity axis, pushing Aschenbach beyond the axis and to his death. The first encounter between the man and the boy offers one of the most memorable moments in the film, as one of the first reviewers notes:

> Aschenbach's first glimpses of Tadzio, the Polish youth who is to dominate his last days, occur during a series of lavish camera movements around the hotel lounge, which convey superbly both the oppressiveness and the stimulation of the setting in which he finds himself.[40]

Aschenbach's arrival at the lounge is covered in one long take (2'05") that opens up with the camera static next to the orchestra. As he enters the frame (a distant tiny figure in a vast, busy, colourfully decorated and heavily ornamented room) the camera follows his movement initiating an intricate movement involving pans, tracks and zooms, left and right, back and forth, accompanied by the rolling melody of the soundtrack. His motion provides a cue for the camera, constituting a complex sweeping reframing movement that offers an exhilarating, if spatially disorientating, exploration of the stunning set, décor and costumes. Nevertheless, this is not a typical reframing shot, as the unclear direction and purpose of his actions, combined with the spectacular setting (a multitude of colourful objects and people dominate the view, often obscuring Aschenbach; at other times the camera meanders freely leaving him out of frame), undermine the agency of his movement and heighten an 'independent' exploration of space within which he becomes yet another object of observation.

The shot that follows is a close up of Aschenbach reading a newspaper and then turning away from it, glancing around the room before directing his look straight ahead. His scanning gaze is replicated in the next shot that, in its panning movement, explores one after another the faces of a group of people, concluding with a first view of Tadzio, and is thus clearly signalled as coming from Aschenbach's point of view. This is further reinforced by the reverse shot that returns to his inquisitive gaze. A cutaway to the orchestra is followed by yet another close up of Aschenbach's face as his gaze emerges from the newspaper and repeats the glancing around routine before it gets fixed on the same off-screen direction. A medium shot of Tadzio comes next as the camera moves again around the room. This time, however, the circular movement eventually discovers Aschenbach and briefly keeps him in the frame before pulling out, turning its attention to other guests. The film cuts to a shot of one such group, starting another circular movement that passes Tadzio before concluding with another distant view of Aschenbach.

Thus, the segment's initial alignment of point of view with Aschenbach's gaze is short lived. Pivotal in that respect is the shot that starts with Tadzio but returns and passes Assenbach, performing a centrifugal movement that, instead of fixing the subject/object, observer/observed relationship, opens up a series of imperfect and never-ending circuits of exploration. In this series of vertiginous exchanges of position Aschenbach is as much captive as initiator. His passion for Tadzio expressed as an act of visual obsession becomes a force that overwhelms and destroys. The initiation of movements of exploration (the journey, the scanning of the eyes over spaces and bodies) places the doomed hero not in a position of mastery but at the mercy of uncontrollable forces. As in the museum scene in *Voyage to Italy*, the mobility of the frame interrogates the agency of the observer and disturbs the linear and unidirectional movement of exploration, mobilising thus the dialectic of activity↔passivity.

Both films, albeit in drastically different ways, reject the binary nature of activity/passivity, certainty/uncertainty, treating them as dynamic fields where the 'negative' terms (passivity, uncertainty) are productive in a dramaturgic sense. *Voyage in Italy*'s uncertain vision of Italy resists the commodified appropriations of tourism, inviting a more interactive experience. Similarly, uncertainty acts as a great power that first rejects the false certainties of marriage and then leads to the discovery of a more open, honest and truthful relationship. *Death in Venice* punishes its tragic hero not for one but for two 'crimes': not just for the utter surrender to his passion for Tadzio but also for the arrogant and ill-founded belief in complete creative agency. Aschenbach's fault is not his extreme passivity but even more so his blinded faith in activity, in other words, his inability to comprehend and abide by the dialectics of activity↔passivity. Visconti's cinematics, however, in its methodical deployment of frame mobility, editing and performance, places its hero in a circle of perpetual exchange of positions that fully explores his failure, displaying in the process a perfect understanding of the dialectic that tragically eludes Aschenbach.

The films mobilise the axes in different ways, with *Voyage to Italy* privileging certainty↔uncertainty, whereas *Death in Venice* revolves around activity↔passivity. This might partly account for the startling difference in the representations of Italy that Rossellini and Visconti (directors whose reputation was built on their neorealist oeuvre) offer in their respective films. *Death in Venice* erodes the agency of spatial exploration but generously indulges the spectator in atmospheric and lavish views of Venice, obliterating its hero but preserving the seductive attraction of the place and inviting an unashamed tourist gaze. *Voyage to Italy*, in contrast, turns its back to the commercial and spectacular exploitation of the landscape by destabilising its exploration and by turning uncertainty into a force that restores the psychological health and integrity of its protagonists. Beyond its critical significance this divergence provides a clear indication of the wide-ranging semantic, emotive and representational possibilities of the two axes activated by/in cinematic movements of exploration, discovery and revelation.

NOTES

1. David Bordwell, *Narration in the Fiction Film* (London: Routledge, 1990), pp. 120–5, p. 124.
2. Ibid. pp. 120–1.
3. Alison Griffiths, '"Journeys for Those Who Can Not Travel": Promenade Cinema and the Museum Life Group', *Wide Angle*, 18.3 (1996), pp. 53–76.
4. Richard Dyer, 'Entertainment and Utopia' [First published in *Movie*, 24 (Spring 1977), pp. 2–13], in Rick Altman (ed.), *Genre: The Musical* (London, Boston & Henley: Routledge & Kegan Paul, 1981) pp. 175–89.
5. Ibid. pp. 177–8.
6. Ibid. p. 179.
7. Arnheim suggests that camera movement was introduced in 1897 by Lumière's cinematographer Alexandre Promio when he mounted the camera on a moving gondola in Venice. Rudolf Arnheim, *Film as Art* (London: Faber & Faber, 1958), pp. 138–9. Gunning supports the claim in his entry on 'camera movement' in Richard Abel (ed.), *Encyclopedia of Early Cinema* (Abingdon, Oxon, and New York: Routledge, 2005), p. 92.

8. See, for example, also Anne Friedberg, *Window Shopping: Cinema and the Postmodern* (Berkeley, CA, and London: University of California Press, 1993); Vanessa R. Schwartz, *Spectacular Realities: Early Mass Culture in Fin-de-Siècle Paris* (Berkeley, CA, and London: University of California Press, 1998); Giuliana Bruno, *Atlas of Emotion: Journeys in Art, Architecture, and Film* (London and New York: Verso, 2002).

9. Tom Gunning, 'The whole world within reach', in Jeffrey Ruoff (ed.), *Virtual Voyages: Cinema and Travel* (Durham, NC, and London: Duke University Press, 2006), pp. 25–41. This is strikingly similar to the way that Balázs talks about 'panoramic shots' (Béla Balázs, *Theory of Film* [London: Dobson, 1952], p. 139).

10. X. Theodore Barber, 'The roots of travel cinema: John L. Stoddard, E. Burton Holmes and the nineteenth-century illustrated travel lecture', in *Film History*, 5.1 (1993), pp. 69–84. See also Jeffrey Ruoff, 'Around the world in eighty minutes: the travel lecture film', *Visual Anthropology*, 15 (2002), pp. 91–114; Jeffrey Ruoff, 'Show and tell: the 16mm travel lecture film' in Ruoff (ed.), *Virtual Voyages*, pp. 217–235; Genoa Caldwell (ed.), *Burton Holmes: The Man Who Photographed the World, 1892–1938* (New York: Abrams, 1977).

11. Charles Musser, *The Emergence of Cinema: The American Screen to 1907* (New York: Macmillan, 1990), p. 38.

12. Lauren Rabinovitz, 'From *Hale's Tours* to *Star Tours*: virtual voyages, travel ride films, and the delirium of the hyper-real', in Ruoff (ed.), *Virtual Voyages*, pp. 42–60. See also Tom Gunning, 'The world as object lesson: Cinema audiences, visual culture and the St. Louis world's fair, 1904', *Film History*, 6.4 (1994), pp. 422–44.

13. Rabinovitz, 'From *Hale's Tours* to *Star Tours*', p. 45.

14. Rick Altman, 'From lecturer's prop to industrial product: the early history of travel films', in Ruoff (ed.), *Virtual Voyages*', pp. 61–76.

15. Ibid. p. 76.

16. Gunning, 'Whole world within reach', p. 35.

17. Holmes quoted in Jeffrey Ruoff, 'Introduction', p. 7, in Ruoff (ed.) *Virtual Voyages*. Paula Amad, in her essay 'Between the "familiar text" and the "book of the world": touring the ambivalent contexts of travel films', in Ruoff (ed.) *Virtual Voyages*, pp. 99–116, examines the case of Albert Khan who 'spoke of travel as means to an end in which "life's path and the universe's functioning principles" would finally be made known to humanity' (p. 99).

18. Lynn Kirby in her discussion of the railroad as a technology of mobile vision that prefigures cinematic movement suggests that 'the ambivalence towards the railroad is interiorized by early cinema' (Lynn Kirby, *Parallel Tracks: The Railroad and Silent Cinema* [Exeter: University of Exeter Press, 1997], p. 7).

19. Louis Althousser, *For Marx* (London: Alan Lane, 1969).

20. The scene is entitled 'A Shocking Discovery' in the breakdown of the film into scenes in the DVD.

21. Charles Baudelaire, *The Voyage*. Robert Lowell (ed.) *The Voyage & Other Versions of Poems by Baudelaire* (New York: Farrar, Straus and Giroux, 1968).

22. See Antoine Compagnon, 'Mapping the European mind', in Duncan Petrie (ed.), *Screening Europe: Image and Identity in Contemporary European Cinema* (London: BFI, 1992).

23. Walter Benjamin, *The Arcades Project* (Cambridge, MA, and London: Harvard University Press, 2002), p. 456.

24. Frederick Engels and Karl Marx, *Manifesto of the Communist Party*, *Selected Works* (London: Lawrence & Wishart, 1980), pp. 31–63, p. 38.

25. Arthur Rimbaud, *Rimbaud Complete Works, Selected Letters*, (Chicago and London: University of Chicago Press, 1966), pp. 303–5, p. 303.

26. Cees Nooteboom, *Nomad's Hotel: Travels in Time and Space* (London: Vintage, 2007), pp. 93–4.

27. Amad, in Ruoff Ruoff (ed.), *Virtual Voyages*, p. 114.

28. See Wolfgang Schivelbusch, *The Railway Journey: Trains and Travel in the Nineteenth Century* (Oxford: Blackwell, 1980), for a detailed discussion of the articulation of the two views in the railway journey.

29. Pierre Sorlin emphasises the 'documentary side' of neorealist films: 'As most of them unfold their plot against a rural or urban background, it would be simple to ascribe to them an almost complete picture of Rome, or Milan, or of some sectors of the country side' (*Italian National Cinema: 1896–1996* [London and New York: Routledge, 1996], p. 94). Marcia Landy argues that Rossellini's early neorealist films (such as *Rome Open City* or *Paisa*) register an 'uncertainty about the relationship of the character to their milieu' (*Italian Film* [Cambridge: Cambridge University Press, 2000), p. 136) but they still offer exhaustive visual explorations of urban space in particular, leading Deleuze to describe them in the following terms: 'this is a cinema of the seer and no longer of the agent' (Gilles Deleuze, *Cinema 2: The Time-Image* [Minneapolis: University of Minnesota Press, 1989], p. 2).

30. See John Urry, *The Tourist Gaze* (London: Sage, 2002).

31. Thomas Mann, *Death in Venice; Tristan; Tonio Kröger* (Harmondsworth: Penguin, 1975), p. 74.

32. See, for example, Michel Foucault, *Discipline and Punish* (London: Alan Lane, 1977), and *The History of Sexuality, vol. 1, The Will to Knowledge* (London: Penguin, 1978).

33. The activity↔passivity dialectics involved in creativity and in the production of art works is arguably best demonstrated in Martin Heidegger's seminal essay 'The Origin of the Work of Art', *Poetry, Language, Thought* (New York: Harper and Row, 1970). It is also extensively discussed in J. Hillis Miller, *Topographies* (Stanford: Stanford University Press, 1995), esp. pp. 9–56.

34. Arthur Rimbaud, *Rimbaud Complete Works, Selected Letters*, pp. 304–6

35. Initiated by Laura Mulvey, 'Visual pleasure and narrative cinema', *Screen*, 16.3 (1975), pp. 6–18.

36. This invites a direct comparison with Rimbaud's 'derangement of the senses'.

37. Margaret Hinxman, 'Death in Venice', *Sight and Sound*, 39.4 (1970), pp. 199–200, p. 199.

38. Ibid.

39. Mann, *Death in Venice; Tristan; Tonio Kröger*, p. 9.

40. Philip Strick, 'Death in Venice', *Sight and Sound*, 40.2 (1971), pp. 103–4, p. 103.

PART II

Cinematic Journeys

CHAPTER 4

Quests

4.1 JOURNEYS OF EXPLORATION, DISCOVERY, REVELATION

In this chapter I will concentrate on three recent travel films that in their cinematic journeys and quest narratives mobilise in typically modern ways the full emotive potential of the activity↔passivity and certainty↔uncertainty axes. In their distinctive and varied textual practices they combine visual explorations of travelled space with investigations of psychological processes of change and transformation. The narrative trajectories of these films place the heroes in situations which test and challenge their certainties, preconceived ideas and beliefs, by setting them in motion through journeys of exploration, discovery and revelation – not only of the world, the land and its inhabitants but also, and fundamentally, of the self. It is the characteristic interaction between travelled space and self-transformation and its cinematic articulation through frame mobility that constitutes the specific focus of this chapter. More specifically two key aspects of that interaction will be addressed in detail.

First, I shall look at the textual specificities of 'views on the move', that is, mobile images of the travelled space and of the travellers in it. Particular attention will be paid in the relationship between the two, which is largely (but not exclusively) constructed through movement in and of the frame and from shot to shot. Views on the move are central to travel films as they combine pleasurable explorations of the landscape with concrete visual articulations of the psychological processes of self-discovery that permeate the quest narratives.

Second, the role of the cinematic body of the traveller as a mediating agent will be studied. While the traveller's vision is an essential component of views on the move, his or her body becomes a site of inscription of the materiality of the journey and provides a physical anchor for the spatial exploration of the films. This enables an embodiment of vision and a visual manifestation of the impact of the experience on the traveller, constructing the body as a powerful instrument of mediation between distant views of space as landscape and intimate experiences of it as land.

The three films, with markedly different aesthetics and production backgrounds, articulate the relationship between travelled space and self-transformation in distinctive ways which traverse the spectrum of modern sensibility around mobile vision. *The Motorcycle Diaries* (Walter Salles, Argentina/USA/Cuba/Germany/Mexico/Chile/Peru/France, 2004) is an epic journey across a continent that explores a post-colonial and pre-revolutionary Latin America in the early 1950s. Based on the diaries of Ernesto 'Che' Guevara and his friend Alberto Granado, the film narrates their travels as a life-changing adventure through which a middle-class medical student is transformed into a revolutionary legend. The journey's transformative potential is presented as a gradual but accelerating process of learning, enhanced by deeply felt experiences. This is clearly signalled in the opening scene where Ernesto (Gael García Bernal) explicitly defines the objective of the adventure: 'the goal: to explore a continent we had only known in books'. In the pursuit of the 'real' experience the protagonist is placed in a cycle of reception-reflection-action: images of Ernesto recording his diary (with extracts regularly surfacing as voice-over), writing letters to his mother or reading books about the history and the politics of the continent are scattered across the film, creating meditative moments in between scenes that showcase the kinetic energy of the journey. It is Ernesto's openness to and reflection on his exploration of the continent and its people that ultimately shape his political beliefs and reveal his extraordinary qualities as a revolutionary leader.

Koktebel ((Boris Khlebnikov and Aleksei Popogrebsky, Russia, 2003) places its story in a post-communist Russia that is riddled with political, social and economic instability. The uncertainty of the period forms the background of the journey of the homeless and unemployed ex-aeronautical engineer (Igor Csernyevics) and his eleven-year-old son (Gleb Puskepalis) out of Moscow and towards the Crimean resort of Koktebel. The narrative revolves around two separate but interrelated quests. The father attempts to rebuild his life, to overcome his alcoholism and, in the process, to regain his son's trust – the latter longs for a better life by the sea and a reliable loving relationship with his father. Koktebel becomes a 'promised land', a destination that when reached will confirm the father's promises and, indirectly, the veracity of his accounts of the past and his views on life. The journey also functions as education, with the father teaching the boy about nature, engineering and history, teachings that are tested by the boy's own experiences. In the movement from Moscow to Koktebel the son's emotional, cognitive and perceptual uncertainties are rekindled and confronted and are dispelled only by the conclusion of the journey and the arrival at their destination.

Japón (Carlos Reygadas, Mexico/Netherlands/Germany/Spain, 2002) takes his hero, a middle-aged man played by Alejandro Ferretis, to a journey from Mexico City to the isolated, remote village of Ayacatzintla (Aya) where he plans to kill himself. At his destination he (accidentally but one feels inevitably) comes across an indigenous old woman, Ascen (played by Magdalena Flores, a local amateur actor), who puts him up in the barn of her old stone house at the outskirts of the village. Through his encounter with the place, the villagers and in particular Ascen, the man's attitude, values and emotions are challenged; he eventually rejects the option of suicide and initiates a sexual relationship with his hostess. A relative of the woman makes a claim, based on traditional laws of heredity, on the barn's stones, and fatalistically she complies. Ascen finds her death in a crash as she accompanies the stones to their new destination. The man's journey leads to a discovery of spiritual and emotional serenity and enables the film to explore the sublime landscape of Aya in a contemplative, searching manner.

Thus the three films set their journeys in very specific and divergent chronotopes. As critical literature on the road movie points out, the cultural significance of the journey and the cinematic representations it generates are inextricably linked to the geographical and historical specificity of the travelled space.[1] All three films offer views of the countryside that are testimonies to the hardship and to the economic disadvantage of rural areas in Latin America, Russia and Mexico, respectively. Importantly, all three chronotopes belong to historical times signposted clearly as 'post-' (colonial, Soviet, modern) and geopolitical spaces at the margins of the West. However, the films narrate journeys of exploration, discovery and revelation, which are structured around individual quests for experience, knowledge, truth, ultimate and/or transcendental meaning, activating in the process distinctly European and modern sensibilities around mobility, vision and subjectivity. This leads to a further paradox, as the journeys create the possibility to explore, discover and reveal spaces and lives at the periphery of modernity[2] but do so from positions bound within its discursive limits and emotive registers.

The narratives of self-discovery are fleshed with visual explorations of the space travelled. In the textual deployment of views on the move and the body of the traveller, the films not only fully mobilise the axes of activity↔passivity and certainty↔uncertainty but also very effectively negotiate some of the crucial ideological anxieties and contradictions around travelling. As previously discussed, questions around the authenticity of the traveller's experience are central in this context. There has been a great degree of concern around modern means of transportation as constructing a type of movement that annihilates space itself, reducing the world to a series of destinations and the traveller to a mere 'parcel', and a travelling experience underscored by passivity and indifference.[3] On a theoretical level (and in a variety of disciplines from cultural studies to anthropology and from literary studies to geography) some of these anxieties have been dealt with by the extensive investigation of an opposition between distinct types of mobility and particularly those pertaining to the different cultural practices of tourism and travel.[4]

This is a difference endlessly reworked by a variety of texts (novels, travelogues, films, etc.) that involve travelling as a key aspect. Commenting on the specific case of contemporary travel writing Debbie Lisle notes:

> Because the tourist can go anywhere the travel writer can, the travel writer now secures his/her subject position by producing an other that is easy to hate: the tourist. The traveller/tourist binary is an explicit formation of the identity/difference logic – the former installed as the hero of the text, and the latter disdained as an unfortunate by-product of globalisation.[5]

In *Topographies*, a collection of philosophical thoughts motivated by travels around the world, John Sallis locates his work and the experiences of his journeys in a similarly polarised manner vis-à-vis tourism:

> This genre of discourse, though deployed in relation to travel, has nothing to do with tourism, either ancient or modern; neither is its orientation such as would simply exploit the figure of travel as a metaphor for the movement of development of philosophical thought. Rather, the travel to which such writing submits takes place as a discovery of evocative places, of places that, because they are evocative, give focus to the visit, in contrast to the accelerated distraction of tourism.[6]

As Lisle suggests and Sallis demonstrates, the experience of travelling involves a special relationship of the traveller with space and place. In generic terms a defining characteristic of the road movie is precisely the textual emphasis on (rather than annihilation of) travelled space:

> Car travel in road movies becomes not merely a means of transportation to a destination; rather the travelling itself becomes the narrative's primary focus. The notion of travel as cultural critique becomes both modernized and modernist, as reinvented by the road movie.[7]

In many ways the road movie addresses key aspects of the cultural critiques against tourism: it emphasises the journey rather than the moment of arrival, the experience of space rather than the reduction of the world in 'destinations'; it values places and resists their transformation into a series of 'non-places'.[8] Furthermore, as the quotation seems to suggest, road movies tap into a discourse of radical and oppositional rhetoric (a diegetic world that goes against and beyond the everyday, conventional, regulated and sheltered life in the city), emancipatory character (the freedom and mobility of the road) and, importantly for the concerns of the present work, are profoundly informed by romantic notions of the authentic, the real and the genuine. Such notions find distinctive cinematic expression in articulations of views on the move and representations of the body of the traveller. The travel writer Cees Nooteboom offers a very suggestive description of himself as a traveller:

> Maybe the genuine traveller is always positioned in the eye of the storm. The storm being the world, the eye that with which he [*sic*] views it. Meteorologists tell us that within this eye all is silent, perhaps as silent as a monk's cell. Whoever learns how to see with this eye might also learn how to distinguish between what is real and what is not, if only by observing the ways in which things and people differ, and the ways in which they are the same.[9]

Nooteboom places in the centre of the 'genuine' travelling experience a romantic (and exclusively male) subject that achieves through vision a privileged relationship with the world. Sallis elaborates further on such (visual) relationship:

> Focusing upon the place would, then, consist simply in becoming receptive to the scene offered. Evoked by the place, this focused receptivity would in turn open our senses decisively to the place's unique power of evocation. Or, more precisely, the place visited may evoke both focused receptivity and, yoked to it, a play of imagination. Through this double interplay, of receptivity and imagination and of both with the scene itself, a new thoughtfulness may emerge, a thinking that draws from the place rather than imposing on it, a thinking that draws from the place by letting itself be drawn to the place.[10]

Significantly, in Sallis's formulation the interplay of receptivity and imagination and the evocative nature of travelled space lead to a 'new thoughtfulness' exemplifying the modern sensibilities attached to processes of spatial exploration, discovery and revelation. The three films discussed here deploy the peculiar dialectics of activity↔passivity and certainty↔uncertainty in views on the move that expressively articulate the transformative impact of travelled space on the traveller.[11] This in turn places the traveller's body in a crucial and overdetermined position as the corporeal dimension of the subject of movements of exploration, discovery and revelation. Orvar Löfgren in his analysis of physical mobility in 'vacationing' makes some crucially suggestive connections between movement, vision and the embodied travelling subject:

Exploring these different modes, from strolling, walking, rambling, hiking and trekking to floating, driving, or speeding through the landscape, it is obvious that we need to discuss the ways in which movement, nonmovement, and experience go together. The cult of the sublime and the panorama made an important connection between motion and emotion. The strong feelings even set your body working, sending a shiver down the spine or making your limbs tremble. The raging storm of the first Eidophusikon or the back-projection illusion of the train and the car explore these connections of moving through a landscape and being moved by the experience.[12]

The journeys of *The Motorcycle Diaries*, *Koktebel* and *Japón* authenticate their respective cinematic experiences of travelled space through overarching narrative trajectories of personal quest that link spatial exploration with self-transformation, views of characters in motion and moving landscapes, and exploit the representational capabilities of bodies as agents and receptors of the travelling experience.

4.2 VIEWS ON THE MOVE

The first shot of Ernesto and Alberto (Rodrigo de la Serna) on the open road, riding the *Mighty One*, the motorcycle on which their journey starts, establishes a recurring convention of the 'views on the move' that *The Motorcycle Diaries* offers which succinctly encapsulates the dialectics that inform its spatial explorations. The shot is organised with precision and symmetry: a road extending from the foreground to a central vanishing point, bordered by vegetation to the sides and a blue sky with few thin clouds at the top of the frame.[13] There is also typical road movie music, a country-like acoustic guitar tune, as Ernesto's voice-over, a letter to his mother, joins in:

> Dear Mom, Buenos Aires is behind us. Gone is this 'wretched life', the uninspiring lectures, the papers and medical exams. All of Latin America is ahead of us. From now on we only trust in 'The Mighty One.'

This clear message that civilisation is left behind is reinforced by the iconography of the landscape with no signs of people, buildings or farmland. Ernesto's voice-over asserts subjectivity, a centre of perception that claims ownership of the mobile point of view implied by the linear movement of the frame towards the vanishing point.

This subjective shot, the view of the road from the perspective of a travelling agent, is an established cinematographic convention of the genre.[14]

However, as the voice-over concludes, the motorcycle with the two protagonists enters from the left and takes central position in the frame, as it cruises on the road. This adds dynamism to the shot (and a utopianism of escape and freedom, values that underpin the road movie) as the speed of the motorcycle exceeds that of the continuing movement of the frame. More significantly though, in the second part of the shot Ernesto's point of view is abandoned for the disembodied gaze of the apparatus, thus turning the subject of the look into an object.

While the travelling point of view shot emphasises 'the *experience* of the landscape',[15] as Barbara Klinger has suggested, the shift of subjectivity that occurs in the shot represents a different (if equally popular) convention that expresses a distinctive logic. It enables the film to strike a fine balance between the subjective experiences of the characters and the presentation of their journeys from a detached perspective. This involves the careful orchestration of views of the characters on the move with their subjective mobile views of the travelled space. On the level of narrative it places the characters in a mediating position that underwrites spatial exploration with personalised narratives, perceptions and emotions. In that respect the shot exemplifies the dynamics of the activity↔passivity axis, attributing movement of the frame to a moving agent but also subjecting that agency to the exploring vision of the camera.

The same dialectics is at play in other uses of movement of/in the frame and in patterns of editing. The film uses a plethora of panning and/or tracking movements that start with spectacular views of the landscape and conclude in a close-up or a medium shot of the protagonists. Numerous other shots undertake spatial explorations that are facilitated by the travellers' vision, either as subjective frame mobility or as movement that follows the trajectories of their gaze as presented in the frame.

Similarly, the film repeatedly edits subjective point-of-view shots that explore the travelled space with views of the heroes as they move within the landscape. In that way, two meaningful spheres and two perceptual objects are defined, the traveller and the landscape, and as movement in and between shots traverses the in-between space it articulates a relationship of interaction and mutual dependence.

The quest narrative of *The Motorcycle Diaries* employs these conventions as particularly effective (and affective) means of expressing on a visual level the film's central theme, that is, the deep impact that the travelling experience has on the heroes, Ernesto in particular. The journey's transformative power lies in the realisation of the activity↔passivity dynamics that permeates the relationship between travelling as self-willed act and as life-changing experience, between the traveller as actant and as acted upon. Within such a dialectic the landscape occupies a privileged symbolic position as it provides concrete and powerful imagery that offers a condensed visual shorthand for the considerably more abstract and diffused nature of the travelling experience. The process of transformation, clearly the effect of a multiplicity of events and factors that the narrative recounts, is often succinctly expressed in movements of the frame that fluctuate between the landscape and the hero (for example, Ernesto and Alberto 'discovered' in the landscape in long panning shots or revealing the landscape through their vision) and patterns of editing which alternate visions of the landscape with views of the heroes in it (placing perceived and perception in a circuit of affective fluidity and exchange).

As the film progresses there is an increasing number of instances where only Ernesto is placed within this visual dialectic foregrounding the process of perception and reflection that leads to the awakening of an increasingly more articulate political consciousness. It is precisely this type of sensibility forged around receptiveness that sets him apart from Alberto and accounts for his legendary revolutionary charisma. Ernesto's journey of exploration is not only a successful quest for self-discovery but also perfectly abides by a Marxist master narrative that sees social transformation as a process that involves human agency (and emphatically so leadership) in a continuous circular movement that links perception, reflection and action. As Ernesto's final flight to a new (revolutionary) future suggests, the film's employment of the activity↔passivity axis articulates a heroic modernist subjectivity that represents the dialectical opposite of the imploded and powerless position of von Aschenbach in *Death in Venice*. Guevara and Aschenbach represent quintessentially modern sensibilities that traverse the same axis of activity and passivity, oscillating between being the subject and the object of frame mobility. They do, however, outline drastically different possible outcomes of the inescapable negotiation between reception and action that the journey initiates, with the movement of interaction becoming the centrifugal force that propels the revolutionary hero ever forward but traps the romantic musician in a vortex of destruction and death.

Koktebel also demonstrates an astute understanding of the dialectics of the activity↔passivity axis, if only to turn its back on it. This is best exemplified by one particular shot that in a simple and effective manner negotiates a series of complex relationships that underpin the film's narrative, aesthetics and emotive register. This comes early in the film as the two travellers hide on a cargo train. The shot opens with a view of the son and the father in a carriage, the former positioned in profile at the centre of the frame facing an open door to the right. Basking in the light that streams from the opening, the boy looks straight ahead at the landscape that is visible through the door. The camera position organises perspective in a way that maximises the depth and breadth of the carriage but renders the side opening flat, creating a virtual screen on which the landscape whizzes by. The father with his eyes closed lies at the dark far end of the carriage. The movement of the train makes the head of the boy rock gently. The camera remains static for 13″ as the rhythmical sound and movement of the train and the monotonous views of 'passing' trees give the shot a contemplative and downbeat feel. Then a slow forward tracking movement that lasts 1′14″ begins and eventually concludes in an extreme close-up of the boy's face, the proximity of the camera amplifying the rocking of his head and rendering visible a rhythmical opening and closing of his eyelids.

The startling effect of the camera movement, paradoxically amplified by its slow pace, is that it gradually, almost imperceptibly, changes the composition of the shot by focusing tightly on the boy and eliminating from the frame both the figure of the father and the flickering views of the landscape. In that way the movement of the frame signals the peripheral role of the father in a narrative that revolves around the boy and leaves in the margins a certain type of movement, the conventionally mobile, travelling views of the landscape. The shot seems to formulate a hierarchy of narrative agencies and to give an early but explicit formulation of the film's aesthetics in relation to 'views on the move'. The camera's movement removes from the frame the object of the boy's gaze and centralises the act of perception, emphasising in that way the subjective nature of the spatial exploration that he is undertaking and pointing towards a possible tension between the traveller's views and views of the traveller.

Koktebel analytically reflects on one of the most prominent visual conventions of travel films, namely, shots that place the traveller against a moving backdrop. This particular type of frame composition involves a play between two planes, that of the immobile in relative terms (but still travelling) passenger and that of the mobile world around him/her. This is of course an optical illusion since it is the movement of whatever vehicle carries the traveller that creates the impression of a 'moving' landscape, a piece of cinematic trickery exploited in its reversal by techniques such as back-projection. This type of shot, which (paraphrasing Julianne Pidduck's eloquent term)[16] we can call the 'traveller at the window shot', is an effective way of offering spectacular mobile views of the landscape and crystallises iconographically the activity↔passivity dialectics that permeates the travel film. Anxieties around the traveller's passivity (Ruskin's parcel)[17] are somewhat dispelled by the spectacular views of the traversed landscape, while the often contemplative tone of such shots (effected through duration, soundtrack and performance) suggests that the traveller is involved in an active recording of and reflection on the experience of the journey. This type of frame composition, with two distinct but interrelated planes, allows a play between the moving, changing landscape and the immobile (but travelling and, importantly, *experiencing*) traveller that, in a manner similar to the shot in *The Motorcycle Diaries* analysed above but involving minimal or no frame mobility, visually articulates the transformative potential of travelling and activates the sensibilities of the activity↔passivity axis.

In *Koktebel*, nevertheless, the convention is rejected by the movement of the frame, as the tracking eliminates the window and the views of the 'moving' landscape. After all, the boy's movement, his journey, is not a quest for experiences or even personal transformation but a search for evidence, assembled with a 'superior' vision that can test and verify his father's teachings, honesty and views of the world and confirm the strength of their bond. The elimination of the landscape (the views of the travelled space) from the frame and the focus on perception itself signal that the film's narrative, its sensibility and mobile vision, are deployed not along an activity↔passivity dialectic but rather across the more pertinent in this case axis of certainty↔uncertainty. The views of the landscape are not transformative but confusing; the movement through the traversed space is not emancipatory and/or pleasurable but prolongs the tortuous uncertainty of the boy by deferring the arrival at the final destination and at a definite and meaningful conclusion.

The partial and subjective views of the landscape, framed by the door of the carriage and passing by as a series of blurred, repetitive and uninspiring images and encoded as movement in the frame, are eliminated by a purposeful and directed movement of the frame. On the level of narrative and from the boy's perspective, the landscape is awash with dangers that can lure his father, diverting him away from the promised destination, immobilised in abandonment either to Mikhail's (Vladimir Kucherenko) vodka or to Kseniya's (Agrippina Steklova) love and kindness. Throughout the film spatial exploration attributed to the boy's mobile point of view is tinted with anxiety that at times becomes reminiscent of a horror film. Subjective mobile shots with jerky handheld camera are used on several occasions (for example, in the first encounter with Tanya [Vera Sandrykina], during his escapade from Kseniya's house, as he stumbles onto the truck driver [Aleksandr Ilyin], and upon his arrival at Koktebel among the crowd of tourists), rendering spatial exploration not only stressful but also potentially perilous.

The film offers a number of instances when the boy determinedly looks for effective visual ways of comprehending his place and movement in the world in which he lives and the space in which he travels: he obsessively reads encyclopaedias and scientific texts, studies geography books and atlases and scrutinises maps of his itinerary. He is particularly fascinated with a hill outside Koktebel that gliders fly from (this is the first place that he visits on his arrival at the resort) and is very interested in the albatross and its ability to fly at a very high altitude and to cover huge distances. All of these suggest a longing for masterful visions of the world structured around high angle vantage points that in their objectivity and omniscience remove all perceptual uncertainty. He idealises aerial points of view, effortless transportation, a mobile vision that glides above the messiness of the terrain at a safe distance from the ambiguities of the land. This is clearly manifested by his self-claimed ability (perhaps a fantasy, but that remains ambiguous) to detach his vision from his body and obtain such views.[18] This occurs at key moments in the film, during his 'date' with Tanya but crucially in the film's final shot. An aerial view of the boy, as he sits at the end of a pier at Koktebel surrounded by the sea with his father approaching, injects a utopian sense of fulfilment, as the shot confirms the reunion and the successful completion of the journey.

While *The Motorcycle Diaries* anchors its mobile vision on an active/passive dialectic that endows the travelled space with a transformative potential, *Koktebel* infuses its 'views on the move' with anxiety and uncertainty, inviting a hermeneutic relationship with the landscape that, through the boy's quest for certainty, foregrounds the opacity of the world as a series of potentially decipherable, mainly enigmatic and occasionally impenetrable signs. Within such a textual system, as the movement of the frame that eliminates that in the frame suggests, mobile vision has multiple possibilities and tracks competing hierarchies.

Japón also situates its mobile vision within a field riddled with tensions. The figure of the Man functions as a narrative anchor whose movement out of the city, on his journey and in and around Aya, is tracked throughout the film or initiates spatial explorations associated with his perception. However, the authority of his vision and the agency of his mobility are consistently undermined by the film's commitment to ambiguity regarding ownership and control of its point-of-view system. Furthermore, movement of the frame tends to follow trajectories that are not strictly dictated by movement in the frame and often unfolds in opposition to it. Overall, the film's spatial exploration and the views on the move that it constructs are attached very loosely to the movement of the traveller and on several occasions even render his presence in and control of the field of vision as a hindrance.

An early example of this tendency is demonstrated in the scene of the man's arrival at Aya. After meeting with the Judge (Rolando Hernández) to arrange his accommodation, Sabina (Yolanda Villa), the woman who will introduce the Man to Ascen, is summoned. Her arrival and subsequent conversation with the Man are shot with a mobile camera in one single long take (1′04″). It opens as a long shot of the Man conversing with several villagers as the camera moves closer to the group. When Sabina's arrival is announced, the Man turns around and looks directly at the camera which first stops and then moves away, panning to the left over the courtyard, the houses and the people, as it eventually discovers the distant figure of a woman which it follows until she stops, framed in a medium shot. The Man enters the frame from the left and, as they discuss arrangements, the camera moves slowly forward and through the gap between them, gradually eliminating them from the field of vision, then pans to the right, where it discovers a water ditch with several children swimming, before turning left again in a movement left incomplete by editing.

In this shot the logic of the camera movement seems to fluctuate indeterminately between placing the Man within the space of the village and abandoning him altogether while it undertakes a spatial exploration detached from his point of view and/or his movement. This is an eloquent and early demonstration of the discomfort that the film demonstrates in following the Man as a centre of perception, a discomfort that is amplified by his diegetic position as the traveller, the agent of spatial exploration and initiator of the journey. Frame mobility seems to be motivated by a desire to free itself from his agency, to roam at will in a visual exploration of the village and its stunning surroundings.

If in *Koktebel* the boy's longing for truth is coded as a search for superior vision, in *Japón* the detachment of mobile vision from the agency of the protagonist becomes not only a spiritual quest but a tangible tension that repeatedly surfaces in the film's frame mobility. In a remarkable sequence right in the middle of the film, the hero's decision to commit suicide seems to be about to be realised. A series of shots showing the Man struggling under torrential rain to climb to the top of a plateau conclude with him standing at a precipice and staring at the steep cliffs of the canyon and the surrounding mountains. He produces a gun which he lifts close to his head but, as the camera tilts up to the whiteness of the sky (possibly a sign of revelation and transcendence), he changes his mind and staggers away from the edge, collapsing in complete abandonment next to a dead horse, with his face and body soaking in the rain. After a brief shot of the rain washing blood off the entrails of the corpse there is a succession of five shots that last 2′15″ in total. Each shot involves circular movements at different speeds and taken from progressively higher camera positions. In the ascending spiral of frame mobility the body of the protagonist becomes smaller and smaller, an insignificant dot in a landscape which, through the upward circular movement, is revealed in its full magnificence for the first time. The sublime iconography (rain, height, mountains, death and life)[19] is re-enforced by the sounds of Bach's *The Passion of St Matthew*[20] (Aria 39, 'Erbarme Dich')[21] and the shots conclude above the clouds in a blank, totally white frame.

The annihilation of the Man's agency, his abandonment to the land, the rain and death, his immobility and diminishing presence in the frame seem to be the necessary prerequisites for the emancipation of the camera which in its ascending spirals reveals a sublime view of the world. In this scene perceptual fulfilment and spiritual transcendence are achieved through mobile vision that is made possible only after the collapse of the hero. In that way movement of the frame is liberated from the conventional restriction to anchor its activity in the agent of movement. The independence and simplicity of such vision and the transcendental subjectivity that it engenders, basking in the spiritual music of Bach and elevated to the sky, is taken to its utopian limit, the complete purity of light that, in the conclusion of the sequence and in the total whiteness of the frame, annihilates the object itself.

Nevertheless, this remains a transient moment that encapsulates the fierce tension around agency and control of frame mobility that permeates the film's spatial exploration. It is Ascen's death, caused by a crash between a train and the tractor carrying her and other villagers, that finally and decisively liberates movement of the frame from the guiding mobility of the Man. This happens in the final scene of the film, delivered in one epic shot that, in terms of its duration (5'22"), the spectacular continuous movement of the camera that explores a landscape littered with the horrific debris of the accident, and the slow, inexorable build up of intensity delivered by the elegiac soundtrack (Arvo Pärt's *Cantus In Memoriam Benjamin Britten*) [22] stands out as arguably the film's most memorable moment.

The movement of the frame is structured around the linearity of the rail tracks which provide a constant visual point of reference throughout the shot. Following an extreme long shot of a valley marked by a road crossing the railway, this shot opens with the camera moving forward at an accelerating pace along the tracks that extend to a distant vanishing point in the horizon. Masonry, tangled and twisted pieces of metal, items of clothing and eventually dead bodies are visible on and around the line. After 32" the camera, while still moving forward, begins an irregular panning movement to the left that reveals not only more debris but also the lush, serene landscape that surrounds the scene of the accident. Using the same composite forward-and-left panning movement, the camera completes four full circles and begins yet another panning but then changes direction to the right completing one more circle that way. Finally, the camera returns to the rail tracks, this time shown at a low angle that minimises perspective and fills the frame with a very short stretch of the line. This is followed by a linear forward and accelerating tracking movement that lasts for 1' which arrives and stops at the spot where Ascen's dead body lies. The frame freezes there for a few seconds before fading out to black as the credits start to roll down.

In this final shot of the film the tension between movement of and in the frame is resolved in a fashion that takes it to an extreme (if predictable) conclusion. While the scene at the top of the plateau extracts freedom of mobility at the cost of the temporary annihilation of the Man as a centre of perception and subjectivity, the concluding shot uses movement in a way that renders any diegetic agency redundant and superfluous. The organisation of movement recreates an affective replication of the crash (the powerful steady forward movement that erupts in chaotic spirals of devastation), returning to a time that precedes the unfolding spatial exploration that the shot also undertakes. In that way the shot overcomes temporal, spatial and narrative boundaries, actualising a perfect and pure vision and a transcendental subjectivity that is longed for throughout the rest of the film.

The startling symmetry of the shot's mobility and its anchoring on the railway tracks make speculation regarding its significance irresistible. On one level, the fast linear movement that destroys the tractor and its passengers and spreads destruction in all directions evokes a symbolism polarised around the progress/tradition binary. More importantly, however, it is the irregular spiral movement rather than the unidirectional forward progression that reveals both the full dimensions of the tragedy and undertakes an emotionally charged visual survey of the landscape and its (now vanquished) inhabitants. Thus the perceptual limitations of views of the world structured around linear movement and narrative transitivity are exposed in the comparison with the holistic qualities of a wandering disembodied vision – a tension that, as we have noted earlier, also permeates the relationship between movement of and in the frame.

The three films articulate different ways in which views of the world are related to the act of travelling. In *The Motorcycle Diaries* movement constructs a reciprocal exchange that glorifies the landscape and exalts its impact in forging the extraordinary personality of Ernesto 'Che' Guevara. In *Koktebel* movement places the boy in a hermeneutic relationship with the space he traverses, emphasising both the anxiety of the process and the importance of an ultimate destination/meaning. In *Japón* a similar anxiety permeates the film and surfaces as a specific textual tension around frame mobility that questions the desirability and effectiveness of the Man as an agent of spatial exploration. All three films, nevertheless, centralise in their textual practices the dynamic relationship between the traveller as a centre of perception and the experience of the travelled space. The affective palette mobilised around each film's quest is profoundly informed by the distinctive ways in which such relationship is articulated but remains within the emotive register of a modern and Western configuration of subjectivity, movement and vision. In the perceptive/reflective/transformative cycle, in the uncertainty of hermeneutics or in the search for completeness through spiritual transcendence, the three journeys traverse in different but complementary ways the axes of certainty↔uncertainty and activity↔passivity that distinctively inform modern subjectivity.

4.3   THE BODY OF THE TRAVELLER

It is obvious from the previous analysis that the narrative agency of the traveller plays a pivotal role in the construction and presentation of the travelled space. The pleasures and anxieties of spatial exploration, the sensual and emotional dimensions of the travelling experience, the intellectual and spiritual challenges of the journey, all are mediated through the vision and the body of the mobile hero. And while the function of the former has been discussed in some detail in the previous section, it is to the latter that we will now turn our attention. The relationship between body and vision surfaces repeatedly and stubbornly in discourses around authenticity, either in the context of actual travelling[23] or in accounts of the virtual journeys of the cinematic experience.[24] Two essential mediations are undertaken by the traveller's body: between the visual and other sensual experiences of the journey, and between the embodied vision of characters and the disembodied vision of the apparatus. The manner in which films negotiate these mediations defines the textual process of authentication of the represented travelling experiences.

The Motorcycle Diaries constructs its 'views on the move' on the basic dialectic of activity↔passivity and deploys its authenticating practices along the same axis. The receptiveness of the hero is articulated as a visual relationship with the landscape reinforced by representational strategies that foreground the full physical impact of the land on the body of the traveller. The most obvious of these strategies is evident in the several instances in which Ernesto and Alberto fall off or crash their motorcycle. The first spectacular, if rather comic, fall comes in the early stages of their journey after an impromptu race with two local horse-riders (in itself a signifier of 'direct' engagement with the land and its inhabitants). With Ernesto's voice-over relating, 'I am glad we've left "civilization" behind and are now a bit closer to the land', the *Mighty One* loses its grip on the dirt track and ends up in a ditch scattering their luggage all over the road. Shots of the two in soaked clothes are part of numerous images throughout the film in which their means of transportation, their bodies and clothing become damaged in the journey by the process of 'coming closer to the land'. A similar authenticating convention emerges in patterns of editing that interrupt long shots of the two heroes traversing the landscape and mobile subjective views of their surroundings with medium or close-up shots of spinning or sliding motorcycle wheels, clouds of dust, arduous footsteps on dry, dirty soil. Thus, while the iconography of the clothes and the appearance of the travellers foreground the imprints of their contact with the travelled space, editing contextualises visual explorations of the landscape with continuous references to the physicality of the journey, rooting vision on a travelling body and grounding it in the land.

The mapping of the emotional and psychological on the surface of the male body is an established textual convention in cinematic constructions of masculinity[25] and the bodies of the travellers[26] comfortably fit within such imagery. However, it is Ernesto's asthma attacks that most clearly place such representations within the characteristic emotive registers of activity↔passivity that the film mobilises. On a semantic and symbolic level his affliction is more than a mere medical condition or a symptom and becomes a sign of his hypersensitivity to the environment. Ernesto's unique ability to open up and absorb the travelling experience, to empathise with the land and its inhabitants, underlies his revolutionary credentials as a man who fully feels and understands the plight of the people. His physical vulnerability made his self-sacrificial heroism even more extraordinary while his death in the Bolivian jungle, in the process of armed struggle, consolidated his legendary status.

Ernesto's first asthma attack happens before the journey itself commences, during the introduction of the main characters. Significantly, it occurs during a rugby game with Ernesto at his most active, in a scene marked by excessive physical movement and sporting iconography that prefigures the relationship between mobility, contact with the land and asthma that become characteristic of his persona as a traveller. Several other manifestations of the condition throughout the journey establish the hold that it has on his body and the danger that it represents to his life. Suffering from asthma, nevertheless, has important dramatic potential and affective value. It establishes Ernesto's empathy with the plight of others as a material force, deeply rooted in his body and part of his nature.[27] In the Peruvian lepers' colony of San Pablo, where he meets Silvia (Antonella Costa), a young patient resisting treatment, it is his difficulty to breathe that initiates their conversation and it is his understanding of suffering that wins her confidence. Particularly effective in persuading Silvia to accept surgery is his description of the experience of the asthma attacks: 'You gotta fight for every breath, and tell death to go to hell.' Suffering becomes the key to empathy.

Particularly significant is Ernesto's night swim across the Amazon and to the south part of the colony to celebrate his birthday with the quarantined patients.[28] This is a pivotal scene that articulates some of the central themes of the film (the authentication of the travelling experience, the mediating agency of the hero's body, the dialectics of activity/passivity and the revolutionary qualities of Ernesto) in his physical movement across the dark, cold and dangerous water. As he swims, his laboured breathing, reminiscent of the asthma attacks, dominates the soundtrack, amplifying the heroic dimensions of the feat as he overcomes not only the adversary current but also the limitations of his own body. Ernesto's 'hypersensitivity' becomes a motivator and motor in the unstoppable movement towards and affinity with the people, provides proof of his determination and makes his triumph over an affliction that otherwise renders him passive and submissive even more heroic. The editing of the scene, with the point of view fluctuating between the mainland (where Alberto, the doctors and the nurses anxiously watch his progress), the river (the arena of the hero's perilous journey) and the island (where the patients excited about the unexpected visit call out his name and cheer him on), places his body in a semantically over-determined position, as it is at once a symbolic bridge between 'civilization' and 'land', the intelligentsia and the people,[29] and the agent of self-propelled movement.

Thus, his unique leadership qualities (and his rapport with people) are established as a composite of natural sensitivity, the ability to learn from experience and the complete determination to overcome physical and other handicaps in the quest for an ultimate goal. Shortly after this scene the film ends by delivering Ernesto 'Che' Guevara to his destiny as he flies off to his revolutionary future. His voice-over outlines the transformative effect of the journey and strongly suggests a newly found confidence and certainty:

> Was our view too narrow, too biased, too hasty? Were our conclusions too rigid? Maybe. Wandering around our America has changed me more than I thought. I am not me anymore, at least I'm not the same me I was.

While *The Motorcycle Diaries*, by grounding its authenticating practices on the body of the traveller, traverses the activity↔passivity axis, *Koktebel* and *Japón* deploy certainty↔uncertainty to achieve similar effects. *Koktebel* revolves around the boy's quest for certainty expressed as a longing for superior vision that can establish a firm view of the world and confirm the father's honesty. Importantly, an intense uncertainty permeates several mobile shots that are attributed to the boy's point of view. Such subjective shots offer restricted spatial exploration but a very intense, tactile sense of the traversed space, constructing a sensual and experiential representation of the landscape. They convey the anxieties and fears of the young traveller through unstable and uncertain frame mobility, by eliminating perspective and by saturating the field of vision with the objects encountered. The landscape is endowed with density, experienced in proximity rather than viewed from distance, represented in material and sensual terms rather than in detached abstraction. In that way, the uncertainty of the boy's mobile vision becomes a potent source for authenticating signs of the travelling experience. In *The Motorcycle Diaries* the mediating agency of the traveller is constructed around images of a receptive body whereas in *Koktebel* the use of handheld camera grounds visions of the landscape in the moving body of the boy. In such shots the point of view is marked by physical movement and vision becomes corporeal, embodied in the mobile traveller, asserting the body's presence in the process of spatial exploration. Where in *The Motorcycle Diaries* the authentication of the experience is facilitated by images of the body in contact with the land, in *Koktebel* the body infiltrates vision itself, registering its presence in subjective views of the travelled space.

The emphasis on the emotional and physical hardship of the journey and its corporeal and sensual qualities in combination with the critique and rejection of conventional travelling views places *Koktebel*'s representation of the travelling experience in sharp opposition to the visuality of the 'tourist gaze'. This is most explicitly articulated in the concluding scene of the boy's arrival at his destination, the Crimean resort of Koktebel. There, the subjective mobile shots used to represent the boy's spatial exploration in search for his aunt's house are claustrophobically crowded with bodies of tourists who obstruct the view and compromise mobility and access, creating a clear conflict of movement and vision between the boy and the tourists. As he enjoys a much-needed meal at a seaside restaurant, an entertainer sings a song that romanticises the road and travelling that provides an ironic counterpoint to the boy's anxious and stressful journey. The same irony surfaces after the meal as the boy appropriates a parasol and a sun lounger, the holiday maker's pleasure props par excellence, as tools of survival during a cold night's sleep on the beach.

While the mental, physical and visual limits of his mobility are contrasted with the plenitude and pleasures of the tourist experience reinforcing the authenticating strategies of the film, his quest for perfect vision is also contextualised, ultimately exposed as utopian. In his brief 'date' with Tanya the boy attempts to demonstrate his ability to obtain detached aerial views – the film provides such a shot but it remains unclear whether this is indeed from the boy's point of view. The boy then proceeds to draw a diagram of the location which seems to correspond roughly to the geography of the place as shown in the aerial view. However, Tanya challenges its accuracy and the boy wipes out his rudimental map. The questioning and rejection of the boy's geographical abstraction can be read as a local's assertion of the right to the land and its representations, and as an indirect but evocative criticism of the narcissistic utopianism of the boy's obsession with perfect visuality. In that way, the film places the boy's mediating agency within a field of contested regimes of vision opening up comparative relationships and complicating the representations of the travelled space.

Japón is structured around, on the one hand, the Man's discovery of life-changing spiritual meaning in the village of Aya and, on the other, the film's quest for pure vision. The utopianism that *Koktebel* relativises is fully embraced in *Japón*'s pursuit of a transcendental experience. Interestingly, Carlos Reygadas articulates his aesthetic commitment to 'purity' of vision as a search for authenticity. Talking about the film's two main actors, Alejandro Ferretis and Magdalena Flores, the director explains:

> When we actually started shooting he started to glamorize himself a little bit, as if he thought we were shooting a French perfume ad. However, he soon learned that I didn't want any of that and that I actually wanted him to do very little . . . Alejandro had never acted before. Magdalena Flores, who plays Ascen, had never acted either. In fact all the cast are non-actors. I wanted to work with pure, real matter, largely for the sake of authenticity.[30]

The film seems to ground its authenticity on 'non-acting', both on the level of performance and on the level of narration. In this case the mediating agency of the travelling hero is, like the glamour of the actor, stripped down to the bare

essentials and provides only a cue rather than a guide to the spatial exploration that the film extensively undertakes. This is evident in patterns of frame
mobility discussed earlier and in the iconography of the body of the Man who
travels light, dresses minimally (he is often shown naked, half-naked or in a
vest) with his physical movement constrained by a pronounced limp.

Within the film's romantic utopianism Ascen is endowed with extraordinary qualities (it is the relationship with her and her land that transforms the
Man) despite, or rather because of, her simplicity and the 'pure', 'real' way
that she approaches life and relates to the world. Although her point of view
is largely excluded from the spatial explorations of the film there is a notable
and structurally significant exemption in the scene that precedes her death.
She requests to accompany the stones of her demolished ancient barn to their
destination and she sits on them as the tractor and the trailer move away. A
series of mobile shots, lasting in total 2′12″, follows, with Ascen's profile in the
foreground and spectacular views of the valley and the surrounding mountains
in the background. The frame is saturated with the warm colours of the trees,
bushes and fields with a cinematography that plays up the warm tones and
offers crisply sharp and clear images.

This series of shots, in the presentation of panoramic views of the landscape,
invites direct comparison with the series analysed in the previous section in
which the Man lies at the top of a plateau. The vivid, warm and detailed nature
of the valley shots contrast sharply with the cold, hazy and rain-soaked views
of the mountains in a manner reminiscent of the beautiful/sublime aesthetic
binary.[31] This dichotomy is often understood as pertaining to qualitatively
different aesthetic experiences, the former appealing to the simple, immediate
pleasures of the body, the latter stimulating the abstract and detached perception of the intellect. Immediacy and attachment to the body are clearly established in the framing of the shots with the foreground dominated by Ascen, as
her face is compositionally linked with the views of the land. The organisation
of the shot also links her vision with the views of the landscape as she is placed
on the left side of the frame facing right, the 'vector' of her gaze covering the
breadth and depth of the frame. Furthermore, her elevated (vis-à-vis the land)
position and the movement of the frame as it tracks her journey, construct her
body and vision as the agent of this spectacular, if conventional, spatial exploration. In marked contrast with the rest of the film, in these five shots the body
of the traveller (who is now Ascen in her brief and fateful journey) remains in
a steady, centred and masterful position that enables the discovery and revelation of the travelled space.

This scene demonstrates that the film's pursuit of authenticity and purity is
ultimately realisable only through the rejection of the agency of the intellectual
outsider, and its replacement with that of the indigenous woman. By exchanging the centre of perception, the subject of spatial exploration, however, the

film turns its back on its own *raison d'être* revealing the Man's journey as a mere narrative excuse and his agency, now abandoned, as an insignificant presence that functions as an entry point that allows glimpses of the purity and authenticity that Reygadas seeks.[32] Alfonso Cuarón, the director of *Y tu mamá también* (Mexico, 2002), articulating the rationale of his own road movie, offers an insight that seems also to inform the textual workings of *Japón*:

> We also saw a reality in Mexico that a lot of people were completely unaware of. But if we had made a documentary then a lot of people wouldn't have cared and consequently wouldn't have seen the film.[33]

While *Japón* involves a far more complex interplay between a documentary aesthetic and its fictional trajectory than Cuarón's film, it certainly exploits the possibilities that narrative situations open up. The agency of the Man and his journey provide the narrative justification for the visual exploration of Aya creating a de facto invasion of the otherwise unapproachable space. The narrative of the film seems to reflect this intrusiveness in the sexual intercourse with Ascen that the Man seeks and achieves, adding a physical and symbolic dimension to the cinematic penetration of the travelled space. It is possible that the tension in frame mobility that the film demonstrates around the figure of the male protagonist is a sign of uneasiness with the film's impossible task (to produce an authentic, real and pure vision out of a fictional situation).[34] It might well be that the film constructs the love-making of the two protagonists, initiated by the Man with Ascen's resigned collaboration, precisely as a way of foregrounding a relationship of power and creating an allegory of the visual penetration of the land by the agency of the traveller and the cinematic apparatus. However, something unsettling, if not disturbing, persists in the realisation that the film uses her death as a means of fulfilling its ambition to achieve the detachment from narrative agency that it desires and the authentic and pure vision that it seeks.

Significantly, after destabilising the agency of the Man and exchanging it briefly for that of Ascen, the film's journey and the camera's liberated epic movement of spatial exploration come to a halt in front of her dead body. The film's anxious search for authentic and pure vision leads inevitably and finally to the discovery of a body. Such a body, the body of the traveller, becomes the inescapable ultimate reference point,[35] the prime authenticating agency of the travelling experience involved in the journeys of all three films. In *The Motorcycle Diaries* the body of Ernesto offers a material and physical demonstration of the impact of the landscape on his subjectivity, a visual manifestation of the dialectics of activity↔passivity that informs the emotive register of the film. In *Koktebel* the views of the travelled space bear the imprints of the traveller's physical mobility; by fluctuating the traveller's vision between the outer boundaries of uncertain subjectivity and utopian certainty the boy's journey traverses fully that axis. Finally, *Japón*'s search for purity is also the search for a suitably pure body on which to attach a certain and authentic vision of its spatial exploration.

NOTES

1. The American road movie clearly attracts the lion's share of critical attention (for example, David Laderman, *Driving Visions: Exploring the Road Movie* (Austin: The University of Texas Press, 2002), extensively discusses 'the road movie . . . as a dynamic manifestation of American society's fascination with the road' (p. 2) before dedicating a final chapter to 'Travelling other highways (*sic*): the European road movie'. See also Jack Sargeant and Stephanie Watson, *Lost Highways: An Illustrated History of Road Movies* (London: Creation Books, 1999). However, Ewa Mazierska and Laura Rascaroli, in *Crossing New Europe: Postmodern Travel and the European Road Movie* (London: Wallflower Press, 2006), set out to 'determine to what extent travel films have engaged with the notion of a changing European socio-geographical space' (p. 1); and Steven Cohan and Ina Rae Hark (eds), *The Road Movie Book* (London and New York: Routledge, 1997), distinguish between 'American roads' and 'alternative routes'.

2. Jason Wood in his exploration of recent Mexican cinema notes the tendency of several films to set their stories outside Mexico City, in rural areas which historically have constituted an off-screen space for Mexican films. He remarks in relation to the groundbreaking in that respect *Y tu mamá también* (Alfonso Cuarón, Mexico, 2002): 'The journey (widely seen as an allegory as well as a literal excursion) brings sexual gratification and rivalry for the boys and a lesson in Mexico's geography, as well as its socio-economic context, for the viewer' (Jason Wood, *The Faber Book of Mexican Cinema* [London: Faber & Faber, 2006], p. 98).

3. See previous discussion in Chapter 1: the clearest accounts are offered by Christoph Asendorf in *Batteries of Life: On the History of Things and Their Perception in Modernity* (Berkeley, CA, and London: University of California Press, 1993), and Wolfgang Schivelbusch, *The Railway Journey: Trains and Travel in the 19th Century* (Oxford: Blackwell, 1980). See also David Harvey, *The Condition of Postmodernity: An Enquiry into the Origins of Cultural Change* (Oxford: Blackwell, 1990).

4. Jonas Larsen in his essay 'Tourism mobilities and the travel glance: experiences of being on the move', *Scandinavian Journal of Hospitality and Tourism*, 1.2 (2001), pp. 80–98, investigates the travelling aspect of tourism, highlighting its discursive exclusion from studies of tourism as a social and cultural phenomenon. The literature on tourism, travel and their relationship is vast – for an extensive bibliography and a comprehensive mapping of debates around mobility and travelling, see Kevin Hannam, Mimi Sheller and John Urry, 'Editorial: mobilities, immobilities and moorings', *Mobilities*, 1.1 (2006), pp. 1–22.

5. Debbie Lisle, *The Global Politics of Contemporary Travel Writing* (Cambridge: Cambridge University Press, 2006), pp. 77–8.

6. John Sallis, *Topographies* (Bloomington & Indianapolis: Indiana University Press, 2006), pp. 1–2.

7. Laderman, *Driving Visions*, p. 13.

8. Larsen, 'Tourism mobilities and the travel glance'.

9. Cees Nooteboom, *Nomad's Hotel: Travels in Time and Space* (London: Vintage, 2007), p. 4.

10. Sallis, *Topographies*, p. 4.

11. Larsen, 'Tourism mobilities and the travel glance', following John Urry (*The Tourist Gaze* [London: Sage, 1990]), proposes a distinction between the stasis and stillness of the 'tourist gaze' and the mobility of the 'travel glance'; 'views on the move' involve aspects of the latter.

12. Orvar Löfgren, *On Holiday: A History of Vacationing* (Berkely, CA, and London: University of California Press, 2002), pp. 69–71.

13. A strikingly similar organisation of the frame surfaces in a number of American road movies, most notably *Easy Rider* (Dennis Hopper, USA, 1969). Laderman analyses the credits sequence of *Detour* (Edgar G. Ulmer, USA, 1945) as a variation of the theme (*Driving Visions*, p. 31).

14. Laderman, for example, suggests: 'one technique road movies tend to mobilize with a certain verve is the traveling shot' (*Driving Visions*, p. 15).

15. Barbara Klinger, 'The road to dystopia: landscaping the nation in *Easy Rider*', in Cohan and Hark (eds), *Road Movie Book*, pp. 179–203, p. 188.

16. In her analysis of costume films Pidduck uses the movement-image of the woman at the window to outline the multiple tensions that inform the genre. Significantly, she discusses such tensions both in terms of activity/passivity and in relation to the mobility of the heroine. See Julianne Pidduck, *Contemporary Costume Film* (London: BFI, 2004), esp. pp. 25–43, and her earlier essay, 'Of windows and country walks: frames of space and movement in 1990s Austen adaptations', *Screen*, 39.4 (1998), pp. 381–400.

17. Schivelbush, *Railway Journey*, p. 195 (note 8).

18. Interestingly, his technique for obtaining such detached masterful views involves the shutting of his eyes, a negation of a form of perception in favour of another, that echoes the effect of the frame mobility in the carriage shot.

19. Clear binaries pertaining to the different aesthetic experiences of the sublime and the beautiful were originally proposed by Kant (Immanuel Kant, *Observation on the Feeling of the Sublime and the Beautiful* [1764; Berkeley: University of California Press, 1960]) and Burke (Edmund Burke, *A philosophical Enquiry into the Origin of Our Ideas of the Sublime and the Beautiful* [1757; London: Routledge, 1958]) and appropriated in the 1980s in the 'postmodern debate', notably by Jameson (Fredric Jameson, 'Postmodernism or the cultural logic of Late capitalism', *New Left Review*, 146 [1984], pp. 53–92) and Jean-François Lyotard, 'Presenting the unpresentable: the sublime', *Artforum*, 20.8 (April 1984), pp. 64–9, and 'The sublime and the avant-garde', *Artforum*, 22.8 (April 1982), pp. 36–43.

20. *The Passion of St Matthew* has been used as the soundtrack in several of Andrei Tarkovsky's films (*The Mirror* [Soviet Union, 1975] and *The Sacrifice* [Sweden/UK/France, 1986] – in the latter the credits sequence is accompanied by the aria used in the *Japón* scene); Tarkovsky is one of the directors whose influence Reygadas openly recognises; see Wood, *Faber Book of Mexican Cinema*, p. 122.

21. The lyrics of the aria are particularly poignant in the context of the scene: *Erbarme dich, mein Gott, um meiner Zähren willen! Schaue hier, Herz und Auge weint vor dir bitterlich. Erbarme dich, mein Gott* ('Have mercy, my God, for the sake of my tears! See here, before you heart and eyes weep bitterly. Have mercy, my God'). The lyrics clearly connect with both the *mise-en-scène* and the high camera positions employed in the scene.

22. The structure of the piece (that Reygadas says informed the 'shape' of the final shot [Wood, *Faber Book of Mexican Cinema*, p. 122]), with silence written into the score,

punctuated by the sound of a single bell ringing at regular intervals and the various string instruments playing the same score but at different and variable pace and pitch, creates both a linear sense of progression and a swirling effect of music building around and diverging from the key notes.

23. Schivelbush, *Railway Journey*; see the discussion around the railway mobile vision in Chapter 1.

24. For example, see Lauren Rabinovitz, 'From *Hale's Tours* to *Star Tours*: virtual voyages, travel ride films, and the delirium of the hyper-real', in Jeffrey Ruoff (ed.), *Virtual Voyages: Cinema and Travel* (Durham, NC, and London: Duke University Press, 2006), pp. 42–60.

25. Starting with Steve Neale, 'Masculinity as spectacle', *Screen*, 24.6 (1983), pp. 2–16.

26. *Thelma and Louise* (Ridley Scott, USA/France, 1991) attracted critical attention for its unusual characters. For example, see, Sharon Willis, 'Hardware and hardbodies: what do women want? A reading of *Thelma and Louise*', in Jim Collins, Hilary Radner and Ava Preacher Collins (eds), *Film Theory Goes to the Movies* (New York: Routledge, 1993), pp. 120–8.

27. It is interesting to compare the effects of asthma attacks that set the lungs into uncontrollable and involuntary motion (spasms) to the hiccups of Uncle Cseklik in *Hukkle*.

28. The Amazon River divides the colony into a north and south side, separating in effect the staff, doctors and nurses from the patients.

29. The scene comes immediately after a speech that Ernesto gives at his birthday party, in which, for the first time in the film, he articulates his political vision: 'We believe, and this journey has only confirmed this belief, that the division of America into unstable and illusory nations is a complete fiction. We are one single mestizo race from Mexico to the Magellan Straits . . . I propose a toast to Peru and to a United America.' His commitment to overcoming borders and barriers, exemplified by the swim that crosses the Amazon and unites him with the segregated patients, is also demonstrated by his refusal to wear gloves when handling the patients; even the name 'Che' is given to him by locals in Chile as an outcome of his contact with the people.

30. Reygadas in Wood, *Faber Book of Mexican Cinema*, p. 119.

31. See note 19 above.

32. On the soundtrack there is a similar struggle between extra-diegetic music, the music that the Man plays in his portable player and bursts of 'real' and natural sounds originating from and within the space of the journey. This is a similar relationship to that articulated through frame mobility as a tension between the movement of the Man and that of the camera – instances of authentic and pure vision surface against and beyond his agency.

33. The director Alfonso Cuarón confirms Wood's suggestion from a slightly different perspective, quoted in Wood, *Faber Book of Mexican Cinema*, p. 105.

34. Not impossible per se but in the terms that Reygadas articulates his quest for purity and authenticity.

35. On one level the 'bird's eye' view of the tiny figures of the boy and the girl provides a perfect example of the use of the body of the traveller as a marker or a yardstick, a concrete individualised unit of comparison that testifies to the vastness of the landscape. Both *The Motorcycle Diaries* and *Japón* provide several similar instances of extremely long shots of the moving figures of the heroes dwarfed by their immense surroundings.

CHAPTER 5

Intercepted trajectories

5.1 ENCOUNTERS

The quests of the heroes of the three films discussed in the previous chapter take them on journeys of exploration, discovery and revelation that also become processes of self-transformation and change. We discussed in detail how the films are informed by a spectrum of peculiarly modern sensibilities activated by mobility in the protagonists' fundamental relationship with the space that they traverse. The focus of that analysis has been almost exclusively on the explored, discovered, revealed landscape with limited reference to the characters that populate that space. The encounters with such figures are crucially important, however, providing density and depth to the landscape and transforming it from spectacular backdrop to meaningful narrative space. In *The Motorcycle Diaries*, the mining couple, the leper colony, the Peruvian boy 'discovered' in the spatial explorations of the journey, all amplify its transformative potential. In *Japón*, Sabina, the Judge and Ascen provide a counterpoint, an alternative view of life and the world that affects not only the Man but also the film's cinematic articulation of space. In *Koktebel*, Tanya, Ksenyia and Mikhail are firmly placed in the land, their presence and narrative agency lending momentum to the hermeneutics of space by contributing to the uncertainty of the boy or by inhibiting the journey's progress.

Despite their narrative significance in all these films, such figures remain within a constrained and bounded space with their agency largely meaningful only in relation to that of the travellers, with their mobility curtailed and with limited opportunity to instigate movement of the frame. Interesting in that respect is Ascen's brief (and final) 'journey' particularly so because it appears to be a rare and exceptional moment when the frame mobility is determined by the agency of a 'discovered', indigenous character. While the short series of shots offers spectacular mobile and panoramic views, the composition and *mise-en-scène* create a natural, 'unforced' and self-evident bond between Ascen and the land, a symbolic unity that is markedly different from the dynamic dialectic relationship with the landscape that otherwise informs the film's mobile vision. In that way Ascen is placed in a privileged bond with nature but outside the representational, emotive and discursive modalities of modern subjectivity that underpins the narrative agency of quests.

This indicates that a rather eclectic and exclusive deployment of the dialectics of certainty↔uncertainty and activity↔passivity is in operation in *Japón*. This is also the case with the two other films discussed – in their movements of exploration, (self-)discovery and revelation, the encounters with the characters that populate the space that they traverse are ultimately one-sided affairs that are textually exploited for their ability to enhance the transformative effect of the journey on the heroes. While the bodies of the travellers are over-invested with mobility and are vital in mediating and authenticating the travelling experience, those of the locals are expendable, meaningful only in relation to a movement that eludes them, their autonomy and agency sacrificed (as Ascen's death eloquently demonstrates) in order to enhance the symbolic and emotive impact of the travelled space.

This tendency is perhaps most clearly demonstrated in the final sequence of *The Motorcycle Diaries*, which includes a succession of black-and-white images of people encountered by the heroes in their journey across Latin America.[1] A close-up of Alberto's face staring offscreen (presumably at Ernesto's departing plane) changes into a blank screen over which we hear Ernesto's voice reading the diary entry that expresses his complete transformation ('I am not me any more'). As the film's musical theme takes over, a series of twelve shots (lasting 1′25″ in total) unfolds followed by a series of intertitles that take the story forward to Ernesto's death and Alberto's new life in Cuba. The image of an aged Alberto, intercut with a departing plane, leads to the roll of the final credits. The syntagmatic position of the black-and-white shots separates them from the main body of the narrative with their temporality resolutely indeterminate as they float suspended between the past (the recordings of the diary) and the future (Guevara's history). The composition of the frame (conventional snap shot portraits) and the cinematography (black-and-white, almost immobile but not completely still images) set them further apart from the rest of the film. At the margins of the film's narrative these images offer a condensed and retrospective summary of key encounters. Editing, soundtrack and iconography strongly frame them as Ernesto's memories, as the human dimension of the indelible experiences of the journey and as an emotive reminder of its transformative power. In that way, the function and value attached to their presence at the conclusion of *The Motorcycle Diaries* reside not in the people themselves but in their narrative use as a causal force in the forging of Ernesto's revolutionary consciousness.

It is striking, however, that these are not photographs or still images but shots animated by minimal but observable movement. One of the effects of the limited yet perceptible mobility is that it endows with connotations of live-ness[2] these representations, turning them into vivid and powerful memories and differentiating them from the reified and anodyne instant photography typical of the 'tourist gaze'.[3] Thus their framed, restricted and controlled movement is exploited as a double mark of authenticity: that of the film and that of the hero's transformative experience. As the strictly limited instance of Ascen's mobile vision also indicates, the trajectories of these other bodies and other lives are essentially insignificant in themselves, unexplored by the films, evocative presences that remain foreign, belonging to unknown, even unknow-able, emotive registers, briefly brought to life by the exploring, discovering and revealing movement of travellers. They constitute part of what the journey reveals,[4] yet these presences are meaningful only in relation to the heroes, with their limited mobility fuelling the forward transformative movement of the travellers. Ultimately these encounters only reinforce a modern dialectics of exploration, discovery and revelation that appropriates and absorbs all other types of mobility.

This chapter, however, will focus on films in which the trajectories of the travelling heroes are intercepted and the dialectics that inform their cinematic articulations are interrogated through a series of encounters that function in a distinct fashion. Not surprisingly such interceptions surface in the context of what critics have variously termed 'intercultural cinema',[5] 'transnational film genre'[6] or 'exilic and diasporic filmmaking',[7] and most evidently across the geo-graphical and historical terrain of 'New Europe' and its periphery.[8] A number of recent films (for example, *Tickets* [Abbas Kiarostami/Ermanno Olmi/Ken Loach, Italy/UK, 2005], *One Day in Europe* [Hannes Stör, Germany/Spain, 2005], *Le Grand Voyage* (Ismaël Ferroukhi, France/Morocco, 2004]) are thematically preoccupied with encounters articulated around different and distinct groups of travellers and types of mobility.

Engrained in the textuality of such films is a process of cultural syncretism within which the sensibilities and emotive registers that inform journeys of exploration, discovery and revelation are substantially contextualised by movements of displacement, exile, diaspora and migration. In *The Motorcycle Diaries*, *Koktebel* and *Japón* the chronotopes within which the travellers operate are situated in a 'post'-era and traverse spaces that are either geopolitically reconfigured or under reconfiguration. The films under consideration here are informed by a different (albeit complementary) dimension of the 'post', articulated not so much in terms of its spatial and temporal nature but mainly as a relation, a profoundly historical and political tension that places mobility in a dynamic field of antagonistic forces. The connotative wealth of the 'post' is explored by Ella Shohat in her detailed and polemical critique of the term 'post-colonial'.[9] Emphasising the relational (rather than spatial) aspects of the term, Shohat identifies 'in-betweenness' as one of its key connotations:

> The operation of simultaneously privileging and distancing the colonial narrative, moving beyond it, structures the 'in-between' framework of the 'postcolonial'. This 'in-betweeness' becomes evident through a kind of commutation test. While one can posit the duality between colonizer and colonized and even neocolonizer and neocolonized, it does not make much sense to speak of postcolonizers and postcolonized. 'Colonialism' and 'neocolonialism' imply both oppression and the possibility of resistance. Transcending such dichotomies, the term 'postcolonial' posits no clear domination and calls for no clear opposition. It is this structured ambivalence of the 'postcolonial,' of positing a simultaneously close and distant temporal relation to the 'colonial,' that is appealing in a post-structuralist academic context. It is also this fleeting quality, however, that makes the 'postcolonial' an uneasy term for a geopolitical critique of the centralized distribution of power in the world.[10]

While Shohat's political reservations around the usefulness of the term are important, her description is all the same striking in the way that the 'post' is endowed with mobility, perceived as a perpetual oscillating movement that underpins the mutual dependency and attraction between two different but inextricably connected historical and discursive poles. The textual practices of the cinematic journeys of intercepted trajectories that this chapter investigates demonstrate a similar, albeit qualitatively distinct in its formal specificity, articulation of mutual dependency and tension between different types of mobility. This involves a relativisation of movement that is often only implicitly political, with the films alluding to rather than manifesting the global 'distribution of power', as Shohat remarks in relation to the lack of 'clarity' of the term 'post-colonial'.

More specifically, the first section of this chapter will consider the theme of 'relational movement' in films directed by Tony Gatlif (mainly *Exils* [France, 2004] but also *Transylvania* [France, 2006] and *Cadjo Dilo* [France/Romania, 1997] and *Swing* [France, 2002]). The focus in the second section is on the convention of 'converging routes' and its articulation in the films of Fatih Akin (*In July* [Germany, 2000], *Head On* [Germany/Turkey, 2004], *Crossing the Bridge* [Germany/Turkey, 2005] and *The Edge of Heaven* [Germany/Turkey/Italy, 2007]). Gatlif's use of relational movement places different types of contemporary mobility in comparative frames of reference, whereas converging routes, journeys and itineraries repeatedly revisited enables Akin to interrogate the self-sufficiency and autonomy of quests.

Both Gatlif and Akin fit quite comfortably in Hamid Naficy's category of 'transnational filmmakers'[11] and their films generally conform to the distinctive features of authorship (and subjectivity) that he sees as surfacing in such work. Although reservations must be raised around Naficy's over-generalising tendencies, his description of transnational directors as being 'in the grips of both the old and the new, the before and the after',[12] in its suggested relational 'in-betweenness', seems to aptly describe the textual practices of the films of Gatlif and Akin (without necessarily accounting for the way in which they operate or perceive themselves as directors).

5.2   RELATIONAL MOVEMENT IN *EXILS*

On a first, obvious but, as we will show, rather misleading view, Gatlif's travelling narratives are quests par excellence. Revolving around stories of personal discovery and structured around explorations (of spaces, people, cultures and emotions) they usually culminate in moments of revelation that confirm and/or reinforce processes of self-transformation. In *Swing*, Max's (Oscar Copp) encounters with Miraldo (Tschavolo Schmitt) and Swing (Lou Rech) change his perspective on life and family and reveal new and exciting cultural alternatives. In *Gadjo Dilo*, Stéphane's (Romain Duris) search for the music that fascinated his father takes him to Romania where he meets and falls in love with Sabina (Rona Hartner), discovers the world of Romany culture and ultimately recognises and rejects the exoticisation of his, foreigner's (*gadjo*), views of that community. Similarly, Zingarina's (Asia Argento) journey in *Transylvania* is motivated by her passion for the musician Milan (Marco Castoldi) but leads to unexpected encounters, a new relationship (with another foreigner, Tchangalo [Birol Ünel]) and the decision to settle down in her new community. *Exils* is perhaps most explicit as it constructs its narrative around the journey of exploration and discovery of the two protagonists, Zano (Romain Duris) and Naima (Lubna Azabal), who search for their Algerian connections on their way from France to Algeria (via Spain and Morocco).

However, the films are quests that systematically contextualise the process of their spatial explorations with mobilities of a different order. This is articulated as a systematic relativisation of the emotive registers that inform the protagonists' movement and surfaces on several levels of the films' textual practices. Narratives are structured around encounters with other moving agents who not only alter the course of the protagonists' trajectories but undermine their motivation and goals.

Furthermore, such encounters are often organised around point-of-view and editing systems that place regimes of looking and observation within relational structures. Stéphane is repeatedly observed by various members of the Romany community that he stays with – the title of the film (that translates as 'the crazy foreigner') indicates the perception of his character from their perspective (and in their language). This is most explicitly articulated in the scene where he cleans the house of his host Isidor (Izidor Serban), with his actions observed (and ridiculed) by Sabina and her friends.

The anthropological dimension of Stéphane's journey (to observe the Romany community and discover the authentic gypsy music that his father adored) is thus problematised and ultimately rejected, as at the end of the film he destroys the recordings of the live performances that he has collected. *Swing*'s narrative revolves around the character of Max but his first foray into the unknown part of the town (where Miraldo and Swing live) is not a spatial exploration that relies on his point of view – instead his arrival is observed by Swing who interrogates him about the purpose of his visit. The arrival of Zingarina, her friend Marie (Amira Casar) and their interpreter Luminitsa (Alexandra Beaujard) in a Transylvanian village at the opening of the film is constructed along similar lines. While the early part of the scene interrupts the 'views on the move' of the three travellers with static, arresting shots of villagers looking back at them, the second part depicts their search for Milan through a series of point-of-view shots that place them as the object of observation and creates a sense of the village as a potentially threatening space beyond their control, rather than as an arena of spatial exploration.

Through such observational structures the agency of the protagonists is consistently 'bracketed' by alternative frames of reference, decentring and denaturalising the trajectories of their journeys. This is reinforced through other mechanisms that further contextualise mobility. A recurring motif in Gatlif's work, for example, is the setting of scenes in forests and woods. The emotive qualities of the movement of the characters within such settings vary considerably, on certain occasions expressing extremes of pleasure and freedom, at other times encapsulating instances of loss, fear and panic. In *Gadjo Dilo* Stéphane and Sabina and in *Exils* Zano and Naima run wildly among the trees as part of their lovemaking; in *Swing* Max and Swing chase each other happily in the woodlands by the river; in *Gadjo Dilo*, after the destruction of the Romany settlement, the protagonists run in the woods in complete despair; in *Transylvania* Zingarina runs maniacally through a forest pursued by the demons that possess her; and Miraldo's death in *Swing* is represented as a flight through the woods. In that way the connotations of movement in that particular setting are rendered ambivalent and unpredictable, inviting comparisons with other instances of similar yet drastically different mobility.

More evocative is a compositional motif in Gatlif's films in which individual shots are organised around two different types of movement that are attached to the different characters that cohabit the frame. In such shots the moving figure of the traveller is framed by the moving figures of significant people encountered in the journey: in *Gadjo Dilo* Stéphane's first encounter with Sabina and her friends is punctuated by a shot in which the outer edges of the mobile frame are occupied by the women moving away from him while he is placed in the centre and moves towards them. This type of frame composition and mobility recurs in Gatlif's films but I intend to focus on a particularly suggestive use of the convention in *Exils*. I will first, however, address some more general aspects of the film's textual construction of movement.

Laura U. Marks in her work on intercultural cinema repeatedly uses the term 'excavation' to describe a textual activity of search for and recovery of history and/or memory. She sees such textuality as profoundly deconstructive:

> [T]he acts of excavation performed by these works is primarily deconstructive, for it is necessary to dismantle the colonial histories that frame minority stories before those stories can be told in their own terms.[13]

Ultimately, they are fruitless as the histories and memories sought are invariably absent or erased.[14] While remaining deeply sceptical about the negativity that permeates Marks's conceptualisation of the term, I find 'excavation' a particularly useful descriptor of key aspects of the textual construction of movement and mobility in *Exils*.

Connotations of 'bringing into light' or 'moving into view' are particularly relevant in analysing some of the film's visual motifs and narrative trajectories, whereas 'excavation' as a culturally and historically situated activity also fits comfortably within the emotive registers of the journey of exploration, discovery and revelation that the protagonists undertake.

Exils opens with Zano asking Naima whether she wants to go to Algeria, offering no special reasons for why he intends to do so. The film's narrative eventually reveals deep personal and historical reasons for such a journey: Zano's French family left Algeria after independence and Naima is involved in a painful negotiation of her Algerian ancestry. The scene starts with an extreme close-up of part of Zano's back, with the camera initially moving closer before it starts a slow tracking-out movement that concludes with a medium shot of his naked body standing in front of an open window that looks out at busy Parisian streets. A breathless, manic female voice uttering fragments of sentences ('It's an emergency', 'we need to talk about democracy', 'we need to talk about those who are absent', 'those who live without democracy', 'freedom', 'it's urgent') to the staccato beat of drums dominates the soundtrack. This adds a sense of powerful physical urge which is layered on the movement of the frame that is rooted in and reveals the body of the hero. This sound–image combination precedes Zano's declaration of his intention to travel to Algeria and offers an eloquent emotive context for his decision.

Thus the scene connects the journey of the protagonists to a political (if not clearly articulated) discourse[15] and it infuses it with a physical urgency, a desire for mobility located in the hero's body. In that respect the movement of the camera away from Zano enacts a symbolic excavation that brings into light an embodied memory[16] and at the same time a revelation of the narrative space that the hero's body occupies, a space that will soon be left behind in the journey to Algeria. Importantly, the film repeatedly scrutinises the protagonists' bodies, exploring their scars in scenes where they recall and reveal personal histories and experiences. Clearly the bodies of the two travellers occupy crucial positions in the film's narrative: they provide the physical urgency that propels them forward in their journey, host the powerful memories that motivate their movement of exploration, discovery and revelation and, in a typical fashion, authenticate the travelling experience.

In a long scene towards the end of the film Naima and Zano participate in a Sufi ceremony that puts them into a state of trance during which they abandon their bodies to the accelerating beat of the music until they collapse, losing control of their mobility but finally finding relief from the physical urgency that motivates their adventure. The film's narrative concludes with the rediscovery of their Algerian connections (Zano visits the old house of his family, Naima accepts her ancestry that she has been stubbornly rejecting) and a new awareness of the historical and cultural context that informs their identities. The end of the journey offers a resolution to the anxious soul-searching and a ceremonial absorption (and exhaustion) of their physical mobility.

Throughout *Exils*, the past as embodied memory is mobilised alongside the movement of the protagonists in their present journey. The film's narrative structure, the motivation and destination of the protagonists and the encounters of different mobile characters in their journey, activate a multiplicity of different but interrelated movements. Naima and Zano's journey is a movement of exploration, discovery and revelation (of contemporary Europe, of Algeria, of a mythical past all but erased from memory) but its trajectory brings into light other movements: mobilities that historically precede and inform the present journey (Naima's diasporic origins and Zano's 'post-'identity are referentially dependent on colonialism and the anti-colonial struggle) but also the processes of contemporary displacement that unfold in the same geographical terrain. The film's opening scene, discussed above, is interrupted by a shot of a mass of people (the clothes and the desert landscape suggesting a North African setting) that form a human stream moving towards the camera – the film's title appears in big, bright red letters over that image.

A similar shot appears later as the two protagonists travel on a train from Morocco to Algeria. A shot of Naima falling asleep is followed by another that looks back at the rail tracks as the train enters a dark tunnel. As complete darkness overcomes the image, a series of shots of Naima and Zano walking against the flow of a mass of people (possibly Algerians, as a flag carried by one of them suggests, and the song 'Algeria' is heard on the soundtrack) conclude with a shot remarkably similar to that of the beginning. While it is unclear whether these shots represent a dream within or the reality of the diegesis,[17] they powerfully relativise the exploring mobility of the protagonists with a reference to movements of mass displacement. Similarly, the shot in which the title '*Exils*' appears offers a movement that in its scale and direction interrogates the overarching narrative trajectory of personal quest.

The descriptor 'exiles' seems to define Naima and Zano (subjects of a historical diasporic displacement) as well as the anonymous mass of people (refugees?) and the various other travellers encountered in the journey (the gypsies, several migrant workers of whom Said [Zouhir Gacem] and Leila [Leila Makhlouf] have a distinct place in the film's story). The semantic fluidity of the term in the context of the film is evident not only in the various types of mobility that underlie the different journeys but also in terms of its organisation of movement of/in the frame. On the level of narrative, Zano and Naima's quest of (self-)exploration is effectively an act of excavation that reveals overlooked, forgotten, marginal or excluded movements and transient spaces of displacement (empty deserted buildings, ruins, old non-functional industrial complexes, ports, borders).

Conversely, the journey of the protagonists is motivated by historically earlier movements (diaspora, exile, migration) while the encounters with alternative mobilities define the context and interrogate the emotive registers of their quest.

The encounter with Said and Laila is of particular importance both in terms of its narrative significance (it is with their family that Zano and Naima will stay in Algiers) and in the way it expresses a specific articulation of relational movement of/in the frame. The four meet in a small town in Spain where Said and Laila, on their way to Paris to 'work and study', have established a temporary residence in a deteriorating empty building where they accommodate the two Parisians. A clear sense of exploration marks the scene, as the camera meanders around the space at the outskirts of a town littered with the ruins of collapsed or collapsing buildings and factories, while Laila asks Naima probing questions about her identity and personal history ('isn't yours an Arab name?' 'are you Arab?' 'why don't you speak Arabic?'), and Zano reveals that the death of his father and mother happened in a car crash as they were on their way to visit Algeria.[18] The scene also maps out the difference between two kinds of mobility: the north-bound trajectory of the migrant workers and the opposite direction of the travellers, the soul-searching, self-discovery purpose of one journey and the anxious desire to study and work that provides the motivation for the other, the pleasurable adventurous passage towards a chosen destination of the couple and the perilous, illegal and necessarily evasive track of the siblings.

The scene concludes with a long (1′25″) mobile shot that opens with the four saying their goodbyes as they leave the town for their separate destinations. The camera is positioned inside the back of a truck where three other passengers are already on board. The truck's dark interior (and the figures of the passengers) frames the bright outside space of the town's post-industrial landscape as Said and Laila jump on, leaving Zano and Naima standing on the dusty road. As the vehicle departs, the camera, mounted on the truck, becomes mobile, continuing to look backwards at the bright opening that forms a frame within the frame in which Zano and Naima start walking towards the same direction. An obvious effect of the frame composition, a double frame of relational movement, is that it binds the two kinds of mobility in a mutually dependent relationship, suggesting a similar trajectory but also highlighting their differences: the leisurely walking of Zano and Naima contrasts with the faster automotive transportation of the group of migrant workers, the freedom associated with the former's mobility (the bright open road, the careless stride) is contextualised by the dark enclosure of the truck and the submissiveness of its passengers (demonstrated by the hypnotic swaying of their bodies in response to the truck's motion).

The speed differential opens up a distance between the two sets of travellers and Zano and Naima's figures diminish, placed in an increasingly expansive space. As the truck takes a sharp turn, the couple momentarily disappear from view but within seconds Naima first and then Zano re-enter the frame as they run towards the truck. When Naima catches up she passes on a piece of paper with a telephone number, advising Said and Laila to call it when (and if) they make it to Paris. In that way, the distance opened-up by the double frame of relational movement becomes a space that Naima, enabled by her freedom of and control over movement, traverses, turning it into a terrain of narrative action and character development as she accomplishes an act of dramaturgic significance and demonstrates a fresh understanding of her identity in realising the affinity with Said and Laila and the connection between their respective journeys.

This instance of a double frame of relational movement offers a clear manifestation of a key ambiguity in the textual practices of *Exils*. On the one hand, journeys, mobilities and movements of/in the frame that involve different types of agency (and ultimately historically different subjectivities) are placed in relation to each other, informing and interrogating their respective values, emotive registers and the narrative forms that underpin their distinct trajectories. In the particular shot under consideration, the image of the bright opening bordered by the darker edges, the double frame of the truck interior and the road, visually evokes an act of 'excavation', the discovery of one type of movement through another. This brings into light individual movements and their historical and emotive relationship, binds them together in a way that inescapably refers the one to the other, undermines the values of autonomy, self-sufficiency, freedom and purposeful self-determined agency attached to quests and journeys of (self-)exploration, discovery and revelation. By placing them into a frame otherwise solely occupied by the travelling protagonists the film brings into attention the movements, trajectories and histories that are blatantly omitted in the quests of the previous chapter.

On the other hand, the numerous binaries (darkness/light, open/closed, freedom/submission) that inform the double frame of the shot point towards a potentially hierarchical organisation of relational movement. Not only is the film structured around the mobility and the agency of the Parisian travellers but the existence of different types of movement is revealed through them. It is Zano and Naima's spatial exploration that makes the interception by people like Said and Laila possible. Furthermore, as the figure of the double frame suggests, relational movement can be rather comfortably mapped along the axes of activity↔passivity and certainty↔uncertainty in a way that subsumes the movements of migration, diaspora and displacement under a modern emotive register. In other words, *Exils* relativises movements of exploration, discovery and revelation, through the intercepting trajectories of other journeys, but it deploys its syncretism in a manner that renders alternative mobilities meaningful only in that particular role, as interrogations of a dominant tendency but ultimately unknown in themselves. While the restricted agency, controlled mobility, uncertain destination, pragmatic motivation of such movements brings into light the privileged nature of the journeys of exploration, discovery and revelation, it remains emotively and semantically dependent on them. Diasporic and migratory mobilities might be employed as a framing device but they are also held captive by the very frame that they set up and the movement that they intercept.

5.3 FATIH AKIN'S CONVERGING ROUTES

The opening sequence of *In July*, the film that brought Fatih Akin into the spotlight of international critical attention, is an encounter between two strangers, a moment of convergence of two separate journeys and two distinct narrative strands. In a long empty rural road the Mercedes Benz that Isa (Mehmet Kurtulus) drives pulls up at the side. The gradual darkening of the daylight, caused by a total solar eclipse seems to have forced the stop. Isa emerges from the car to watch the phenomenon and then opens the car boot where a foul-smelling dead body lies. As he uses air freshener to nullify the smell, a subjective mobile point of view shot indicates the unexpected arrival of Daniel (Moritz Bleibtreu) in the scene. Isa is startled and assaults Daniel who, nevertheless, explains that he is a hitchhiker looking for a lift. Isa initially refuses the request and drives away running Daniel down as he tries to stop the car. After starting and stopping the car several times Isa eventually offers Daniel a lift. Following brief introductions during which Daniel reveals that he travels to Turkey to meet a mysterious woman, he begins to narrate the story of his journey so far. The film reverts to a third-person narrative that presents Daniel's story and his journey with Juli (Christiane Paul) from Germany to Istanbul, across Central and Eastern Europe,[19] that was triggered by a meeting with Turkish Melek (Idil Üner) in his home city of Hamburg. Within such a structure, the opening scene is inevitably revisited as the two temporal orders eventually converge, concluding the film in a unified narration that renders a significant part of the film a flashback.

Thus the opening sequence of *In July* maps out a series of converging trajectories that are, as we will demonstrate, typical of Akin's cinema. In his films stories, characters, journeys, itineraries, temporal orders, narrative strands, points of view, all repeatedly meet and intertwine. It is, however, important to note the violence that underlines the first encounter between Isa and Daniel, their journeys colliding before eventually merging. In fact violence permeates the encounters between many of the characters in Akin's films (for example, the explosive relationship between Sibel [Sibel Kekili] and Cahit [Birol Ünel] in *Head On* and the verbal aggression between Ayten [Nurgul Yesilçay] and Sussanne [Hanna Schygulla] in *The Edge of Heaven*) and continuously emerges in the spatial explorations of their journeys (most obviously in Sibels's horrific beating in Istanbul and in Lotte's [Patrycia Ziolkowska] death in the same city). Routes and destinies converge but do so in conflict and with difficulty, foregrounding and negotiating deeply rooted differences, belonging to different types of travelling and involving different emotive registers. Whereas Isa's journey is an act of desperation that attempts to repatriate for proper burial the dead body of his illegal immigrant uncle, Daniel's adventure is an exploration of his feelings for Juli and, more generally, of his views on life. Isa's is a journey of evasion burdened by a hidden body in the boot of his car, Daniel's is a celebration of the freedom that the road offers. Like Gatlif's relational movements, the converging routes in Akin's films inform and interact with each other placing different types of mobility and travelling in a dialogic, mutually dependent relationship, which is informed by contesting power structures, histories and politics as the thematic violence suggests.

This 'violent convergence' makes particular sense with reference to certain biographical aspects. Born in Hamburg from Turkish parents, receiving his film education and establishing his career in Germany, Akin structures his stories as journeys to and from Turkey (especially Istanbul), exploiting and exploring the cinematic possibilities that cultural difference generates. By the same token, however, Akin places his film-making at a site of convergence that he often experiences as challenging and uncomfortable. Turkey and Istanbul, in particular, have been seen as a space of convergence par excellence, an imaginary area where, as the cliché has it, the West meets the East, a notion amplified and foregrounded by the ongoing process of EU membership negotiations. Akin's films not only offer multilayered and complex interrogations of such clichés but are also marked by ambiguity and often contradiction between their marketing and representational strategies. On the one hand, the DVD of *Crossing the Bridge: The Sound of Istanbul* describes the film as 'an absorbing portrait of the city that bridges Europe and Asia and continues the themes raised in . . . *Head-On* by challenging notions of east and west',[20] establishing and exploiting the liberal, multicultural dimensions of Akin's films' themes that also heavily feature in their critical reception.[21] On the other hand, Akin seems to be acutely aware of what is at stake with clichés of that kind and, as we will discuss, the development of his film-making involves a relentless and uncompromising questioning of the cinematic conventions (including the ones that he himself follows in earlier films) that are employed in the narrative appropriation of the Turkish locations that abound in his films.

A particularly suggestive glimpse of such questioning emerges in the documentary *Fatih Akin: Diary of a Film Traveller* (Monique Akin, Germany, 2007), a commentary on the making of *The Edge of Heaven*. There, Akin explains how an exploratory trip to his grandfather's village of Camburnu on the Black Sea coast of Turkey, as he was researching locations for the film's script, helped him to clarify the eventual storyline. As a result of the trip Akin rejected what appeared to be his original inspiration, namely, to explore the interaction between two emblematic but drastically contrasting film stars: Hanna Schygulla (almost synonymous with Fassbinder's melodramas) and Tuncel Kurtiz (seminal Turkish actor associated with, among others, Yilmaz Güney). Instead he opted for a plot structure that revolves around clearly delineated story strands that keep the two stars apart. As a result Schygulla and Kurtiz share only a few seconds of screen time during which they do not even address each other. In effect Akin's own journey, a spatial exploration that takes him beyond his beloved Istanbul, led him to the revision and rejection of an idea based on a rather banal (if highly marketable) appropriation of the 'West-meets-the-East' tired metaphor and to the inclusion (for the first time in his work) of rural areas of Turkey in the film's diegetic world.

Overall a sense of uncertainty and critical interrogation permeates the discourse on his cinematic relationship with Turkey[22] that leads him to constantly revisit and reconsider practices employed in previous films. In *Fatih Akin: Diary of a Film Traveller*, Akin directly addresses the cinematography and *mise-en-scène* of his films in relation to the narrative space that he sets out and explores:

> When looking at my films, I see a difference between the German and the Turkish locations. The German ones seem arbitrary while the Turkish ones seem special. As I live in Germany, I may lack a visual detachment from the sites. For me Turkey is still virgin soil to be discovered and understood.

Akin articulates an acute awareness of his position and a determination to acknowledge, understand and negotiate his 'outsider's' look. Furthermore, his films demonstrate a progressively increasing realisation that the 'West meets-the-East' cliché, far from being a comfortable convergence of world-views, is in reality a collision of perceptions and visions of Turkey and more specifically Istanbul, the privileged setting of his films. Orhan Pamuk's extensive study of the city,[23] both as the lived place of his childhood and as a space constructed textually in books, paintings and photographs, offers insightful observations regarding the 'convergence' of East and West on the level of representation. In a particularly pertinent chapter, entitled 'Under Western Eyes', Pamuk examines the power that descriptions and evaluations of Istanbul by Western writers, painters and photographers hold over Turkish intellectuals, creating inescapable points of reference that initiate a profoundly dialogic discursive activity. And detailing his own position he writes:

> To see the city from many different points of view and thereby maintain the vitality of my connection to it, I sometimes fool myself. There are times . . . when I worry that my attachment to this place will ossify my brain, that isolation might kill the desire in my gaze. Then I take comfort in reminding myself that there is something foreign in my way of looking at the city owing to all the time I've spent reading the accounts of Western travellers. Sometimes when I read about the things that never change . . . I will lull myself into believing the accounts of Western outsiders are my own memories.[24]

Pamuk describes in operation a similar, if inverted, dialectic to the one that informs Akin's questioning of his use of locations and, more generally, his cinematic practices. On one level his films set out travelling trajectories which are traversed and negotiated by the converging routes of different characters, on another level the evolution of his cinema involves a continuous retracing and reworking of the formal trajectories laid out by/in previous films.

In July (the earliest in the body of work considered here) employs a plethora of stereotypical representations of Istanbul. Early in the film Daniel listens to *Istanbulu* Melek describing her life in her home city. Set in a Hamburg kebab shop, the scene utilises a traditional painting depicting a mosque by a Bosphorus bridge which dominates the *mise-en-scène* and to which the camera zooms-in, in effect illustrating Melek's narration with an orientalist representation. The romantic resolution of the film (involving this time Daniel and Juli) takes place in a tourist hotspot by the Galata bridge,[25] reworking thus the theme of the bridge into a more 'realistic' representation. The film concludes with a panoramic shot of yet another bridge that the car with the four main characters crosses as they are heading to 'the fucking south'.

Of course the exoticisation involved in these representations is to a degree contextualised by the colliding converging routes that take Isa, Daniel, Juli and Melek to Istanbul, adding critical layers to what appears to be an exploitation of the images that the city enables. The orientalist fantasies that inform the painting of the bridge in the kebab shop are on one level romanticising the ultimate destination of the young German lovers' journey but they are also reworked and questioned through the converging narrative strands that transform the two-dimensional image into a meaningful narrative space within which the film's resolution unfolds.

While in *In July* the textual interrogation of the sensibilities that inform the imagery of Istanbul is inconsistent and ambiguous (as evidenced by the final panoramic shot of the bridge/route to the south) it gains momentum and clarity in Akin's later film, *Head-On*. Having met accidentally in a hospital, Cahit and Sibel get married so that she can enjoy the freedom of living away from her conservative and patriarchal Turkish family. The first half of the film is set in Hamburg and traces the complications of the often violent and increasingly more passionate relationship between the two protagonists. When Cahit is imprisoned for the murder of Nico (Stefan Gebelhoff), Sibel decides to move to Istanbul where her cousin Selma (Meltem Cumbul) lives. From that point onwards, Istanbul becomes the location of all narrative events with dramaturgic significance. At the same time, first Sibel and then Kahit (once out of prison and in search of his lover) undertake extensive spatial explorations of the city, discovering and revealing its rich socio-cultural geography.

In terms of its narrative, thus, *Head-On* replicates the trajectory of *In July* (exemplified not only by the Hamburg-to-Istanbul movement but also in the theme of discovering real love). On another level, however, Istanbul as a romantic façade, a symbolic setting and destination, is replaced by a 'deeper' space, within which narrative development unfolds. This is a space with which the characters interact and one that relies on imagery which de facto contextualises and interrogates the flat orientalist representations that abound in *In July*.

It is, therefore, very surprising that *Head-On* is punctuated by a series of (six in total) static shots of a traditional Turkish musical group performing songs at the Golden Horn of Istanbul against the backdrop of the Süleymaniye Mosque. These shots interrupt the narrative flow of the film at regular intervals and, although they roughly relate affectively to the diegetic events that surround them, sometimes linked through a musical bridge with previous scenes, they are clearly situated outside the diegesis of the film. Organised as tableaux these shots have been described as 'postcards of Istanbul',[26] recalling and relying on precisely the 'flat' representational mode that the film's textual practices otherwise confront. While such a formal convention can trigger speculation regarding its textual, emotive and representational functions,[27] it is significant in the context of the present argument in its relationship to both *In July* (resurrecting as it were its orientalist fantasies) and the subsequent documentary *Crossing the Bridge*. The latter, arising from Akin's collaboration with the musician Alexander Hacke, bass player for the German band Einstürzende Neubauten, for the score of *Head-On*, is Hacke's musical travelogue. As he explains at the film's outset:

> The first time I came to Istanbul was for *Head-On*. I recorded a few songs for the film. Since then, this city and its music have fascinated me. For me, Istanbul was and still is a mystery. I decided to capture the sounds of this city in order to figure them out.

Thus, taking its queue from the static tableaux of the previous film, *Crossing the Bridge* revisits the musical scene of Istanbul and explores its vibrant diversity. This is yet another instance where a trajectory tentatively suggested in an earlier cinematic work is reworked by Akin into a new project that traverses a similar journey but introduces a new dimension, initiating a dynamic, syncretic and diachronic process of convergence. A deeply ironic aspect of *Crossing the Bridge* is the discovery that the leading singer of the 'traditional Turkish musical group' featured in the 'postcards' of *Head-On* is in fact the Canadian Brenna MacCrimmon – playfully drawing attention to a whole series of assumptions and prejudices regarding representation and representativeness.

Crossing the Bridge opens with several panoramic shots of the city intercut with shots of some of the musicians that will be encountered later. As the film moves on from this initial interlude, masterful views of Istanbul are systematically withheld and replaced by kaleidoscopic, fragmented and limited views of the parts of the city which are used as the background and the natural or chosen milieu of the fifteen groups and musicians. In that way the representation of Istanbul's musical scene becomes a diverse assemblage and the city itself a mosaic of heterogeneous spaces held together through Hacke's journey of exploration.

The replacement of panoramic and masterful with limited and partial views is textually and politically significant. It questions and ultimately cancels unified positions of control and power over images of Istanbul and in the process enables Akin, through the theme of converging routes and the continuous revisiting and revisioning of his film-making tropes, to develop a cinema of spatial exploration that resists orientalism. The experience of Istanbul produced in that manner is extremely reminiscent in its representational 'ethos' of the much earlier paintings of Melling, which Pamuk praises in the following terms:

> In Melling's Istanbul landscapes it is almost as if there is no centre . . . to see them [his paintings] is for me rather like driving along the Bosphorus

when I was a child: one bay suddenly emerging from behind another, with every bend in the shore road bringing a view from a surprising new angle. And so it is that . . . I begin to think of Istanbul as centreless and infinite . . .[28]

In Pamuk's formulation an all-encompassing vision of Istanbul that can masterfully explore, discover and reveal is rejected in favour of a process of gradual discovery that preserves the city's complex unpredictability. This is an obvious and pervasive theme in Akin's films, as characters with little or no knowledge of the city are repeatedly placed within narratives involving search: in *In July* Daniel explores a limited part of the city as he looks for Juli; in *Head-On* Sibel and Kahit reveal the diversity of the city, as does Hacke in *Crossing the Bridge* and Lotte, Susanne and Nejat (Baki Davrak) in their different quests in *The Edge of Heaven*. Thus, views of the city rather than being readily and instantly offered become integrated in arduous, dangerous and highly subjective processes of investigation. As the routes of the characters converge, the different journeys and individual investigations provide dynamic, fragmented and interactive representations. In Akin's films Istanbul emerges not so much as 'centreless' but decentred as the converging routes destabilise positions and constantly rework and rewrite the experience of the city. Similarly, the modern sensibilities that inform quests are contextualised and problematised by the broader spectrum of mobility involved in Akin's cinematic journeys.

A striking shot in *The Edge of Heaven* aptly encapsulates the multiple ways in which the theme of converging routes operates in Akin's films. The first part of the film ('Yeter's Death') concludes with a mobile shot clearly signalled as coming from a moving vehicle. Parts of the road and the landscape are visible and as the field of vision widens we can see another road at an angle to the direction of the moving camera. A car, a white VW, is visible on the second road. The two vectors of movement and the two roads gradually converge and, as we get closer to the white car, we can recognise Nejat as the driver. As the two routes finally merge, a collision seems inevitable but the shot is interrupted by a close-up of Nejat inside the car. The scene continues with shots of his journey across Turkey towards his father's village. It is this journey that structurally frames *The Edge of Heaven*, as it appears in the opening scene with Nejat arriving at a petrol station and in the conclusion with the repetition of the arrival at the petrol station before continuing with the drive to his ultimate destination. The shot at the end of 'Yeter's Death' is thus one that belongs to a series of shots, surfacing at the beginning, middle and end of the film, presented as converging parts of a journey fragmented by the narration but temporally uninterrupted.

One effect of this fragmentation is that the journey is structurally dispersed among other narrative events inviting a hermeneutic contextualisation of its significance. Thus, Nejat's journey is connected to the journeys of the other characters: Yeter's emigration and the return of her dead body to Turkey; Ali's emigration and repatriation; Ayten's political exile, return to homeland and redemption; Lotte's crusade to rescue her lover and Susanne's search for a meaning in her daughter's death. In that way Akin places the sensibilities that inform Nejat's quest in a syncretic relationship to the spectrum of emotive registers and historically specific types of mobility that underpin the different journeys of the Turkish, German and Turkish-German characters of *The Edge of Heaven*.

But as in the opening scene of *In July*, the merging of the routes in the shot under discussion takes the form of a virtual collision, avoided in the final instance by cutting to the car's interior. On one level the narrowly avoided collision can be seen as pointing towards the representational violence involved in spatial explorations undertaken under the aegis of a powerful cinematic apparatus perfectly aligned with the actions and vision of a traveller on a quest, as exemplified by the specific organisation of movement of/in the frame that permeates the 'views on the move' discussed in the previous chapter. By setting the trajectories of the cinematic apparatus and Nejat on a course of potential collision, *The Edge of Heaven* foregrounds the positional and relational nature of the representations on offer and alludes to Akin's personal difficulties in undertaking the spatial explorations that the film demands. As discussed earlier, *The Edge of Heaven* is informed by Akin's own exploration of his relationship with Turkey and his family's history. As *Fatih Akin: Diary of a Film Traveller* reveals, Akin undertook a journey almost identical to that of Nejat, along the same route and with a similar destination and purpose. Thus, another level of convergence, between film and autobiography, is in operation. The romanticisation of a creative fusion of the *auteur*'s life and his fiction is, however, resisted by exposing the difficulties of such convergence as it is open to the same conflicts, contradictions and difficulties that Akin's films investigate in the diasporic experiences and the multifarious journeys of the characters.[29]

Akin's thematic use of converging routes constitutes a formal convention that intercepts the autonomous and self-contained trajectories of quests. The diversity of the ways in which the same route can be traversed and experienced, a repetition that brings into attention difference, places the cinematic journeys of his characters in relationships of mutual dependence and contextualises the emotive registers that inform them. Moreover, the convergence of routes becomes a politically charged and effectively employed aesthetic tool as Akin explores his way around a complex web of representational legacies and pitfalls and continuously questions and revises his own spatial explorations. In such a context converging routes are not unidirectional trajectories leading to the discovery of cultural roots or celebrating the 'homecoming' journey of a diasporic filmmaker but map a field of historical tensions around mobility, vision and subjectivity. The violent collisions that always lurk just underneath the surface of his films but erupt with a disturbing regularity, provide a stark reminder of the explosive conflicts that riddle the 'postcolonial'. The cinematic journeys in the films of Fatih Akin and Tony Gatlif offer a testimony to the impossibility of discovering or recovering pure historical and cinematic roots and manifest the profoundly impure, inescapably hybrid nature of contemporary life and experience.

NOTES

1. While some of the shots are of characters whose encounter with Ernesto is included in the diegesis, others appear to be characters not recognised by the narrative, presumably because they constitute 'typical' representations of encounters omitted by the narration.
2. In a characteristically modern way that equates movement with life and stillness with death.
3. See John Urry, *The Tourist Gaze* (London: Sage, 1990).
4. In some ways this showcases an important political characteristic of a certain type of road movie, which uses the road as the 'locus of revelation of [the] people . . . a cinematic vehicle for the coming-to presence of the people', as Bennet Schaber has argued in '"Hitler can't keep 'em that long:" the road, the people', in Steven Cohan and Ina Rae Hark (eds), *The Road Movie Book* (London and New York: Routledge, 1997), pp. 17–44, p. 19.
5. Laura U. Marks, *The Skin of the Film*: *Intercultural Cinema, Embodiment, and the Senses* (Durham, NC, and London: Duke University Press, 2000).
6. Hamid Naficy, 'Phobic spaces and liminal panics: independent transnational film genre', in R. Wilson and W. Dissanayake (eds), *Local/Global* (Durham, NC: Duke University Press, 1996), pp. 119–44.
7. Hamid Naficy, *An Accented Cinema: Exilic and Diasporic Filmaking* (Princeton, NJ, Oxford: Princeton University Press, 2001).
8. Ewa Mazierska and Laura Rascaroli, *Crossing New Europe*: *Postmodern Travel and the European Road Movie* (London and New York: Wallflower Press, 2006).
9. Ella Shohat, *Taboo Memories, Diasporic Voices* (Durham, NC: Duke University Press, 2006).
10. Ibid. pp. 142–3
11. Naficy, 'Phobic spaces and liminal panics: independent transnational film genre'.
12. Ibid. p. 125.
13. Marks, *Skin of the Film*, p. 25.
14. Ibid. p. 21.
15. It is worth noting the lack of political clarity that the film demonstrates. While this supports Shohat's critique of the 'post' it should not necessarily be used to condemn *Exils* critically. Not interested in clarifying the tensions of the 'post' the film sets its diegesis within that context, exploiting its dynamism for dramatic and aesthetic purposes.
16. Marks also identifies the excavation of memories from objects and the importance of embodied memories as key features of intercultural films and videos (*Skin of the Film*). The scene under discussion here seems to offer a powerful combination of the two.
17. There is a strong suggestion that this is a dream, as a rhythmical beat, similar to a train's noise, is heard on the soundtrack before the song starts. In an earlier scene Naima talks about a dream in which she saw the road to Algeria covered in blood.

18. The way that this particular incident is constructed in terms of editing and frame composition strongly evokes 'excavation'. A shot of a dark interior with the bright reflection of water on a wall is followed by a shot of an overwhelmingly black frame at the centre of which there is a small bright patch on which we see the reflections of Zano and Naima as the former narrates the death of his parents and concludes on a bright close-up of Zano's face as he finishes the story. Here 'bringing into light' as an act of remembrance is reinforced by the gradual revelation, in a frame edged with darkness, of Zano's face.

19. Interestingly the trajectory of Daniel and Juli's journey almost replicates the path of the total solar eclipse of the summer of 1999 that attracted remarkable pan-European attention as a unique end of the millennium phenomenon.

20. DVD distributed by Soda Pictures, 2006.

21. See, for example, Nick Pinkerton, '*The Edge of Heaven* can wait: storylines and cultures crash – and isn't it arty?', *Village Voice* (20 May 2008); or A. O. Scott, 'Tying knots that bind lives despite the divisions of generation and nationality', *New York Times* (11 August 2008).

22. I had the opportunity to discuss this particular aspect of Akin's cinema during the 'Tenth New Directions in Turkish film studies Conference: Cinema and Fantasy', held in Istanbul (7–9 May 2009). Both Ahmet Gürata and Çetin Sarikartal noted textual conflicts in the films. Savaş Arslan read Akin's films as fantasies about the possibility of imitating an 'old' Turkish cinema style.

23. Orhan Pamuk, *Istanbul: Memories of a City* (London: Faber & Faber, 2005).

24. Ibid. pp. 217–18.

25. Geert Mak in his *The Bridge: A Journey between Orient and Occident* (London: Harvill Secker, 2008) discusses the cultural significance of the Galata bridge and notes: 'almost everyone on the bridge finds themselves suspended between two worlds and all have dreamed of making that great leap forward.' (p. 41).

26. Asuman Suner, 'Dark Passion', *Sight & Sound*, 15.3 (March 2005), pp. 18–21.

27. Suner, for example, reads it as 'a self-reflexive Brechtian strategy' (ibid.).

28. Pamuk, *Istanbul*, p. 60.

29. The case of Akin's cinema and his strategy of converging routes seems to question the simplicity of the formulation proposed by Naficy that diasporic cinema demonstrates a nostalgia expressed in 'home-coming' journeys (Naficy, *Accented Cinema*, pp. 222–36).

CHAPTER 6

Movement beyond the axes

6.1 THE LIMITS OF EXPLORATION, DISCOVERY, REVELATION

The intercepted trajectories discussed in the previous chapter place a check on the pleasures of exploration, discovery and revelation that abound in quest narratives. However, the journeys of Zano, Nejat et al. are meaningful in relation to two distinct and competing emotive registers: the pleasures of individual quests and the anxieties glimpsed in the encounters with refugees, exiles, diasporic and nomadic travellers. There is an implied hierarchy between these two types of sensibility which, despite a contextualisation of quests, still creates the possibility of 'othering' alternative types of mobility. The relational double framing in *Exils* offers a clear demonstration of that tendency in Gatlif's films in the aesthetic organisation of the shot around formal binaries informed by modern values. Akin's case is slightly more complicated as the cinematic tales that he spins are burdened with a historical baggage of signification, a representational burden that he is conscious of and attempts to offload by retracing his routes and reinventing his cinematic style. His films become journeys of discovery of a different order, a simultaneous symptom and critique of the modern romantic investment in exploration.

The previous chapter also expanded a conceptualisation of the 'post' from simply referring to explorations of the chronotopes of the changing historical and geopolitical landscape of New Europe to accounting for journeys involving encounters with new (or newly recognised) mobilities. Hence a second semantic possibility of the 'post' emerged, that of a historical relationship, a tension. The present chapter moves to discuss the 'post' as a historical, geopolitical and cultural terminus that points towards a 'beyond'. In the two films examined here, *Ulysses' Gaze* (Theo Angelopoulos, Greece/France/Italy/Germany/UK/Yugoslavia/Bosnia/Albania/Romania, 1995) and *Blackboards* (Samira

Makhmalbaf, Iran/Italy/Japan, 2000), the discourses and sensibilities that inform modern subjectivity, notions of agency, epistemologies of movement and vision, fantasies of complete knowledge and control, and the pleasures of journeys of exploration, discovery and revelation, all have either completed and concluded their historical trajectories or are irrelevant within a referential context that involves different configurations of the subject and mobility.

Angelopoulos's film places itself at the end point of a series of historical, political and cultural processes: the end of modernity and modernism, the collapse of communism, the crisis of nation and the national, the disintegrating Balkans, the death of cinema.

Critical opinion perceives Angelopoulos as the ultimate and final modernist auteur. A collection of essays[1] on his work that appeared shortly after *Ulysses' Gaze* not only refers to him as the 'last modernist' but also identifies the film as a prime example of a cinematic practice that represents a final frontier in the defense of the values of modernism and modernity. David Bordwell, for example, concludes his contribution by asserting:

> Often majestic, sometimes mannered, almost always melancholic, Angelopoulos demonstrates that, contrary to what prophets of postmodernity keep telling us, cinematic modernism can still open our eyes.[2]

Desperately seeking an aesthetic and politically progressive alternative to the dying modernist project, Fredric Jameson comments on *Ulysses' Gaze*:

> Grand things – such as the sculptured head of Lenin on its way to sale in the West – or the set pieces . . . recall older moments of a late modernism from which something new is seeking convulsive emergence.[3]

As my analysis will demonstrate (focusing on the scene that Jameson refers to) *Ulysses' Gaze* obliterates the subject and object of the spatial exploration that the film undertakes. And by doing so it puts an end in the most melancholic manner to the dialectics of certainty↔uncertainty and activity↔passivity, failing to rescue modern subjectivity from a profound and irretrievable defeat that dissolves the hero and his journey into complete passivity and uncertainty.

In contrast, the textual practices of *Blackboards* turn their back on such dialectics articulating different types of mobile vision and subjectivity. The film is structured around journeys of perpetual motion with uncertain origins and with borders as their destination involving subjects whose mobilities emerge as movements of displacement, dispossession and dislocation. Like *Ulysses' Gaze* Makhmalbaf's film obliterates the landscape as the visual attraction of spatial exploration, most obviously through the lack of panoramic, masterful shots and the inseparability of the body of the traveller from the land. Here, mobility is experienced not as an extension of being (the ever increasing knowledge of the self and the world effected by quests or the increase in the sum of human knowledge through explorations and discoveries) but as a condition of being. That and the different treatment of the relationship between traveller and landscape, makes problematic, if not unattainable, diegetic and extra-diegetic positions (exemplified in the modern *repertoire* by figures such as the observer, the *flâneur*, the explorer, the self-discovering artist) that infuse the travelled space with the values and emotive registers of modern mobile vision.

However, despite the fact that *Ulysses' Gaze* laments the end of a particular configuration of modern (and modernist) subjectivity and *Blackboards* defines its referential field beyond such boundaries of Western modernity they both ultimately succumb to European cultural hegemony in their dependence on the Cannes Film Festival as a definitive arbiter of aesthetic value and marketablity. Since the critical acclaim for *The Travelling Players* (Theo Angelopoulos, Greece, 1975) brought him international prominence, Angelopoulos presents (and usually opens) his films in Cannes, aiming for awards that will enhance their critical standing and marketability. That festival is clearly important for Makhmalbaf, too. *How Samira Made 'The Blackboard'*, a documentary directed by her brother Maysam and included in the DVD of the film,[4] is neatly divided into two intertwining parts, Samira's cinematic technique (primarily in relation to *Blackboards*) and the film's extraordinary reception at Cannes, creating a sense in which Makhmalbaf's hard work in the Kurdish mountains finds its just reward in the festival.

Importantly, Hamid Dabashi in his study categorises contemporary Iranian cinema according to three locations: Tehran, Cannes and the USA. Positing Cannes as the site of truly great Iranian cinema (where Makhmalbaf, Ghobadi and Hasan Yektapanah put Iranian cinema on the map in 2000) Dabashi argues:

> In Iran, the old masters are indulging in self reflection, and, in doing so take their ego for the world. In Cannes, the new masters are measuring themselves in and against the world. In Iran, the old masters are big fish in a small pond; at Cannes, the new masters are sizeable fish in an ocean . . . These children [Makhmalbaf, Ghobadi, Yektapanah] conform to an entirely different hope. They have seen the world celebrate and embrace their youthful dreams and deposit their fathers' overwrought works – now grandiloquent claims on our credulity – safely in the Museum of National identity. Alterity is this generation's choice.[5]

Ironically the alterity of the film-makers and their subjects does not prevent Cannes, an institution quintessentially European and modern, from providing a desired critical seal of approval for their films. It is a testimony to an enduring hegemony that *Ulysses' Gaze* and *Blackboards*, despite placing their cinematic journeys beyond the values of European modernity, eventually submit themselves to its discursive authority.

6.2 *ULYSSES' GAZE*: OBLITERATING THE SUBJECT AND OBJECT OF SPATIAL EXPLORATION

Ulysses' Gaze, a film about the journey of Greek-American film director A (Harvey Keitel) through a war-torn Balkan peninsula, was received by the press and promoted by its director as an ambitious cinematic comment on such vital and topical issues as the state of Europe, the disintegration of the Balkans, the end of communism and the death of cinema. Angelopoulos, who in interviews refused to acknowledge the relevance of any awards as a meaningful judgement of his film's value, was reportedly outraged[6] that *Ulysses' Gaze*, a firm favourite with the Greek press to win,[7] was awarded the Grand Prize of the Jury, losing the prestigious Golden Palm to Emir Kusturica's *Underground* (France/Yugoslavia/Germany, 1995). The critical controversy notwithstanding, the film's title and subject matter (the allusion to a special gaze, that of a legendary traveller, and the journey through a chronotope of grave historical significance) resonate with some of the key concerns of this book.

A is travelling from Greece through Albania, Macedonia, Bulgaria, Romania, Yugoslavia before ending his journey in Sarajevo,[8] in search of undeveloped film stock shot by the Manakia brothers, pioneering film-makers, photographers and entrepreneurs, who lived in the Balkans in the early part of the twentieth century and whose films are credited as the first produced in the area. He repeatedly refers to his quest to find the three Manakia reels as a search for a cinematic 'glance': the 'first glance', the 'lost glance'. The theoretical suggestiveness of the term invites closer scrutiny.

Clearly, although A talks about the three reels as containing the 'lost glance', the implied loss cannot be understood in literal terms. The Manakia brothers were pioneering ethnographic film-makers but also travellers themselves: their films recorded the everyday lives of the people of the Balkans, the broad terrain within which A's journey unfolds. Their films belong to a cinematic tradition and a mode of film-making that is conspicuously absent in Greek film history, as travelogues and fictional films involving the spatial exploration of 'foreign' lands were and still are extremely rare: the value attached to the missing reels motivates A's epic quest and provides a fictional testimony to their uniqueness. In historical terms the 'loss' (of the films and of the gaze) refers to a structural dislocation, Greece's marginalisation from the economic and political discourses and the technological and aesthetic practices that shaped nineteenthth-century European mobile vision and found a powerful expression in early travel cinema. In other words, the 'lost glance' has not been simply misplaced with the Manakia reels, but it never really existed – the film's overwhelmingly nostalgic journey ends with a return that discovers and reveals nothing.

Ulysses' Gaze, as a road movie par excellence holds the promise to redress the balance and compensate for the historical 'loss' by delivering a Greek view (mediated by A's travelling gaze) on the important international historical events of the period and the expansive spatial arena within which they unfold. Pardoxically, the film turns its back on the pleasures of travel cinema by constructing a formal system that obliterates both the subject and the object of spatial exploration. In *Ulysses' Gaze* the traversed space, the potentially spectacular and definitely attractive (in Tom Gunning's sense of the word)[9] historical setting of the disintegrating Balkans is constantly obscured or completely obliterated from the film's field of vision. Furthermore, A as a traveller and agent of exploration, discovery and revelation is rendered utterly powerless, the helpless subject of overwhelming historical forces.

Ulysses' Gaze's representational strategies minimise spatial depth and detail. A's journey seems to unfold against landscapes that are barely visible: the prologue in Florina takes place at night in the dark streets of the city, the taxi ride into Albania is through snow-covered land and contains several tracking shots of dark figures (possibly refugees heading south) scattered across an almost blank expansion of space, while, in the final part, the cityscape of Sarajevo is covered by the smoke of fire and guns and is eventually dissolved into a thick fog that covers everything.[10] The composition of the frame, with the camera positioned low, reduces perspective and flattens the image, systematically diminishing the vividness and attraction of 'views on the move'. Thus the construction of the landscape deprives the journey of spatial depth that can enhance the affectivity of exploration, becoming instead a flat, non-descriptive backdrop, a bland theatrical set, an empty screen[11] that A traverses but remains remarkably unmoved by, lost in his thoughts and memories.

An even more extreme erasure of 'views on the move' is evident in the 20'-long journey that A shares with Kali[12] (Maia Morgenstern) which starts in Macedonian Bitola (or Monastiri, where the Manakia brothers lived and ran a cinema), goes through Macedonia and Bulgaria and ends in Bucharest. The editing of the scene eliminates any external views, apart from a few shots at the Macedonian/Bulgarian border which are mainly inside buildings as A is interrogated by police, or in very dark exterior sets in which he enacts scenes of the life of the Manakia brothers. Instead it focuses on the relationship between the two characters that involves a conversation recounting the brothers' ethnographic film activities and explicates A's investment in the search. In that way, although the journey traverses the entire breadth of the Balkan Peninsula from west to east, passing spectacular and historically significant places and landmarks, several of which are mentioned in the soundtrack by A, those remain resolutely withheld from the field of vision. Within such a system the material and historical specificity of the landscape and its visual affect are entirely lost, the 'views on the move' becoming obsessively and increasingly inward. As Ann Rutherford, in her appreciative essay on the film, suggests:

> While it is vision that propels the narrative of the film . . . vision, the gaze itself is constantly undercut, prefigured or superseded by sound . . . It is vision that collapses finally in Sarajevo . . . It is as if the whole film has led, inexorably, to the collapse of vision . . . [13]

The indecipherability of the landscape is amplified by the film's narrative. The characters are unable to recognise the space that they travel and almost every arrival at a new place is enshrouded in doubt. When the old woman, to whom A offers a lift in the taxi, arrives at the Albanian city of Korçë (Korytsa), she wonders, 'What's this place?' and A exclaims, 'Is this Sarajevo?' as he enters the city. Andrew Horton notes that an unused shot from *Ulysses' Gaze*, that eventually found its way into the *portmanteau* film *Lumière & Company* (Angelopoulos et al., France/Denmark/Spain/Sweden, 1995),[14] involves

> An actor playing Ulysses/Odysseus, crawling out of the sea after his escape from Calypso's island. He stares at the camera and thus at us . . . and a title card appears echoing Homer's line: 'On what foreign shore have I landed?'[15]

The uncertainty of the image and in the characters, in relation to space, location and place, but also time (now and then, the past surfacing in the present, the Manakia brothers' journeys overlapping with those of A and Odysseus), and the systematic obliteration of the landscape compromise spatial exploration and eliminate its pleasures from the emotive register of the film.

While A's journey is in narrative terms an archetypal (albeit an ultimately unsuccessful) quest, it is also, as a critic called it, 'a walk on the blind side',[16] during which the hero moves like a somnambulist, following predetermined routes rather than charting his own itinerary and interacting with the space that he traverses. As A arrives at the train station in Bucharest, Kali asks him, 'So why have you come?', to which he responds, 'my footsteps, somehow they led me here'. In itself the encounter with Kali is denied the potential of romance precisely because of A's inability to fully 'experience' the journey; 'I am crying because I can't love you' are his final words to her. A is a traveller devoid of agency, completely surrendered to forces far more powerful than himself, passive in the most extreme sense of the word.

The uncertainty of/in the spatial exploration and the utter passivity of A as a traveller are most clearly demonstrated in the film's most memorable scene, the journey on a barge on the Black Sea from the Romanian port of Constanja and along the Danube all the way to Belgrade. The scene (a good example of Angelopoulos's use of long takes) is 15′30″ long and consists of fifteen shots organised around four segments: the first (four shots in all, including an epic 5′40″ shot) is set at the port where a gigantic statue of Lenin transported from Odessa is loaded onto the barge as A and Kali tearfully part company; the second shows the barge travelling in the Danube; in the third, at the tripartite control point (a border shared between Bulgaria, Romania and Yugoslavia), a patrol boat intercepts the barge to check its load; in the final part, the boat arrives at Belgrade. I will focus my analysis on the second segment of the scene (five shots, 3′21″ in total).

The segment opens with an extremely long shot of the barge, on which the massive statue now lies horizontal, floating slowly but steadily on the river. The camera slowly zooms in and pans to the left, following the barge's movement and picking out A's figure. The 1′ take ends with a closer (but still distant) shot of A at the bow of the boat with the statue's massive feet just behind him. This is followed by a 54″ tracking shot to the right (replicating the barge's movement and suggesting that it is coming from it) which shows large groups of people running to line up or standing still at the river's bank. Several of them begin to make the sign of the cross and kneel. The film cuts back to the end of the first shot, with A standing at the front of the boat, but the camera remains static for the full 25″ seconds allowing A to disappear out of frame as Lenin's statue subsequently passes in front of the camera. The fourth shot is similar to the second (but shorter at 36″), as the tracking continues revealing more people standing at the bank or running to follow the boat, again, several make the sign of the cross. The concluding shot (35″) is similar to shots one and three, but here the camera is positioned behind A, momentarily follows the movement of the barge with a pan to the left and zooms out before stopping to let first A and then Lenin disappear out of the frame.

It is worth considering in more detail the relationship between movement of and in the frame in the segment. The opening shot is in some ways a typical reframing with the panning movement following the motion of the boat while the zooming brings A closer and places him in a central position in the frame. However, A is essentially still as his motion is predicated upon that of the boat (in itself following the flow of the river) and remains a central but miniscule figure, dwarfed by the statue of Lenin. Thus, the movement of the frame primarily follows that in the frame but also defines A's position (on the barge and at the feet of the statue) that will remain the same throughout the segment.

Shots 2 and 4 appear to come from A's point of view but this proves not to be the case as he remains staring directly ahead, never turning his glance to the side. The shot-reverse shot pattern, therefore, is not structured around A's vision but as an interaction between the gathering crowd and the barge (or, to be precise, its cargo). This is reinforced by the fact that the movement and actions of those who line up along the bank are clearly motivated by the spectacle of the statue, a response to the procession that they witness. The editing, frame mobility and composition are also organised around the movement of the barge and the inescapable presence of a gigantic Lenin. In this scene (as in several others in the film) A becomes marginal in the process of spatial exploration and his agency is dissolved by the progression of a totalising meta-narrative (Marxism is unambiguously suggested by the iconic statue). The gaze that organises the cinematic apparatus is usurped by forces that are larger and more powerful than A and his movement is eclipsed by that of history.

A's powerlessness and lack of agency are amplified by several layers of irony that permeate the scene. His insignificance is articulated in relation to the figure of Lenin, completely powerless itself, a fragmented, decommissioned statue, lying on its back and carried as cargo for sale. The crowd react to its presence as that of a corpse in a funeral procession, compounding the irony by crossing themselves, a religious and thus totally inappropriate and alienating reaction to one of the founders of historical materialism. Lenin's new historical status of irrelevance is confirmed at the tripartite control point where the question 'have you got anybody on board?' is answered by the captain with 'nobody'. The shot, coming from behind the enormous statue's head, renders the leader of revolutionary socialism visually present but diegetically irrelevant and historically insignificant. This is an unambiguous and poignant image that expressively articulates the death of one of the most influential grand narratives of modernity, the Marxist-Leninist tenet of social progress that collapsed with the historical defeat of communism. The statue's index finger that once pointed straight ahead to revolutionary triumphs is now turned aimlessly at the sky, the promise of a bright future broken like the statue itself.

A's journey is not one of exploration, discovery and revelation but a predetermined trajectory that he helplessly follows and during which he becomes an empty vessel, a conduit for other people's lives and memories (the Manakia brothers, the Greeks of the Balkan diaspora). His movement in space is determined by forces that crush him as he carries on his shoulders the dead weight of history. The image of A at the feet of the fallen, stone statue of Lenin, following the relentless flow of the river and the inescapable movement of time, is tragically eloquent. The death of the modern meta-narrative that the film laments goes hand in hand with the end of a specific configuration of vision, mobility, subjectivity and history.

In that respect Angelopoulos takes no prisoners. *Ulysses' Gaze* also pronounces the death of Greece, as the taxi driver who takes A to Albania declares:

> Greece is dying. We're dying as a people. We've come full-circle. I don't
> know how many thousands of years among broken stones and statues

> . . . and we're dying. But if Greece is to die she'd better do it quickly . . .
> because the agony lasts too long and makes too much noise.

This is particularly poignant as it comes from the lips of Thanassis Vengos, an actor who entertained generations of filmgoers, a comedian synonymous with the glorious days of popular Greek cinema and widely seen by critics and public alike as encapsulating the most positive aspects of Greek identity: humour, generosity, resilience, inventiveness, improvisation, compassion.[17]

The film indirectly yet explicitly suggests that cinema is also dying. It is not only the constant reference to the lost reels, the 'lost glance' and the 'lost innocence', but also A's story on the train to Bucharest where he describes the mysterious event of taking photographs that fail to develop: 'blank negative pictures of the world; as if my glance wasn't working'. This is most obviously and powerfully expressed at the very end of the film where A watches the discovered film stock which is projected on a black, empty screen. At the end of his odyssey, after his traveller's gaze has dissolved into the Sarajevo fog, the vision of the cinematic apparatus also pitifully disintegrates as the persistent but ultimately futile flickering of the projector gives place to A's desperate sob.

Angelopoulos litters his film with references to the Greek urtext of *Odysseia* but his travelling hero is almost the semantic opposite of Odysseus. The latter not only defies the gods, defeats monsters and suitors and wins back his wife but, importantly, is the resourceful and canny[18] agent of an amazing journey that explores, discovers and reveals fantastic lands and creatures, turning a ten-year ordeal into a fabulous feast of the imagination. Instead, *Ulysses' Gaze* systematically obliterates the pleasures of spatial exploration and annihilates the subjectivity of the traveller, the *nostos* of Odysseus that defines the emotions of the hero and functions as a motivating force to complete the most spectacular adventure and to be rewarded with *nostimon emar*, the day of return, the arrival at the journey's end that addresses and removes the loss. A, in contrast, is abandoned to a *nostalgia* that is not any more a mobilising force but a permanent deprivation, an incurable pain (*algos*), experienced during and at the end of a fruitless journey. The inescapable grip of such pain annihilates not only the traveller but also modern subjectivity and delivers to their historical death Greece, the Balkans, Europe, cinema and the pleasures of mobile vision.

6.3 *BLACKBOARDS*: JOURNEYS OF PERPETUAL MOTION

Blackboards was Samira Makhmalbaf's second feature following the critically acclaimed *The Apple* (Iran/France, 1998). The film was very successful at the 2000 Cannes Film Festival and, as Hamid Dabashi points out,[19] together with Bahman Ghobadi's *A Time for Drunken Horses* (Iran, 2000) and Hassan Yektapanah's *Djomeh* (France/Iran, 2000), it signalled the arrival on the international scene of a new generation of Iranian film-makers. The relationship with Ghobadi's films is particularly significant for our purposes. *Blackboards*, like *A Time for Drunken Horses*, *Marooned in Iraq* (Ghobadi, Iran, 2002) and *Half Moon* (Ghobadi, Austria/France/Iran/Iraq, 2006), is set in the Kurdish areas of Iran and Iraq and involves journeys between the two countries; as in *Turtles Can Fly* (Ghobadi, Iran/France/Iraq, 2004), *Blackboards*'s action takes place near the Iran/Iraq border and children play an important part in the film's story; furthermore, Ghobadi himself was one of only two professional actors used in Makhmalbaf's film. While this section focuses on *Blackboards*, it will use Ghobadi's films as a comparative framework in order to flag up some formal similarities and differences between Makhmalbaf's travel movie and those of the Kurdish film-maker.

The film, set in an unspecified time at the immediate aftermath of the 1980–88 Iran-Iraq war,[20] is structured around the intertwining journeys of three sets of travellers: a group of wandering teachers forced by the destruction of their schools to search for peripatetic pupils, a large group of old men (and a solitary woman and her child) in search of Halabja (Helepçe), their town that was notoriously attacked by Iraq's chemical weapons, and, finally, a group of young children smuggling goods. Two of the teachers, Said (Said Mohamadi) and Reeboir (Bahman Ghobadi) join the groups and share their journeys which end at the Iran/Iraq border.

Blackboards is defined against a referential backdrop of mobility as displacement. This is diegetically expressed by the film's differentiated journeys, undertaken by nomadic teachers, children gaining a living via contraband and elders returning to their birthplace. These travellers are mobile only because their settlements, villages, homes, schools and work places either have been destroyed or never existed, their mobility instigated not by a self-willed decision but out of necessity, as the direct consequence of homelessness. A sense of 'out-of-place-ness' permeates the film's diegesis: none of the characters belongs to the roads and paths that they traverse and their itineraries lack both origin and destination. The image of the blackboards carried on the backs of the teachers is particularly eloquent in that respect: torn out of the classroom, removed from their natural discursive (education, the acquisition of knowledge) and spatial contexts (school as built environment and institution), they become signifiers of a violent uprooting and dislocation. In Said and Reeboir's journeys the blackboards are transformed from objects of instruction and education to fluid objects whose function is subjected to the contingencies of the journey as they become in turn protective cover from overflying helicopters, an item of dowry, support for a broken limb, and a partition wall for creating an improvised and desperately needed domestic space. But the uprooted blackboards, a physical burden, a distant echo of a lost stability and a hopeless attachment to an impossible alternative, also transform their bearers, turning them into strange birdlike creatures and creating a decidedly 'out-of-place' image for a teacher.

Extra-diagetically, the film is set in Kurdistan, a homeless nation par excellence. Spread between several countries (mainly Iran, Iraq and Turkey but also Syria and Armenia) Kurds have been historically denied the sanctity of a unified, independent nation-state and continue to exist without the security and permanence of a homeland. In this context the chemical attack on Halabja becomes a crucial and recurring reference not only in *Blackboards* but also in Ghobadi's films. Simultaneously referring to a historical event and a place, 'Halabja' constitutes the scene of a historical trauma[21] and becomes emblematic of the plight of a homeless nation. Caught up in the middle of a war involving two other nations but unfolding partially over their land, the Kurds had no stakes in the Iran-Iraq conflict and no recourse to a protective state apparatus. The poignant irony is that the attack was carried out not by an enemy from across the border but by the government in control of Halabja. The nature of the event, the genocide of thousands of helpless people with chemical weapons, further emphasises de-territorialisation and homelessness not only because it rendered the town utterly uninhabitable but also because it was not the outcome of military defeat following territorial struggle but a clinical and systematic mass assassination inflicted by a distant, invisible and unknown enemy. Thus, the attack on Halabja, a spatio-temporally specific event, becomes in Ghobadi's and Makhmalbaf's films a condensed but abstract symbol of the homeless and powerless existence of the endlessly travelling characters of the narratives. The detachment of the signifier of 'Halabja' from its historical and material referent is powerfully and tragically emphasised by the inability of the old men in *Blackboards* to recognise their birthplace when they eventually reach it at the end of the film, their arrival becoming the re-enactment of trauma rather than an act of return or resolution.

The inconclusive character of the film's ending, with the groups of travellers and the teachers hovering around the border never reaching a concrete destination, epitomises the nature of their travelling in the dramatic and the spatial sense. *Blackboards* is structured around narratives of perpetual motion with the characters involved in journeys with no origin and no destination. The introduction of the three groups of travellers is particularly significant in that respect. The opening shot of the film, a long shot of a mountain dirt track, shows the teachers emerging out of the turn of the road, walking towards the camera in a steady and arduous pace. This is succeeded by a mobile shot that follows their progress from behind, emphasising the blackboards and the effort involved in carrying them. The next shot introduces Said as he talks to another teacher while walking, with the camera following their movement and occasionally panning to frame more centrally one or the other of the two interlocutors. A series of shots follows in which the group momentarily stop, clearly alarmed by something, until the noise of a helicopter engine sets them into a panicked run for cover. Even in these shots, where the teachers' progress is temporarily halted, there is an abundance of movement in the frame: the men are nervously moving as the howling wind makes their clothes shake and rattle violently. Importantly, stillness is in this scene associated with danger as it is imposed by the invisible overflying helicopter that terrorises them.

It is after a succession of shots in which Reeboir climbs a narrow and rocky path that he comes across an individual child (probably a member of the group of boys that he joins shortly afterwards). During the initial phase of the encounter both Reeboir and the boy are standing still but are placed in precarious positions: the former half way up a steep slope (further amplified by the high angle of the camera), the latter at the edge of a cliff. Their conversation continues over a shot of a group of old men emerging from a mountain and descending a slope. While the soundtrack renders the two scenes (and groups) contiguous it is never clear in the film how close the two groups are. Through this cutaway the film eliminates the temporary cessation of Reeboir's movement by introducing yet another group of travellers who are in motion.

A scene in which Said enters a village looking for pupils follows, before the film returns to Reeboir's encounter with the full group of boys. The children, moving down a path and carrying their load of contraband, reject Reeboir's offer to teach them and, more significantly, protest against his attempt to curtail their mobility, urging him to let them pass and complaining that the burden is unbearable when they are standing still. Thus, all the groups of mobile travellers are introduced as already in motion and although the causes of their mobility are understandable (harking back to the fundamental homelessness of the Kurds) their movement is not connected either to processes of self-transformation and development or to the pleasures of spatial exploration, discovery and revelation.

Blackboards systematically resists or renders irrelevant the subjectivity embodied in the mobile vision of the travellers involved in quests. This involves the rejection of a detached, masterful and objectifying position that, in conventional cinematic journeys of spatial exploration, renders pleasurable the views of the landscape and which would result in a de facto aesthetic exploitation of the Kurdish mountains and valleys. The rejection of such an exterior position is made possible by visualising the distinct travelling narrative of the film through a particular combination of spatial composition, camera position and frame mobility.

In *Blackboards* the significant binary oppositions that inform quest narratives (such as home and the road, origin and destination, before and after the journey) are dissolved in a framework of perpetual motion. Instead of exploring coherent and individualised trajectories of self-transformation the film offers fragments of incomplete stories involving a multitude of mobile characters which in their totality construct an exposition of the conditions of their existence. As we discussed in Chapter 4, processes of self-transformation are textually articulated through a carefully orchestrated dialectic relationship between the body of the traveller and views of the landscape; 'views on the move' combine the visual pleasures of spatial exploration with narrative processes of character development and change. By contrast, *Blackboards* remains largely unconcerned about individual trajectories (without being in the least dispassionate or indifferent to their lives), merging the bodies of the travellers with the land that they travel, forging an unbroken bond that circumvents the dialectics of certainty↔uncertainty and activity↔passivity.

The perpetual motion of the film's characters is echoed by the relentless movement of and in the frame. The scenes in which the travelling groups are introduced are characteristic of the representation of the characters as continuously mobile; the occasional short pauses in their journeys are always marked by other types of movement within the frame. The camera is hand-held throughout the film with no use of steadicam or tripod, a choice possibly dictated by the mountainous terrain but also pointing towards an aesthetic decision to follow moving characters rather than capture their movement from a fixed position. However, this results in permanent shaking (paradoxically more noticeable when the camera or the characters are otherwise motionless) that renders the limits of the frame uncertain and transient. A lack of fixity permeates the image creating a potentially disturbing fluidity in what is seen and what appears in the scene. This not only creates hermeneutic uncertainty but also undermines security about creative agency. Is the movement of the frame intentional or accidental? When does a randomly shaky frame become a 'meaningful' panning shot?

The constantly moving camera is usually placed close to the characters and that necessarily restricts views of the landscape. The proximity of the camera to the body and the persistent tracking of its motion emphasises the physical aspect of the travellers' movement. Long shots that place the characters in open space are very rare and in that way *Blackboards* does not turn landscape into a vast narrative space within which the freedom of mobility is celebrated. Thus some of the most powerful visual pleasures of the conventional road movie (the images are familiar: vehicles gliding across the scenery in clouds of dust or bathed in the glorious light of sunsets, travellers at the foot of a majestic mountain) are denied and replaced with restricted views and visceral images of bodies involved in slow, arduous and inescapable movement.

The prominent place of the body(ies) of the traveller(s) within the frame limits the field of vision, creating the landscape as an uncertain and often indiscernible backdrop and flattens the image by abandoning perspective and the attendant illusion of depth. Such an approach to framing distinguishes sharply between foreground and background, with the levels of exposure adjusted to privilege clear and detailed depictions of the traveller(s) – as a result the landscape often dissolves into a bright haze. On other occasions (and increasingly so as the group of old men approach the border and Halabja) the traversed space is covered by mist and disappears completely from view.

A startling implication of these techniques and conventions is that any sense of spatial orientation and comprehension of direction of movement becomes problematic if not impossible. Even on the rare occasions of long shots of bodies of travellers in the landscape the views are limited and partial (a fragment of the slope of a mountain, as in the shot of the appearance of the group of old men discussed above). The film does not provide maps or any masterful aerial or panoramic shots that could identify and/or describe the area within which the journeys unfold, and the itineraries of the travellers remain resolutely uncharted. The space that *Blackboards* reveals is primarily experiential, enabled by the corporeality of the film's agents of mobility rather than by the abstract geographical or panoramic delineation of an expansive terrain. In his first encounter with the boys Reeboir asks for directions but he receives the answer 'all paths lead somewhere', a response that eloquently expresses an understanding of space as polymorphous and personalised and in that sense resisting navigational rationality.

The film's editing system is mostly organised in a way that rejects conventional point-of-view structures and shot-reverse shot patterns.[22] The scene in which Reeboir explains the benefits of education to one of the boys (at the outset of their shared journey) provides a clear demonstration of this trend. A long shot of the group, led by the teacher and moving towards the camera, is succeeded by a medium shot of Reeboir from behind, following his forward motion and then by another mobile medium shot of the boy from the front. The two shots represent the two parties involved in the conversation and are repeated in the same order four more times until the end of the scene. In its focus on the two interlocutors such a pattern seems to be similar to the shot-reverse shot convention but it is significantly different as there is no eye-line match connecting the shots. Reeboir never turns back to look at the child and the shots of the back of Reeboir's head come from a camera position considerably higher than the boy's height. In that way the succession of shots is one between two separate fields of vision within which the characters appear but is disconnected from personalised points of view.

Importantly, the shots are marked by the same forward movement with the camera following the relentless advance of the group, overwriting in that sense the individual agency with a collective mobility. The subject matter and the form of the dialogue replicate both the editing and the movement of/in the frame. Reeboir and the boy express diametrically opposing views on the usefulness of education (the former exalting its benefits and the latter rejecting its relevance to his life) while remaining in constant motion:

> REEBOIR: Listen my child, with education you will be able to read a book, or, even better, a newspaper when you are travelling . . . Learn to read and write! You'll know what's going on in the world.
> BOY: Doing the accounts that's great for the Boss. Us, we are mules. Always on the move. How do you expect us to read? To read a book, you have to sit down. Us, we never stop moving.

Throughout the film the camera moves along with the characters but does not adopt their point of view, unlike in *Koktebel*, for example, where the boy's hermeneutic anxieties are expressed through subjective camera movement. Thus, the limited and restricted views of the landscape are divorced from individual perception which, combined with the cinematography, composition and movement of/in the frame, renders the dialectic between traveller and landscape irrelevant. The possibility of such dialectic is based on a meaningful separation between the two that allows the dynamic affectivity of certainty↔uncertainty and activity↔passivity to unfold.

The formal system of *Blackboards*, however, links inextricably the bodies of the travellers with the land that they travel. An implication of such aesthetic is that it creates a bond between the Kurdish people and the land that provides the space, the expanse of their stateless existence. Furthermore, such existence is fundamentally, necessarily and perpetually mobile, a de facto nomadism dictated by structures of power and forces of history that lie beyond possibilities of individual or collective acts of choice and journeys of exploration, discovery and revelation. *Blackboards* treats perpetual motion as a mode of existence, in marked contrast with the mobility celebrated by the quest movie and by post-structural critics such as Rosi Braidotti, for whom nomadism becomes an act of evading power, a 'kind of critical consciousness that resists settling into socially coded modes of thought and behaviour'.[23]

Braidotti proposes the openness of the land as a fundamental oppositional aspect of nomadic existence:

> *Noumos* is a principle of distribution of the land, and as such it came to represent the opposition of the power of the *polis* because it was a space without enclosures or border. It was the pastoral, open, nomadic space in opposition to which the sedentary power of the city was erected. Metropolitan space versus nomadic trajectories.[24]

Blackboards directly contradicts such a sense of nomadism and rejects the romanticism that is very thinly disguised in the association of the land with freedom and 'openness'. As the previous analysis demonstrated the film employs a number of formal conventions that reject the construction of an 'open' and border-less space and, through corporeal proximity and limited access to views of the landscape, negate the pleasures of panoramic vision.

While Makhmalbaf's film is extremely consistent in its treatment of space this is not always the case in Ghobadi's films. It is clearly not the case that the latter is not acutely aware of what is at stake in representations of Kurdish landscapes, an awareness that he demonstrates in an interview about *A Time for Drunken Horses*:

> The two defining characteristics of Kurdish life are suffering and hardship. I have always seen the Kurds suffering from agony and pain. At the same time, Kurdistan's nature is so exquisite with beautiful landscapes. This poses a problem for me as filmmaker depicting the suffering of the Kurds. If I parade characters like Ayoub or Maadi across Kurdistan's gorgeous landscapes in the spring or fall, my viewers' eyes will be stunned by the postcard beauties of Kurdistan, and people with their miseries will disappear in the landscapes. I felt snow was the best element to use to cover the landscapes.[25]

Ghobadi's formal and political dilemma repeatedly surfaces in his films. *Marooned in Iraq* is in many ways similar to Makhmalbaf's film in the partial and bounded views of the land - on the other hand, *Half-Moon* treats the viewer to magnificent and often folkloric representations of Kurdistan.[26] *A Time for Drunken Horses* is clearly divided into two parts with the first part offering several panoramic views of the stunning landscape while the final part uses the strategies that the director outlines above. Asuman Suner also notes the inconsistent representational practices of *A Time for Drunken Horses* in a critical investigation that unfortunately remains trapped in Naficy's concepts of the 'open' and 'third-space' chronotopes:

> Consistent with open chronotopes, the *mise-en-scene* favors ' . . . external locations and open settings and landscapes, bright natural lighting, and mobile and wandering diegetic characters' . . . The entire film, with the exception of a few indoors scenes, is shot in open spaces. The mountainous landscape with its snow covered hills, curving roads, spectacular constellations of sunlight is elegantly depicted by Ghobadi's camera.[27]

In Naficy and Suner, as in Braidotti, 'openness' seems to be a natural property of landscapes unmediated by the representational practices of texts.[28] In contrast, the present analysis of *Blackboards* has suggested that the film's articulation of space revolves around several complementary formal devices marked by closeness and proximity that infuse the relationship between travellers and travelled space with a distinct aesthetic.

Such aesthetic makes particular sense in the context of Kurdish history and in particular the special place that the land occupies in the imaginary of a homeless nation. In that respect it is more than a mere coincidence that *Blackboards*, as do all of Ghobadi's films, ends its narrative around or at a border. The border, by definition a manifestation of power (to mark the land and claim ownership and control), is a particularly poignant symbol of Kurdish homelessness.[29] For nation-states borders constitute protective boundaries, symbolic walls that defend the homeland and define its spatial unity, while for the Kurds, they become signs of arbitrary segregation separating families and communities, physical scars on the land and emblems of a violent de-territorialisation.

Two further formal aspects of the film point towards its cultural and historical specificity and its self-positioning beyond the boundaries of the axes of activity↔passivity, certainty↔uncertainty that underpin modern sensibilities in relation to movement. In *Blackboards*, the fundamental types of modern mobile vision, linear and incremental revelation of space (best demonstrated in the numerous versions of the tracking shot) and circular exploration of objects and or landscapes (panning), give place to a perpetual movement of/in the frame. This ceaseless mobility lacks identifiable origin, destination and purpose, does not contribute to an overarching cognitive trajectory and remains fundamentally incomplete. Furthermore, while in cinematic journeys of exploration, discovery and revelation, enhanced knowledge (of the world and/or of the self) is the desired effect of the heroes' mobility, *Blackboards* rejects the epistemology of progress and transformation. Instead of changing and organising the lives of others, the teachers' own journeys become subordinate to the mobility of the nomadic groups as the academic knowledge that they wish to impart to the travellers is rendered irrelevant and useless. In the process, the blackboards, initially instruments of instruction and emblems of self-improvement and knowledge, become tools for survival, their function constantly revised and subjected to the contingencies of a perpetual and incomplete journey.

NOTES

1. Andrew Horton (ed.), *The Last Modernist: The Films of Theo Angelopoulos* (Trowbridge: Flicks Books, 1997).
2. David Bordwell, 'Modernism, minimalism, melancholy: Angelopoulos and visual style', in Horton (ed.) *Last Modernist*, pp. 11–26, p. 25.
3. Fredric Jameson, 'Theo Angelopoulos: the past as history, the future as form', in Horton (ed.), *Last Modernist*, pp. 78–95, p. 92.
4. DVD distributed by Artificial Eye.

5. Hamid Dabashi, *Close Up: Iranian Cinema Past, Present and Future* (London and New York: Verso, 2001), pp. 280–1.

6. It was widely reported that when Angelopoulos was presented with the Grand Prize of the Jury at Cannes, he gave a cursory speech declaring that he had nothing much to say because he had prepared an acceptance of the Golden Palm Prize! See *Ta Nea* (29 May 1995), *Eleftheros Typos* (30 May 1995), *Ethnos* (29 May 1995).

7. *Ta Nea* (25 May 2009).

8. The Sarajevo scenes were actually shot in Mostar.

9. Tom Gunning, 'The cinema of attraction: early film, its spectator and the avant-garde', *Wide Angle*, 8.3–4 (1986), pp. 63–70.

10. Such strategy might be justified for pragmatic reasons as the location is not Sarajevo. In the original script of the film (dated on the director's official website [http://www.theoangelopoulos.gr/] from 27 April 1993), however, Angelopoulos describes the scene with specific reference to dense mist: 'a fog makes the exterior space impenetrable' (my translation from the Greek original).

11. Comparable to the empty screen of the film's end.

12. Her name is never revealed in the film but identified in the script.

13. Ann Rutherford, 'Precarious boundaries: affect, *mise-en-scène* and the senses in Angelopoulos's Balkan epic', *Senses of Cinema*, 31 (2004), <http://archive.sensesofcinema.com/contents/04/31/angelopoulos_balkan_epic.html>, visited on 2 June 2009.

14. For an analysis of the film in terms of its conceptualisation of history and in the context of the centenary celebration of the 'birth' of cinema, see Dimitris Eleftheriotis, 'Early cinema as child: historical metaphor and European cinephilia in *Lumière & Company*, *Screen*, 46.3 (Autumn 2005), pp. 315–28.

15. Andrew Horton, 'Preface', in Horton (ed.), *Last Modernist*, p. vi

16. Adam Mars-Jones, 'A walk on the blind side', *The Independent* (15 February 1996).

17. See, for example, the analysis of Vengos's star image and the values that it expresses in Yannis Soldatos, *History of Greek Cinema*, vol. 3 (Athens: Aigokeros, 1990), esp. pp. 5–16, and Yannis Soldatos, *Enas Anthropos Pantos Kairou* ('An all-weather man', my translation) (Athens: Aigokeros, 2000).

18. Odysseus is described in *Odysseia* as *polymichanos*, i.e., resourceful and canny.

19. Hamid Dabashi, *Close Up*, p. 260.

20. This is an assumption and not a certainty. The film makes repeated references to the chemical attack on Halabja, an event that took place in March 1988, towards the very end of the Iran-Iraq war.

21. See, for example, Cathy Caruth, 'Unclaimed experience: trauma and the possibility of History', *Yale French Studies*, 79 (1991), pp. 181–92; Nancy K. Miller and Jason Tougaw (eds), *Extremities: Trauma, Testimony and Community* (Urbana and Chicago: University of Illinois Press, 2002).

22. A notable exception is the scene where Said 'reads' a letter to an old man working in a field. A clear shot-reverse shot exchange forms the main part of the scene.

23. Rosi Braidotti, *Nomadic Subjects: Embodiment and Sexual Difference in Contemporary Feminist Theory* (New York: Columbia University Press, 1994), p. 5.

24. Ibid. p. 27.

25. Ghobadi in *Interview with Director Bahman Ghobadi*, included in the DVD (distributed by Wellspring) of *Marooned in Iraq*.

26. The cinematography in *Half Moon* is noticeably different, possibly because of the impact of Nigel Bluck whose previous credits include second unit director of photography for *The Lord of the Rings* trilogy.

27. Asuman Suner, 'Outside in: "accented cinema" at large', *Inter-Asia Cultural Studies*, 7.3 (2006), pp. 363–82, p. 369.

28. Suner, however, places the open chronotope in the context of a third-space (that of the border in Ghobadi's film) relationship that introduces an 'agoraphobic experience of space' (Ibid. pp. 368–70).

29. In *Interview with the Director* feature of the *DVD* of *A Time for Drunken Horses* (released in the *UK* by Tartan Video, 2002) and *How Samira Made*, Ghobadi and Makhmalbaf are explicit about the importance of borders in their films and for Kurdish people: describing borders as 'dirty' (the former) and as dangerous minefields (the latter).

PART III

Travelling Films

CHAPTER 7

Films across borders: Indian films in Greece in the 1950s and 1960s

The second part of this book considered in some detail the specific ways in which cinematic journeys often unfold along the lines of narratives of (self-)transformation in which the unfamiliar and 'foreign' environments that heroes are placed in act as catalysts for personal change. This chapter, focusing on a specific case study, will consider the transformations effected upon films themselves in the process of crossing borders that is characteristic of internationally circulating commodities. The examination will continue in the final chapter where subtitles, as a marker of difference, will be used as a way of conceptualising a speculative theoretical category, that of the 'foreign spectator'.

Considering films as travelling cultural products raises crucial questions in relation to key political, critical and historiographical discourses and practices. Conventional international histories privilege certain flows of import/export that represent only a small number of the journeys involved in the global migration of film: Hollywood's domination, the unexpected popularity of Italian Neorealism, the French New Wave's aesthetic impact – a long but limited list. At the same time, critical discourses of national cinemas and protectionist policies perceive national cultures and identities as threatened by exposure to certain foreign products while engagement with others is seen as desirable and enlightening: the politics of cultural imperialism unfold along such lines. Finally, the polysemic potential of films in encounters with 'foreign' audiences challenges critical and theoretical understandings of the complete and unique nature of texts.

The popularity of Indian films in Greece in the 1950s and 1960s offers an interesting challenge to such assumptions. In terms of historiography it represents an aberration, a cultural flow that escapes the radar of conventional histories.[1] It also presents a clear threat to models of Greek national cinema and points towards a profound discursive anxiety around Greece's European identity. The critic and writer Nestor Matsas denounced the 'illegitimate' infatuation of Greek audiences with Indian films in revealingly loaded terms: 'It is not acceptable, at a moment when we are trying to establish ourselves in the European arena, to have become a cultural colony of India.'[2]

His reaction is depressingly typical of the critical denial of the key role played by Indian cinema in Greek film culture in the 1950s and 1960s. In that period many Indian films were imported and screened in a variety of theatres ranging from small neighbourhood operations to large city centre cinemas and encompassing both open-air and conventional venues. While the Greek-Indian cinematic affair is now recognized as a historical event, there have been no attempts to analyse and theorise the phenomenon in a convincing and rigorous way. This chapter will attempt to 'tell the story' of the Indian cinematic presence in Greece, to account for the popularity and success of the films, to indicate ways in which the 'crossing borders' of the films changes them and to speculate about the causes of the persistent critical reticence surrounding this remarkable cultural exchange.

There is no accurate or substantially reliable documentation of the exact dimensions of the importation of Indian films. Important research has been undertaken by Helen Abadzi and Emmanuel Tasoulas that led to the publication in 1998 of their book *Indoprepon Apokalypsi*.[3] Their research is a painstaking troll through a huge number of primary sources (newspaper articles and reviews, distributors' publicity material, items in the popular press, etc.) which are not always accurate or reliable. Despite the best efforts of the authors it is impossible to construct a precise and accurate historical picture of the phenomenon but, thanks to their work, we can at least understand the broad dimensions of it.

7.1 INDIAN CINEMA IN GREECE

Abadzi and Tasoulas identify 'at least 111 Indian films exhibited in Greece'[4] in the period from 1954 to 1968. While very precise about the 'moment of origin' of the Greco-Indian engagement, they are rather vague about its end (they do not offer any real evidence that no Indian films were shown after 1968). The screening of *Aan* (Mehboob Khan, 1952) on 17 January 1954 is posited as the first time that an Indian film was shown in Greece ('until that day [Indian cinema] was unknown to the movie goers'),[5] but the end of the affair is never firmly set. It is difficult to find corroborative evidence regarding their data or the accuracy of the periodisation that they propose. Another researcher, Panos Kouanis,[6] offers the following figures[7] for imported Indian films: thirteen in 1959–60, thirteen in 1960–1, fifteen in 1961–2, six in 1963–4 and nine in 1965–9, giving a total of 56 films in the period 1959–69. The volume of relevant publicity material, newspaper articles, as well as testimonies, private accounts and personal memories, is significant enough, however, to enable us to claim justifiably that Indian films had an important, lasting and all-pervasive presence in Greece.

The importers/distributors of the films were primarily small companies or individuals who obtained copies from a variety of sources: there are stories of entrepreneurs travelling to Bombay (Mumbai) to buy prints and thus owning the complete right to the distribution of the movies, whereas others used British distributors as their first point of contact. There are also anecdotes of distributors 'discovering' Indian cinema through their links with and travels to the Greek diasporic communities of the Middle East and North Africa.[8] The suggestion that minor independent distributors spearheaded the importation of Indian films is not only supported by the study of the publicity material but also makes sense in the context of international distribution practices at the time. Brian Larkin, for example, details the role played by Lebanese distributors/exhibitors in the import of Indian films into Nigeria in the 1950s,[9] while Christopher Wagstaff, in his investigation of Italian genre films in the world market in the 1960s, alludes to the key role played by small production and distribution companies.[10] Small or independent distributors importing large numbers of low-cost films appears to be the way that the international film markets of the period operated, even in the usually hermetically controlled by the Majors American market.[11]

In the Greek context such distribution practices were very much unsolicited by the Indian film industry. There is no evidence, with the exception perhaps of major films such as *Mother India* (Mehboob Khan, 1957), that Indian exporters played a particularly active role in facilitating the incredible popularity of Indian films in Greece. On the contrary, what appears to be the case is that there was very little awareness on their part of the significance or even the existence of the Greek market. What makes the Greco–Indian relationship particularly fascinating is that it seems to be a rather spontaneous infatuation happening at the margins of established national and international distribution/exhibition practices but occupying a central place in popular culture and imagination.

The Greek engagement with the Indian films, nevertheless, was very much subjected to obvious processes of manipulation and translation. The titles of the films were invariably changed, often beyond recognition;[12] for instance, *Aan* was distributed as *Mangala the Rose of India* and *Mother India* as *Land Soaked with Sweat*. A closer comparative examination of the Greek and Indian titles suggests that the 'translation' process consistently, and undoubtedly deliberately, identified, foregrounded and marketed two key aspects of the films, promoting a particular 'appeal' to the Greek imagination around the melodramatic (as suggested by the *Mother India* example, but also with titles such as *Our Love Will Never Fade* [*Babul*], *My Child I Didn't Sin* [*Kala Pani*], *Not Even Death*

Can Separate Us [*Mirza Sahiban*]) and the oriental/orientalist (as suggested by the *Aan* example but also in *The Siren of Bombay* [*Amar*], *Storm over India* [*Chandralekha*], *The Flower of Kashmir* [*Junglee*]) or a combination of the two (*The Flame of India* [*Amrapali*] or *India My Love* [*Pardesi*]).[13]

The melodramatic/orientalist axis that informs marketing strategies is particularly suggestive as it embodies the dynamics of a familiarity/foreignness dialectic. While, on the one hand, the melodramatic clearly connects with the popularity of Greek melodramas and the familiarity of the audiences of the period with the trope,[14] on the other hand, the exoticisation of the films activates distancing orientalist fantasies of mythical, far-away lands. As I will explore later, the fundamental underpinning of the Greco-Indian relationship is a cultural empathy that is continuously counteracted by a multitude of surrounding framing discourses of objectification and distanciation.

The Greek distribution/exhibition sector's modus operandi did not interface with the Indian films in any rational or well-organised way. The time that the films were imported very much depended on when individual distributors/entrepreneurs spotted the movies or realised their commercial potential, and had very little relevance to their actual release date. As a result, the order in which the films were presented to Greek audiences was typically unchronological, creating a fragmented and a historical experience totally isolated from the actual flow of production: *Babul*, made in 1950, was released in Greece in 1964, whereas *Aan*, made in 1952, was released in 1954. The 'time lag' between Indian and Greek release presented distributors with additional challenges as it was deemed deeply problematic for the categorisation of the first, second and third run cinemas that structured the distribution/exhibition practices.[15] *Mother India*, released in Greece a good three years after its Indian opening, was exhibited in a mixture of venues ranging from traditional first-run venues (such as the Kotopouli in the centre of Athens) to suburban and provincial second- and third-run venues.

The length of the Indian films (in general considerably longer than their Greek or American counterparts) had to be adjusted in order to fit better with the regular two-hour screening slots of most cinemas and with the viewing habits of the spectators. The result was that narrative suffered, as the musical and other spectacular numbers were considered to be the main attraction. This had the additional advantage of simplifying somewhat the onerous task of subtitling which was already strewn with considerable obstacles. There was very limited linguistic expertise in the industry and subtitlers relied heavily on English subtitled versions of the films (or English scripts that often accompanied the films). Correspondence between source and target texts was open to numerous semantic errors and often to complete lack of synchronisation. This was not, however, an insurmountable difficulty, not only because a significant number of the audience were illiterate or semi-literate anyway[16], but also because there was familiarity with key aspects of the Indian melodramatic mode and particular fascination with the music, singing and dancing involved in the films.

Although it is very difficult to obtain hard evidence of the commercial success of the films there are some strong indicators of their undoubted popularity. Panos Kouanis offers lists of the Greek box office returns of films in the 1939–99 period, in which we discover that in the 1959–60 season *Mother India* was in eighth place in the Athens area with 87,216 admissions.[17] Abadzi and Tasoulas offer a collection of newspaper reports that document the obsession of the press and of film fans with Indian stars. An excellent example is offered by the coverage of the event of the short visit of Nargis and her husband Sunil Dutt to Athens airport in September 1962. While Nargis spent only about half an hour at the airport (changing planes on her way to Zurich) every Greek newspaper had lengthy features on her career and extensive coverage of the mini press conference that was hastily organised. Ironically, on the same day, Robert Mitchum was passing through Athens airport; reports of his visit, however, were comprehensively eclipsed by those on Nargis.[18]

7.2 EXPLORING SIMILARITIES

In order to investigate the factors that enabled and sustained the popularity of Indian cinema in Greece, I will turn to the work of scholars such as Ravi Vasudevan, Rosie Thomas and Lalitha Gopalan in order to explore some of the defining characteristics of Indian cinema, and to establish a series of structural correspondences between the two cultures and cinemas.

In his 1995 essay, Vasudevan discusses the popularity of Indian cinema in the international market, noting its presence 'in countries of Indian immigration as in East Africa, Mauritius, the Middle East and South East Asia', as well as in other places such as North Africa, the USSR and China, and speculates about the possibility of a wider 'sphere of influence'.[19] Importantly, Vasudevan proposes a link between textual aspects of the Bombay 'social' and defining transformations in Indian society at the time, that can have currency beyond the Indian national context:

> Such a sphere of influence makes one think of a certain arc of narrative form separate from, if overlapping at points with, the larger hegemony exercised by Hollywood. From the description of cultural 'peculiarities' of the Bombay cinema which follows, one could speculate whether its narrative form has a special resonance in 'transitional' societies.[20]

Following Vasudevan's suggestion, I will focus on four areas of possible 'resonance' between Indian and Greek cinema, culture and society: textual affinities in the melodramatic mode, comparable exhibition contexts, similarities in the organisation of the entertainment sector, and structural correspondence in the 'transitional' aspects of the two societies.

Defining the salient peculiarities of the Indian melodramatic mode, Vasudevan notes:

> The diegetic world of this cinema is primarily governed by the logic of kinship relations, and its plot driven by family conflict. The system of dramaturgy is a melodramatic one, displaying the characteristic ensemble of manichaeism, bipolarity, the privileging of the moral over the psychological, and the deployment of coincidence. And the relationship between narrative performance sequence and action spectacle is loosely structured in the fashion of a cinema of attractions. In addition to these features, the system of narration incorporates Hollywood codes of continuity editing in a fitful, unsystematic fashion, relies heavily on visual forms such as the tableau and inducts stable cultural codes of looking of a more archaic sort.[21]

While one needs to recognise that undertaking a wholesale comparison between Indian and Greek melodramatic forms involves a considerable danger of overgeneralisation, simplification and reduction, it is also equally important to acknowledge the resonance of the above description in the context of popular Greek cinema in the 1950s and 1960s. Niki Karakitsou-Dougé, for example, describes Greek melodrama in remarkably similar terms, foregrounding the Manichean binary opposites that inform the dramaturgy (guilt/innocence, honesty/dishonesty, betrayal/faithfulness, corruption/purity) and which are also based on moral rather than psychological values.[22] Karakitsou-Dougé also refers to the key role played by fate/destiny for the resolution of dramatic conflict, echoing, thus, Rosie Thomas's discussion of Hindi melodramatic themes.[23]

Indian cinema's centrality of the tableau, frontality and iconicity also corresponds to the visual organisation of popular Greek films[24] although no research has as yet been undertaken into the possible presence of 'dormant' mobilisation in the static tableau that defines the 'social', according to Vasudevan's argument. Similarly, the structure of looking that characterises the Bombay 'social' and contrasts with 'formulations about looking which have become commonplace in the analysis of Hollywood cinema . . . the figure looked at is not necessarily subject to control but may in fact be the repository of authority'[25] rhymes with the analysis of Greek masculinity that I have undertaken elsewhere, with specific reference to the leading star of Greek melodramas, Nicos Xanthopoulos.[26] Again, while it is not the process of 'residual sacralization'[27] that informs the structure of looking in the Greek cinema, access to the hero's image (whose virtue is either beyond doubt or proven by the dramaturgy) is offered liberally to the spectator and is invested with a moral authority comparable to that of the male hero of the Bombay 'social'.

Even more striking is the similarity in the use of musical numbers in Greek and Indian melodramas: not only do they stand apart from the narrative but also they are commodities in their own right, with a commercial life that extends beyond the popularity of the films from which they originated.[28] The similarity is so striking that it leads Karakitsou-Dougé to a very unusual (for a Greek) critical assertion:

> The presence of popular music, of the bouzouki kind, is characteristic of many melodramas. In all of the Apostolos Tegopoulos films, the talismanic star Nicos Xanthopoulos plays the bouzouki and sings about his frustrated love and sufferings as a victim of fate and social injustice. These are long-winded songs full of passion, emotional upheaval, sadness, melancholy, desperation and hopelessness. *Greek melodramas offer them the same inflated position as Indian cinema.*[29]

Interestingly, Lalitha Gopalan, describing the typical viewing experience of Indian cinema in India, identifies as one of its defining characteristics a constellation of interruptions, focusing on 'three different kinds of interruptions that brand the narrative form of Indian cinema: song and dance sequences, the interval and censorship'.[30]

Gopalan notes that the interruptive nature of the song–and–dance sequences is twofold. Not only do they interrupt the narrative in a variety of ways but also, crucially, they stand as self-contained units that 'often outlast the film's own story in the popular memory'.[31] It is important to note that perhaps the most important consequence of the popularity of Indian cinema in Greece was the use of Indian film songs as source material for thousands of Greek popular songs. In fact, it is primarily this phenomenon (the extensive 'copying' of Indian tunes by Greek musicians, uniformly condemned as plagiarism) that motivates the research of Abadzi and Tasoulas and others[32] and constitutes, in the opinion of many Greek critics, a 'shameful' event in the history of Greek popular culture. I will return to this issue in the concluding section of this chapter but it is worth noting the phenomenon as an indicator of the popularity of Indian cinema in Greece and of the fact that the positional autonomy of the song-and-dance sequences allows for a closer and affectionate relationship between the viewers and the films and their music.

The description of the interval by Gopalan[33] and that of the overall viewing experience by Thomas ('audiences clap, sing, recite familiar dialogue with the actors, throw coins at the screen [in appreciation of spectacle], "tut tut" at emotionally moving scenes, cry openly and jeer knowingly')[34] is strikingly similar to the viewing experience typical of a very popular venue in Greece in the 1950s and 1960s: that of the open-air, neighbourhood cinema where the majority of Indian films were exhibited.[35]

Textual similarities and affinities in the nature of the viewing experience are reinforced by a number of shared characteristics between the Indian and Greek popular entertainment sectors, and more specifically in the television and music industries that are crucially related to cinema. The histories of Greek and Indian television in the 1960s are remarkably similar. They both started as state initiatives branching out of established radio services and with early experimental phases. Grigoris Paschalidis in his history of early Greek television suggests that the first experimental broadcast took place in September 1960 with a limited area of transmission. He also notes the low take-up of the technology until 1966 (13,000 receivers) and the acceleration that occured at the end of the decade (96,000 receivers in 1969).[36] In the Indian context, K. Viswanath and Kavita Karan state:

> *Doordarshan* [the Indian state TV] started as an experiment in 1959 in New Delhi, primarily for educational purposes, with All India Radio providing its programming. Regular broadcasting on a very small scale started in 1965 in New Delhi and spread to fewer than a dozen other cities in the next decade. The growth of the new medium was stalled, in stark contrast to radio, until 1982.[37]

The absence of television as a serious competitor to cinema in India and Greece goes hand-in-hand with the crucial importance of the music industry. In both countries there are significant links between the film and music industries both in terms of the former providing an outlet and a strategically important marketing instrument for the latter, and in terms of enhancing the earning potential of a film through the sale of its music. The close interconnection between the two sectors is reflected by the explicit references that Indian and Greek films of the period make to the music industry as they dramatise storylines that involve, for example, the ambition of characters to become music stars or to accumulate wealth through the sale of records.[38]

Vasudevan's speculation about the attraction of Bombay cinema in 'transitional' societies is very much constructed around the close examination of Indian films against their specific historical background, suggesting that there exists a link between the textual practices of the films and a negotiation of social 'transition'. In Indian society at that time, this transition was seen in three overlapping areas. On the political level, there is the passage to independence, the movement to post-coloniality and the attendant construction of the 'national' as a meaningful category. Vasudevan notes that such a process involves a hegemonic relationship between central privileged identities and peripheral marginalized ones. On the level of social modernisation particularly significant are the processes of secularisation, urbanisation and industrialisa-tion, the emphasis on social mobility, and the reconfiguration of patriarchal authority in the family. Attached to such processes are moral and ideological values that are negotiated, as Vasudevan explores, through the textuality of the Bombay 'social' film.[39]

Importantly, Greek society underwent similar changes in the 1950s and 1960s. The bloody and divisive civil war that ended in 1949 left a significant proportion of the population (communists or more generally left-wing liber-als) completely disenfranchised by the state.[40] The victory of the nationalists was very much facilitated by the military involvement of British and US forces (it was a widely held belief for people on the left that Greece experienced two occupations in the 1940s, first by the Germans and then by the British and Americans). A major component of the political project of the nationalist governments of the 1950s was the creation of a durable pro-Western, anti-communist national identity, as well as the limitation of the endemic depend-ency on foreign aid for the economic survival of the country. From the mid 1950s to the late 1960s, there was a succession of governments whose agenda was clearly to modernise Greek society along lines similar to those of India: the period was marked by urbanisation and industrialisation and the process of gradual replacement of the extensive by the nuclear family.

The structural similarities between Greek and Indian societies make pos-sible a mode of textual address that can appeal to both audiences, and confirms in that way Vasudevan's speculation regarding the relevance of Indian films for transitional societies. By discussing the much celebrated (by Indian cinephiles) opening sequence of *Shree 420* (Raj Kapoor, India, 1955), I will identify ways in which the musical number 'Mera Joota Hai Japani' resonates with meanings that correspond to specifically Greek sensibilities and social dynamics that revolve around perceptions of national identity in the early 1960s.

Thanks to Abadzi and Tasoulas it is easy to establish the popularity of the film in Greece. They indicate that in three weeks in the Thessaloniki cinema Alcazar and in a week in Aigli the film made 37,000 tickets, an impressive but by no means exhaustive figure as it is based on the limited and eclectic data that the researchers managed to collect which excludes the rest of Greece where, and other periods in which, the film was exhibited.[41] Furthermore, the tune of the musical number that I will consider here, 'Mera Joota Hai Japani' ('My shoes are Japanese'), provided the basis for at least two popular Greek songs – several other Greek songs also appropriated tunes from the film.[42]

The setting of the number, on the road to Bombay, is in itself suggestive of transition. Not only in terms of the road as a space of transition par excel-lence, but also articulated by the film's narrative as Raj's (Raj Kapoor) passage from rural to urban, from countryside to city, from an existence marked by honesty and innocence to one of dishonesty and corruption, from the values of tradition to those of modernity. As already discussed such processes of transformation inform the social dynamics of both India and Greece. The end of the road, the ultimate destination of the transition, is clearly suggested by the numerous shots that come from a camera placed behind Raj as he walks down the road and that, in their composition, open up the perspective of what lies ahead – the city. This is re-enforced by the appearance towards the end of the sequence of images of Bombay superimposed over shots of the road. The agenda of transformation/modernisation is also clearly set out by the lyrics: 'Foolish are those who sit on the sidelines/With little care for their country's fate/To forge ahead is like life/To stand still is like death.'

The choice of Raj's costume in the sequence is also crucial: as a result of his success as the tramp in *Awaara* (Raj Kapoor, India, 1951), Kapoor presents himself in a more Chaplinesque fashion, establishing thus an essentially international frame of cinematic reference. Of course Chaplin's tramp has been adopted in a variety of popular forms in almost every country in the world, including Greece where, as early as 1920, Kimon Spathopoulos was impersonating Chaplin (known as 'Charlot' in Greece) in his films. The figure of Kapoor as tramp/Charlot internationalises the appeal of the film not only by recalling a legendary type but also by activating transnational processes of imitation and copying. Furthermore, it reveals similarities between Greek and Indian self-perception of national culture as existing in a distinctly subordinate position in relation to a hegemonic culture capable of producing and circulating global icons such as Chaplin/Charlot.[43]

The national/international dialectic of the musical number is further amplified by the lyrics: 'My shoes are Japanese/My pants are from England/the cap I wear is Russian/but my heart is Indian.' Greece in the 1960s was (and arguably still remains) a country with very limited exports, relying heavily on imports for many everyday-life consumerist goods, and depending heavily for political and financial support on her powerful allies. The 'Greekness' of the national identity (certainly in its cinematic, melodramatic form) did not revolve around a confident sense of belonging to a powerful and self-sufficient nation but depended on emotional bonds between people who 'make do' under adverse conditions – as the song suggests, to be Greek (like being Indian) means to possess a heart but not much more.

The number's narrative content, Raj's journey to Bombay in search of employment, has poignant relevance to Greek society during the early 1960s when masses of Greeks migrated to wealthy industrial European countries. Almost every Greek family at the time had emigrant relations, and references to migration abound in the popular songs and films of the period.[44] The following lyrics would have particular resonance with a broad spectrum of Greeks: 'I venture into the big world/I walk with my head held high/Where does my destination lie?/Where will I ever settle?'

7.3 CRITICAL DENIAL

The *mise-en-scène* of the 'Mera Joota Hai Japani' number, nevertheless, also provides a lavish display of assorted exotica (ethnic costumes, camels, snakes, elephants, palaces and parades), offering to Greek spectators the possibility of objectifying distance as a counterpoint to the cultural empathy with the film's sensibilities. Greek critical discourse is very much informed by a similar fundamental ambivalence. There is first of all outright and deafening silence. Apart from rare in-passing comments about the presence of Indian films in Greece there has been no serious attempt to address the phenomenon in its multitude of dimensions. Greek film scholarship manifestly overlooks the theoretical and historical urgency to pursue research questions around the shared genealogies of Greek and Indian (more generally Asian) cinema.

At other times, we witness a tendency to shroud the Greek-Indian transnational relationship in a vestige of exoticism and idiosyncrasy, and explain it as an anomaly or 'exception' which is characteristic of the unpredictable, anarchic and unbridled imagination of Greek culture rather than a logical manifestation of cultural and social similarities. An interesting and very common variant of this critical line is the exoticisation not of the Indian films but of the Greek spectators watching them. Unfortunately, because in general their work is motivated by the desire to investigate and gather data and to address the issues, Abadzi and Tasoulas offer several examples of such elitism, with the most outspoken example referring to audiences of Indian films in the derogatory terms *kosmakis* ('little or lesser people', my translation) and *tsemperia* ('headscarves', my translation, a term used to describe 'poor women' and dependent on a rather suggestive orientalist image).[45] In that way the audience are effectively divided between middle-class enthusiasts whose engagement with Indian cinema takes place under the aegis of either irony or exotic thrills and working-class, poverty-stricken victims of ideological (mis)recognition and identification, disavowing, in both cases, the danger of cultural affinity with Asian culture. Within such discourse Indian films remain profoundly and undeniably 'other': either as strange, exotic products of an alien culture or as the source of base entertainment for 'other' people.

For Abadzi and Tasoulas, as well as for the majority of critics, nevertheless, the fundamental issue is not the cinematic relationship between Greece and India but its implications for the music industry. In fact, the musical dimension is the one that attracts critical attention and discursively demonstrates another manifestation of denial. The debate revolves around the 'illegitimate' use of Indian tunes by Greek musicians (invariably presented as 'plagiarism') and focuses on issues regarding copyright, unfair competition[46] and negative effect on Greek musical traditions and on Greek audiences. Once again a critical position of distance is established but this time in political and moral terms:

the appropriation of music violates codes of fair trade but also contaminates Greek popular culture and heritage. Surprisingly what is overlooked in the critical debate is the fact that the success of such 'plagiarist' activity depends crucially on the similarities between Greek and Indian music and culture. The plagiarising musicians had such astonishing success in passing off their songs as Greek only because they did not stand out as markedly different. By focusing the debate on issues of authenticity and copyright, property and theft, Greek and 'Indian-like' songs, the truly astounding dimension of a background of similarity is lost.

It seems to me that the Western orientation that powerfully informs the Greek political and critical discourse (manifested by the 'we belong to the West' political imperative of the 1950s and 1960s that evidently still has currency today) makes it extremely difficult to address the profoundly hybrid and impure nature of Greek cultural and national identity. Interestingly, both Abadzi and Tasoulas and Papadakis are resorting to a historical review of the Greek-Indian relationship which, they argue, originates with Alexander's invasion and is circular in nature: the recent popularity of Indian culture in Greece is explained away as the repayment of a debt, as the ancient Greeks are credited with the export of key scientific and cultural ideas that benefited Indian civilization.[47]

Greece's social transition was (and still is) crucially informed by the conceptualisation of the process as one of 'Europeanisation', of 'becoming Europe', and it is that perception that informed Greek politics throughout the second half of the twentieth century. In such discourse, 'Europe' was (and to a lesser extent still remains) perceived as a desirable 'other', as a political and cultural entity distinct from Greece but one that constitutes the ultimate destination of the journey of modernisation. By the same token, 'Asia' becomes linked with an undesirable past (associated with centuries of Ottoman occupation) that must be negated and expelled from the popular imaginary.

The temptation to reduce the wealth of messy cultural exchanges into teleological outcomes of a glorious ancient Greek civilisation appears to be hard to resist. Equally difficult to accept is the fact that while the politicians were working hard to commit Greece to Europe and the West, and film and cultural critics were striving to educate and enlighten the masses, audiences cried and laughed and sang with Indian melodramas rather than with the great works of the Western canon. The popularity of Indian films across borders and in a foreign national cultural terrain marked by ambiguity and anxiety was facilitated by cultural and social similarities but unfolded against hostile critical reception. Within such a context the journey of films initiates on the one hand a process of textual and cultural transformation through translation and appropriation and, on the other, it reveals the violence involved in the enunciation of national cinemas and identities. Thus, the transformative potential of travelling engulfs not only its mobile agents but the discursive articulation of the arena that they traverse.

NOTES

1. For a more general consideration of the historiographical challenges that the international popularity of Indian cinema poses, see the special issue 'Indian cinema abroad: historiography of transnational cinematic exchanges', *South Asian Popular Culture*, 4.2 (2006), in which an earlier version of this chapter appears.

2. As quoted in Helen Abadzi and Emmanuel Tasoulas, *Indoprepon Apokalypsi* (Athens: Atrapos, 1998) p. 44.

3. The title of the book translates loosely as 'Revelation of the Indian-like' and it refers to popular songs imitating the tunes of Indian films. The book proposes causal links between imported Indian films and the popularity of an 'Indian-like' music: the imported films offered the raw material for the (imitating or plagiarising) composers who exploited the popularity of the films (and their tunes) with Greek audiences.

4. Abadzi and Tasoulas, *Indoprepon Apokalypsi*, p. 111.

5. Ibid. p. 36.

6. Panos Kouanis, *I Kinimatografiki Agora stin Ellada, 1944–1999* ('The Film Market in Greece, 1944–1999', my translation) (Athens: Finatec, 2001), pp. 238–9.

7. Kouanis's figures are equally unreliable and are assembled from a variety of sources, including magazines and official (but not necessarily accurate) statistics.

8. Abadzi and Tasoulas, *Indoprepon Apokalypsi*.

9. Brian Larkin, 'Indian films and Nigerian lovers: media and the creation of parallel modernities', *Africa*, 67.3 (Summer 1997), pp. 406–41.

10. Christopher Wagstaff, 'Italian genre films in the world market', in Geoffrey Nowell-Smith and Steven Ricci (eds), *Hollywood & Europe: Economics, Culture, National Identity 1945–95* (London: BFI, 1998), pp. 74–85.

11. See Thomas Guback, *The International Film Industry: Western Europe and America since 1945* (Bloomington, IN, London: Indiana University Press, 1969), esp. pp. 82–90. Guback notes that small distributors in America were getting 'squeezed out' in the late 1960s after a period of significant activity.

12. Abadzi and Tasoulas offer an illuminating table comparing the original titles of the 111 films that they have identified as exhibited in Greece with the Greek titles; the vast majority of the Greek titles are often completely unrelated to the originals: *Indoprepon Apokalypsi*, pp. 171–5.

13. In fact an Indian/USSR co-production; see Sudha Rajagopalan, 'Emblematic of the Thaw: early Indian films in Soviet cinemas', *South Asian Popular Culture*, 4.2 (2006), pp. 83–100.

14. See, for example, Yannis Soldatos, *Istoria tou Ellinikou Kinimatografou* ('History of Greek Cinema', my translation), vol. 2 (Athens: Aigokeros, 1989); and Athina Kartalou, 'Protasi gia ena Plaisio Anagnosis ton eidon ston Elliniko Kinimatografo' ('Proposing a framework for the reading of genre in Greek cinema', my translation), *Optikoakoustiki Koultoura*, 1 (2002), pp. 25–35.

15. New releases were usually exhibited in first-run cinemas with the second- and third-run venues showing older films. The system was very similar to the Italian one detailed by Chris Wagstaff, 'A forkful of westerns', in Richard Dyer and Ginette Vincendeau (eds), *Popular European Cinema* (London: Routledge, 1992), pp. 245–61.

16. Soldatos suggests that in the 1960s illiteracy was running at 18 per cent and semi-literacy at 35 per cent (*Istoria tou Ellinikou Kinimatografou*, p. 15).

17. This only refers to Athens and the first- and second-run venues; one can assume a much better overall performance if third-run venues and the rest of Greece as well as the considerable re-runs of the film are taken into consideration. There were only two foreign films that exceeded *Mother India* in the box office that year: *Solomon and Sheba* (King Vidor, USA, 1959) in fifth place and *Some Like It Hot* (Billy Wilder, USA, 1959) in seventh place (*I Kinimatografiki Agora stin Ellada*, p. 249).

18. Abadzi and Tasoulas, *Indoprepon Apokalypsi*, p. 39.

19. Ravi Vasudevan, 'Addressing the spectator of a "third world" national cinema: the Bombay "social" film of the 1940s and 1950s', *Screen*, 36.4 (1995), pp. 305–24.

20. Ibid. p. 306.

21. Ibid. pp. 306–7.

22. Niki Karakitsou-Dougé, 'To Elliniko melodrama: i aisthitiki tis ekplixis' ('Greek melodrama: the aesthetic of surprise', my translation), *Optikoakoustiki Koultoura*, 1 (2002), pp. 37–52.

23. Rosie Thomas, 'Indian cinema – pleasures and popularity', *Screen*, 26.3–4 (1985), pp. 116–31.

24. See Dimitris Eleftheriotis, *Popular Cinemas of Europe: Studies of Texts, Contexts and Frameworks* (London and New York: Continuum, 2001), p. 186.

25. Ravi Vasudevan, 'Addressing the spectator of a "third world" national cinema', p. 314.

26. Dimitris Eleftheriotis, 'Questioning totalities: constructions of masculinity in the popular Greek cinema of the 1960s', *Screen*, 36.3 (1995), pp. 239–40.

27. Ravi Vasudevan, 'Addressing the spectator of a "third world" national cinema', pp. 314–17.

28. There is a vast bibliography on the role of song-and-dance sequences in Indian cinema (see, for example, Vasudevan, 'Addressing the spectator of a "third world" national cinema', and Thomas, 'Indian cinema – pleasures and popularity'). Equally the 'arbitrary', 'autonomous' nature of musical numbers in Greek cinema has been identified by many critics. See, for example, Eleftheriotis, *Popular Cinemas of Europe*; Soldatos, *Istoria tou Ellinikou Kinimatografou*; Karakitsou-Dougé, 'To Elliniko melodrama'.

29. Karakitsou-Dougé, 'To Elliniko melodrama', p. 48, my emphasis and my translation.

30. Lalitha Gopalan, *Cinema of Interruptions* (London: BFI, 2002), p. 18. While censorship is not considered in the present essay it is worth noting that the practice of 'trimming' films to fit screening schedules (as discussed above in relation to Indian films) was wide spread in Greece.

31. Ibid. pp. 18–19.

32. See, for example, Giorgios Papadakis, 'Indika . . . ki agirista', *Difonon*, 54 (1999), pp. 48–51; the title of his article can be loosely translated as 'Indian and unpaid', a pun on the slang expression 'daneika ki agirista', referring to unpaid debts.

33. 'The "Interval" is the ten-minute break in every Indian popular film after eighty minutes of film screening. Lights are turned on, the projector is turned off, and viewers step out of the theatre to smoke a cigarette, eat a snack, or visit the restroom' (Gopalan, *Cinema of Interruptions*, p. 19).

34. Thomas, 'Indian cinema', p. 129.

35. For a very similar description of the open-air cinema viewing experience, see Dimitris Eleftheriotis, *Popular Cinemas of Europe*, pp. 189–92.

36. Grigoris Paschalidis, 'Elliniki Tileorasi' ('Greek Television', my translation), in Nicolas Vernicos, Sofia Daskalopoulou, Filimon Bantiramoudis, Nicos Boubaris and Dimitris

Papageorgiou (eds), *Politistikes Viomihanies: Diadikasies, Ipirisies, Agatha* ('The Culture Industries: Processes, Services, Products', my translation) (Athens: Kritiki, 2004), pp. 173–200.

37. K. Viswanath and Kavita Karan, 'India', in Shelton. A. Gunaratne (ed.), *Handbook of the Media in Asia* (New Delhi and London: Sage, 2000), pp. 84–117, p. 91.

38. It must be recognized, however, that the dependency of the Indian music industry on cinema was far more extensive than was the case with Greece: 'Until the early 1980s, these film songs were the only form of popular music in India that was produced, distributed, and consumed on a mass scale, and even today film music accounts for the majority – nearly 80 percent – of music sales in India' (Tejaswini Ganti, *Bollywood: A Guidebook to Popular Hindi Cinema* [New York and London: Routledge, 2004], p. 78).

39. Ravi Vasudevan, 'Addressing the spectator of a "third world" national cinema'.

40. Thousands of Greek communists and 'sympathisers' were imprisoned or exiled in remote islands of the Aegean.

41. Helen Abadzi and Emmanuel Tasoulas, *Indoprepon Apokalypsi*, p. 191.

42. Abadzi and Tasoulas categorise Greek versions of Indian songs according to degrees of similarity. One version of 'Mera Joota Hai Japani' released in 1963 is characterized as a '3' ('versions where Indian and Greek musical themes co-exist') whereas a 1964 version is a '1' ('significant similarities'). They also identify another five Greek songs with clear links to *Shree 420* (ibid. pp. 178–88).

43. For a more extensive analysis of the international orientation of Greek popular culture in the 1960s, see Dimitris Eleftheriotis, *Popular Cinemas of Europe*, pp.188 and 193–5.

44. See Fotini Tomai-Konstantopoulou (ed.), *I Metanasteusi ston Kinimatografo* ('Emigration in Cinema', my translation) (Athens: Papazisi, 2004).

45. Helen Abadzi and Emmanule Tasoulas, *Indoprepon Apokalypsi*, p. 38.

46. Vasilis Tsitsanis, perhaps the most respected composer of popular and 'rebetiko' songs, in Greece, is quoted as saying: 'I was trying my hardest to write songs to compete with theirs. How could I know that their songs were Indian? Despite all my efforts I couldn't compete. Nobody can compete against Indian music because it is infinite' (Giorgos Papadakis, 'Indika . . . ki agirista', p. 51).

47. Abadzi and Tasoulas, *Indoprepon Apokalypsi*, esp. pp. 117–37; Papadakis, 'Indika . . . ki agirista'.

CHAPTER 8

Reading subtitles: travelling films meet foreign spectators

8.1 'WORLD CINEMA' AND FOREIGN SPECTATORS

The previous chapter pointed out that the journeys of films across borders have potentially destabilising effects that transform the travelling text itself and challenge the (imagined) unity of the 'host' community. Thus, the mobility of films as cultural products places them within a dialectics of cultural interaction and exchange and into the relatively new but rapidly developing field in film studies that is variably defined as 'transnational', 'intercultural' or 'world' cinema.[1] The differences between the terms are of course significant but perhaps more important is the observation that the body of films studied under the one or the other title tend to overlap considerably. This is in many ways understandable within the context of a (politically, economically, institutionally and technologically) changing international audiovisual culture: not only the easier, faster and increased circulation of films (in a variety of formats) around the world makes inevitable inter- or trans-cultural transactions but the very essence of the 'world' in 'world cinema' assumes the interaction and interrelation of different communities and texts.[2]

But the term 'world cinema' instantly introduces questions of position. It issues an open invitation to investigate closer the semantics and politics of the relations of opposition, exclusion or similarity that this new umbrella term enters into with other longer established categories of 'cinema'. From a critical perspective 'world' can be seen as referring to the opening up of a certain type of theoretical/historical discourse to cinemas and films that exist beyond hegemonic canons. At the same time, if we approach the term from the perspective of the audience, 'world' may well refer to the multiple and different cultural/national origins of films that form the cinematic universe of spectators around the world.[3] What informs both understandings, however, is a sense of positionality, more specifically a position marked by difference, the difference between an established common ground (critical, historical and theoretical in the first case, national and cultural in the second) and what lies beyond that.[4] Furthermore, both understandings directly or indirectly suggest that such positions surface and operate within a field of complex and variable forms of national and transnational power structures and relations: the influence of the canon, the hegemony of certain cinemas over others, the limits and limitations of critical discourse. More importantly for the purposes of the present work, 'world cinema' implies a position of foreignness. A film is a 'world film' for some not all of its spectators: one assumes that Chinese cinema can only be 'world cinema' to non-Chinese audiences. Thus, 'world cinema' is a discursive space occupied de facto by foreigners, foreign films and foreign spectators,[5] as they meet each other in encounters made possible by the journeys of cultural products.

Subtitles (or alternatively dubbing) accompany such journeys and become an unambiguous sign of foreignness, a visual testimony (like visa stamps on a passport) that the film that bears them has travelled and has crossed borders. Subtitles also succinctly encapsulate some of the positions and relations outlined above. In my own personal experience, subtitles, in their unavoidable presence, represent an obvious cultural imprint and constitute the most widely shared characteristic of 'world cinema'. From a perspective forged by the years of my childhood and adolescence in Greece, films from the 'world' come with subtitles. With that comes an awareness of occupying a specific position in 'world cinema', the position of a member of a minority linguistic constituency which is also determined by the specific distribution/exhibition practices of a national film industry.

Subtitles bring with them an awareness of position and that is a fundamental discursive mode of 'world cinema' that transcends local variations. This is not to deny the significant differences that exist, both qualitative (dubbing rather than subtitles, for instance) and quantitative (the number of subtitled/dubbed films spectators have access to and watch) but to tentatively and polemically suggest that it is possible to propose the 'foreign spectator' as a theoretically productive conceptual category.[6]

By focusing on subtitles this chapter aims to first map out and delineate critical positions as emerge within film theory and 'world cinema' in order to investigate their limitations. Within such mapping subtitles will not be considered as primarily an issue of linguistic translation, as it has usually been approached,[7] but as an integral component of the machinery of film. Such an approach will have to revisit some of the influential theorisations of the cinematic apparatus and to consider the conceptual implications of the insertion of subtitles in that discourse.

In this concluding chapter of *Cinematic Journeys* I shall propose an understanding of 'foreign spectators' as characters encountered in the travels of films but I intend to explore this metaphor with a shift in point of view away from that of the traveller. Subtitles will be seen as the marks of a journey, imprinted on the bodies of travelling films and read by the spectators that they encounter. The reading involved has a double frame of reference: it is an act of consumption of the literal meaning that the subtitles provide but also a critical and productive act that reads the subtitles as incomplete signs and instigates cultural syncretism and semiotic engagement with the films. I shall then be able to propose in a deliberately provocative and polemical way an understanding of subtitles that not only challenges hegemonic critical assumptions but also constructs a paradigm of dynamic, interactive, transnational spectatorial possibilities.[8] I shall use the film *Black Cat, White Cat* (Emir Kusturica, Germany/France/Yugoslavia/Austria/Greece, 1998) to posit the engagement of a fictional character, Grga Pitić played by Sabri Sulejman, with *Casablanca* (Michael Curtiz, USA, 1942) – for him a subtitled text – as an idealised and emblematic instance of the 'foreign spectator'.

8.2 SUBTITLES AND THE CINEMATIC APPARATUS

What is still fascinating about the 'apparatus theory' of the 1960s and 1970s is the obsessive attention to the minutiae of the constituent components of cinema and the viewing experience on a determinedly abstract level that excludes individual films or indeed individuals. This fascination should not stand in the way of recognising the theoretical and political value of the numerous critiques of such abstractions which have primarily targeted the notion that subject positions constructed by the apparatus are inescapable and transcend demographic or any other kind of difference between spectators as members of an audience. There are, however, two issues that I want to raise in this context.

First, that despite the sustained critique of the generalisations and abstractions of the 'apparatus theory' subsequent theorisations of spectatorship and/or audiences remain largely indifferent to the transnational experience of cinema and the specificities of the engagement of spectators with 'foreign' films.

Second, that the detailed analysis of the apparatus still offers useful insights into the 'raw' experience of cinema and forces a constant reconsideration of the role and function of the 'basics' of viewing films. From this perspective and for this author the exclusion of subtitles (or dubbing, for that matter) from theorisations of the apparatus is totally surprising – not only subtitles are an integral part of the 'basics' of my personal experience of cinema but surely they must also have been part of the experience of the French theorists who analysed in such detail the apparatus. This paradox will be examined later, but at this point I want to insert subtitles as a missing but fundamental component in the discursive construction of the cinematic apparatus. Such insertion will help me to ascertain a model of transnational spectatorship that goes someway towards a delineation of the dynamics involved in the relationship between spectators and foreign texts.

An initial consideration of subtitling practices outlined in guides and manifestos of best practice appears to suggest that subtitles are meant to function in a fashion consistent with the 'ideological effects of the basic cinematographic apparatus' as outlined by Jean-Louis Baudry.[9] For instance, Fotios Karamitroglou in his article 'A proposed set of subtitling standards in Europe',[10] is guided by the principle that subtitles must be unobtrusive but clear, respecting all aspects of the film form and communicating meaning in an economic and effective mode. They must cover as little area of the image as possible, respect the pace of the film and show consideration to the coherence of shots and scenes:

> Subtitles should respect camera takes/cuts that signify a thematic change in the film product and, for this reason, they should disappear before the cuts. Different camera shots, fades and pans that do not indicate a major thematic change (e.g. a change from a long shot to a close-up and back) should not affect the duration of the subtitles at all as they do not signify thematic change.[11]

The 'Code of Good Subtitling Practice', proposed by Mary Carroll and Jan Ivarsson and adopted by the European Association for Studies in Screen Translation, further explains:

> Language distribution within and over subtitles must consider cuts and sound bridges; the subtitles must underline surprise or suspense and in no way undermine it . . . Spotting must reflect the rhythm of the film . . . There must be a close correlation between film dialogue and subtitle content; source language and target language should be synchronized as far as possible.[12]

It is this ideological function of subtitles that Abé Mark Nornes attacks in his call for abusive subtitling that would counteract the 'corruption' involved in subtitled films. Subtitling, Nornes claims, is a corrupt practice:

> Ever since the subtitle's invention in that chaotic babel of the talkies era, translators confronted the violent reduction demanded by the apparatus by developing and maintaining a method of translation that conspires to hide its work – along with its ideological assumptions – from its own reader-spectators. In this sense, we may, in a sincerely playful spirit, think of them as *corrupt*. They accept a vision of translation that violently appropriates the source text, and in the process of converting speech into

writing within the time and space limits of the subtitle, they conform the original to the rules, regulations, idioms, and frame of reference of the target language and its culture. It is a practice of translation that smoothes over its textual violence and domesticates all otherness while it pretends to bring the audience to an experience of the foreign.[13]

While the desire of professional subtitlers to keep their intervention to a minimum and to adhere to the values of transparency, continuity and effortless unity that the ideological logic of the apparatus dictates is beyond any doubt, the successful outcome of their efforts is rather uncertain. Clearly Nornes's assumptions and the objectives of the codes of professional practice are very much in line with the apparatus theorists' conceptualisation of spectatorial positioning as totally determined by the operations of the cinematic apparatus.

A defining characteristic of the ideological nature of the apparatus is, according to Baudry, the 'denial of difference.'[14] First, the difference between different kinds of reality: the reality of the profilmic event and the reality of the camera's recording of it, the reality of *decoupage* and editing and the reality of projection and viewing. Also, the corresponding difference between all the above different temporalities. The difference between frames that the illusion of cinematic movement entails. The difference between the transcendental subjectivity of Renaissance perspectival systems and the individualised subjectivity of the spectator. Finally, the denial of the symbolic that renders the imaginary transparent,[15] the denial of *discours* in favour of *histoire*,[16] the denial of the performative dimensions of projection in favour of a mythical original and uniform text.[17]

The insertion, however, of subtitles, the mere presence on the screen of the lines of symbols imprinted on celluloid, reintroduces undeniable difference. The multiple differences listed above reveal themselves in a way that opens up the film's unity as *discours*, carves out the peculiar space and time of subtitles and alludes to a journey across borders that bridges those spatio-temporal gaps and brings the foreign film to the audience. Subtitles also offer a clear manifestation of the multiple existence of films as texts by demonstrating the material difference between the forms in which the same film can appear to audiences: for example, with or without subtitles, dubbed or subtitled in different languages and with varying degrees of technical and/or interlinguistic competence.

Subtitles bear witness to the fact that texts form specific relationships with audiences and are experienced differently by different audiences.[18] If we accept, for a moment, Metz's argument that the ideological effect of the apparatus lies in the illusion that the film is produced by/in the spectator as *discours*, as naturally unfolding in front of his or her eyes as

> . . . a story from nowhere, that nobody tells, but which, nevertheless, somebody receives (otherwise it would not exist): so, in a sense, it is the 'receiver'

(or rather the receptacle) who tells it and, at the same time, it is not told at all, since the receptacle is required only to be a place of absence, in which the purity of the disembodied utterance will resonate more clearly . . . [19]

these films must be different for different audiences. Subtitles reveal the multiplicity of filmic texts and profoundly challenge notions of originality and authenticity. In that respect, to prioritise a mythical original as the location of ultimate 'meaning' for analytical/critical/theoretical purposes constitutes an act of violence, a powerful, imperialistic closing-down of possibilities that ignores the extensive transnational life of filmic texts.

Furthermore, the unity of the spectator, which, according to apparatus theory, is the effect of the alignment of the viewer with the subject of the text, is deeply problematised in the interlingual experience of film. As Ella Shohat and Robert Stam suggest:

> [T]he interlingual film experience is perceptually bifurcated: we hear another's language while we read our own. As spectators, we forge a synthetic unity which transcends the heteroglot source material.[20]

Interestingly, this complex mode of spectatorship is also described as limited, less satisfactory and, ultimately, incomplete:

> The linguistic mediation of subtitles dramatically affects the film experience. For audiences in countries where imported films predominate, subtitles are a normal, taken-for-granted part of the film experience. Literalising the semiotic textual metaphor, spectators actually *read* films as much as they see and hear them, and the energy devoted to reading subtitles inevitably detracts from close attention to images and sounds.[21]

From the practitioner's point of view there are also material constraints that make the experience of the subtitled film incomplete:

> One of the chief aspects to be considered is the amount of reduction it [subtitling] presupposes. This is due to the fact that the number of visual verbal signs on the screen is restricted, on the one hand, by the space available and, on the other hand, by the time available. The constraints of space and time lead into the problem of selection as the translator has to analyse the source text material carefully to decide what should be transferred to the target text and what can or must be left out.[22]

As with the 'original' discussed above, the notion of a complete or perfect relationship between spectator and text is politically suspect and theoretically insupportable. In fact, 'limited understanding' is the only way in which such a relationship can be properly and rigorously conceptualised.

This sense of limitation and incompleteness will be considered later, but at this point I want to invert the metaphor suggested by Shohat and Stam and propose the thesis that the viewing experience of subtitled films is akin to a semiotic rather than a literal act of reading. At the most obvious level the presence of subtitles in the projected frame demands that viewers actively construct causal links between the written text and the image and the soundtrack – words, for example, need to be attributed to the person who utters them. This involves a constant oscillation in the spectator between the narrative depth of the film and its surface where the subtitles reside. Far from being sutured into the imaginary, the spectator of the subtitled film constantly resorts to the symbolic[23] in his/her process of making sense of the film. The viewing experience of the subtitled film is marked by a dialectic relationship, a mutual dependence between the soundtrack, the images, the overall conventions of the film and its subtitles.

Importantly, as the frustration of critics demonstrates, subtitles can never really succeed in the impossible double task of translating accurately the source language and of avoiding intrusion. This is further aggravated by the fact that there seems to be always something wrong with subtitles: there is either too much or too little of them, they mistranslate, they are unable to distinguish between different languages in the source text, they appear on screen too soon or too late, they stay on screen for too long or for not long enough, they obscure the image or the image renders them unreadable, and so on. While all these 'faults' do frustrate spectators they also make the presence of subtitles obvious and undeniable.

The engagement with the subtitled film demands that the spectator undertakes a number of actions and makes important decisions. For example, he/she must attribute subtitles to the right person and to the right narrative space and moment, might want (or have) to consider the appropriateness of the translation, and can choose whether to read closely the linguistic text or to dedicate his/her attention to the image. Spectators are acutely aware of the 'reduction' that subtitles entail and try to compensate for that loss by scrutinising the image and the soundtrack for clues: generic conventions, codes of framing, aspects of the *mise-en-scène*, performance styles can all provide information that bridges omissions and gaps in linguistic understanding.

In fact, far from passively consuming the subtitles provided, spectators often perform the kind of work that Nornes describes as characterising his first experience as a subtitler:

> It was an experience filled with surprises. Here was an extraordinarily close form of textual analysis where every element of verbal and visual language is read off the image, repeatedly, line by line, even frame by frame.[24]

Nornes, however, places such active textual engagement in the body and mind of the translator/subtitler who seems to have complete control over the spectatorial mode of engagement. This is perhaps understandable as Nornes is not only himself a translator but also because his approach focuses too narrowly on translation as the most important mediation between text and viewer. It is not a coincidence that his book begins by reflecting on the damage inflicted by incompetent translators and concludes by asserting that 'global cinema is the translator's cinema'.[25]

It is my contention that like conscientious and enlightened subtitlers, spectators perform constant comparisons and translations as they cross-reference words, images and sounds, and, in that respect, undertake complex and often unpredictable negotiations between what is familiar and what is strange. It is important to recognise that the familiar/strange dialectic does not narrowly correspond to a source/target language binary or to a domestic audience/ foreign film opposition. The sphere of familiarity includes aspects of the subtitled film (such as audiovisual codes and conventions, generic stylistics, star image or authorial attributes), which transcend linguistic competence, overcome the barriers of language and infiltrate and undermine the cultural foreignness of the text. In the experience of the subtitled film linguistic unfamiliarity activates a process of close scrutiny of the foreign film for familiar signs and conventions that can be utilised to bridge gaps of understanding.

Laura U. Marks's work on intercultural cinema while attempting to identify a visuality peculiar to such cinema refuses to engage with subtitles, perhaps the most obvious sign of interculturalism. This is particularly frustrating as her analysis seems to be highly suggestive, especially in the distinction that she proposes between haptic and optical visuality as different 'inclinations' of the viewer towards the image:

> The works I propose to call haptic invite a look that moves on the surface plane of the screen for some time before the viewer realizes what she or he is beholding . . . Such images offer such a proliferation of figures that the viewer perceives the texture as much as the objects imaged. While optical perception privileges the representational power of the image, haptic perception privileges the material presence of the image . . . In most processes of seeing, both are involved, in a dialectical movement from far to near . . . The haptic forces the viewer to contemplate the image instead of being pulled into narrative.[26]

This is not only as close as you can possibly get to a description of the experience of watching a subtitled film but also relates to the dialectics of familiarity/ strangeness discussed above. The reading of subtitles is in itself an act of scanning, exploring and visually caressing the 'skin' of the film, the outermost layer of the image, but it is always accompanied by an engagement with its 'depth'. Subtitles constantly aid the spectator to make sense of the film but at the same time function as an unmistakable signifier of the materiality of film. Thus, haptic visuality surfaces again and again in the engagement of the spectator with the foreign subtitled film. For Marks such engagement has profound political implications as it involves a 'non-mastering visuality'[27] but it is also erotic: 'What is erotic about haptic visuality, then, may be described as a respect of difference, and concomitant loss of self, in the presence of the other.'[28] It is worth noting the profound 'otherness' of subtitles as they belong to a different spatio-temporal and representational order from the image; they are a sign of the film's foreignness and yet they speak to the spectators in the language that they understand. Read in that way subtitles involve a peculiar and erotic dialectic that animates the 'foreign spectator'.

8.3 CRITICAL AND SPECTATORIAL POSITIONS

A key issue in academic studies of 'world cinema' is the conceptualisation of difference. Not just the difference between kinds of films or the difference of certain neglected traditions from those well covered in film studies, but also the position of difference between spectators and 'world cinema' texts. The previous consideration of subtitles as part of the cinematic apparatus reveals three distinctive critical attitudes: the denial of their existence as demonstrated by the apparatus theorists; the outright condemnation of subtitles as distorting and deeply ideological, explicitly expressed by Nornes and implicit in the views of the practitioners; and, finally, one modelled on the embracement of subtitles as dynamic, even erotic interactions between spectators and 'foreign' texts. If, as I argue here, subtitles encapsulate key aspects of the transnational experience of cinema, these three attitudes also inform critical positions vis-à-vis cultural/national difference and conceptualisations of transnational spectatorship.

Although the first two positions appear to be diametrically opposite, they are in fact two sides of the same coin, two manifestations of a Eurocentric view of difference. The position of the apparatus theorists renders subtitles invisible and as such it dismisses and denies difference as a factor in the relationship between texts and audiences. It is surprising that the French apparatus theorists had nothing to say about subtitles – how did they watch the Hollywood films that they so extensively write about? Metz opens his influential essay 'Story/discourse: notes on two kinds of voyeurism' on a personal note:

> I'm at the cinema. The images of a Hollywood film unfold in front of me.
> It doesn't even have to be Hollywood: the images of any film based on
> narration and representation – of any 'film', in fact, in the sense in which

the word is most often used today – the kind of film which it is the film industry's business to produce.[29]

The fact that it does not occur to him that subtitled films might communicate differently is of course just one of the many ways in which difference escapes the consideration of apparatus theorists. Their stubborn refusal to consider that subtitles might be theoretically significant or to at least acknowledge their existence has two implications that define key aspects of that critical position. The first is a logical extension of the apparatus theory rationale and suggests that films operate by constructing universal positions that transcend difference, in other words, that the cinematic apparatus and its effects are universal and immune to national/cultural variations. The second is the apparatus theorists' inability to acknowledge the specificity of their own position, as one of necessarily partial and limited understanding rather than perfect mastery over the 'foreign' text. Ultimately, such a position resides in the realm of a politically suspect fantasy and typifies modern sensibilities as discussed in Chapter 1 above, sensibilities that value the possibility and desirability of universal knowledge that transcends national and cultural specificity. It is profoundly elitist as it elevates the theorist to a level of immense cultural and epistemological power.

From the second position, that of the frustrated but conscientious practitioner, difference appears to be unbridgeable; the experience of the foreign text is always already inescapably reductive and marred by incomprehension. The foreignness of the text is absolute and the subtitles are all too visible – in Anglo-American film culture subtitled films are seen as a genre in themselves. A slightly different version of such a position surfaces within film criticism. The issue for many (American in particular) critics is the difficulty involved in the study of the films of foreign cultures. Prima facie, such a concern is a legitimate and possibly sensitive reaction to the denial of difference demonstrated by the apparatus theorists. However, this position is also problematic as it is informed by a tendency to overcompensate which results in a valorisation of difference that surfaces in the work of many difference-sensitive critics. A pertinent example is the encounter between Fifth Generation Chinese cinema and American critics that initiated a lengthy and acrimonious debate around 'cross-cultural criticism'.[30] While the sensitivity to cultural difference demonstrated by critics such as E. Ann Kaplan is commendable, there is also something disturbing in the manner that it gives way to anxiety if not fear:

> Cross-cultural analysis is difficult – fraught with danger. We are forced to read works produced by the Other through the constraints of our own frameworks/theories/ideologies . . . How are we to arrive at a method, a theory for reading texts from Other worlds until we have first answered some of the questions about how different cultures think

about representation in the first place? Until we know more about the unconscious of different cultures as it might pertain to the level of the imaginary?[31]

Despite the best of intentions, here the foreign text is condemned to be alien and difference becomes a condition of all-consuming distance. What also informs this position is the desire to create (or restore) between critic or spectator and foreign text a relationship of perfect understanding that is expressed in the unmistaken unhappiness about occupying a position of inadequacy, of failed mastery, and of accepting limits and limitations.

Nornes offers a more complex variant to that position. His call for an 'abusive' practice of subtitling[32] is made in the name of counteracting the (false and ideological one assumes) completeness of corrupt subtitling and that involves a foregrounding of its own activities. As such it is very much in line with the modernist critiques of cinema as an illusionist and ideological apparatus, exemplified by Metz, Baudry et al., as discussed earlier. But abusive subtitling remains conceptually trapped in an impasse by romanticising 'fidelity' to the 'original' text or culture but conceding that it is unachievable. In fact the opening-up of unbridgeable cultural chasms is for Nornes in itself positive:

> We must not reject impossibility, but embrace it. Moments of untranslatability – a nearly constant condition for the subtitler – are times for *celebration*, for not only are they privileged encounters with the foreign, but they are also opportunities for translators to ply the highest skills of their craft. They are moments crying for abuse.[33]

The defining characteristic of the third position is an embracement of incompleteness, imperfection, limits and limitations, but not of impossibility in the encounter between spectators and 'foreign' texts. This position is marked by awareness of one's own relation to the foreign text/culture and of the limitations and imperfect understandings that it entails. It is also characterised by an active reading both of the subtitles and of the formal codes of the film and by a constant oscillation between familiar and strange that cuts across the domestic/foreign binary. It is a form of engagement that accepts gaps and lacunae in the experience while at the same time strives to overcome cultural and linguistic barriers by a semiotic reading of the filmic text alongside the literal reading of the subtitles. A cross-cultural critical practice that corresponds to such model would be one of modest and limited claims, acute awareness of the position from which the critic analyses and speaks, openness to the possibility of errors and misunderstandings, painstaking attention to textual and contextual detail but also a determination in the pursuit and acknowledgement of the value of such partial knowledge.

A brief consideration of *Black Cat, White Cat*[34] will illuminate some of the issues raised above. The film is transnational in a number of different ways and on many levels: a co-production involving companies from five European countries, it is located in a non-nationally specific area by the Danube (one of the main routes of international trade in Central and Eastern Europe); it populates its diegesis mainly (but not exclusively) with Romany characters (a nation or rather a people that exists across national boundaries) and saturates its story with continuous references to a multiplicity of different cultures and/ or nations. The profound transnationalism of the film problematises in itself any simple distinction between domestic and foreign audiences as there seems to be no obvious position of familiarity with the diegetic world of the film, at least not one that can be delineated across national boundaries.

Viewed as a subtitled text (VHS tape distributed in the UK by Artificial Eye, with English subtitles by Ian Burley, processed by Eclair Vidéo) the film presents the spectator with many of the typical difficulties, mistakes and faults usually associated with subtitles discussed earlier. The subtitled film succumbs to the inability to register the linguistic shifts between the different languages spoken by the characters. There is no doubt that the understanding of the viewer (any viewer bar an exceptional polyglot) of the subtitled text is limited by all these difficulties. Although linguistic incompetence might not make it possible to identify precisely the moments of language change, the film still finds ways to flag up the fact that differences (linguistic, cultural, national) do exist and are important. A clear example is the scene in which Matko (Bajram Severdžan) meets for the first time his Serbian friend Dadan (Srdjan Todorović): very early into the scene Dadan scolds his entourage for being racist towards gypsies because they offer Matko a small glass of whiskey.

The rich texture of the film with its deep-shot composition and chaotic movement alludes and contributes to the complexity of the intricate relation-ships between different formal components as well as between different char-acters. In an interview Kusturica described his aesthetic strategies for the film as follows:

Q: A lot of the shots looked like very complicated orchestrations of camera and blocking movements?
A: It is always. I'm just a troublemaker. I do it always more than I can bear at the moment and I always fight for this. Because I strongly believe that background, midground, and foreground are equally important . . . The use of wide lenses means that you really have to open it and orches-trate so many things at the same time.[35]

The film's form with its continuous cross-referencing between frame planes reflects the incessant transcultural/transnational referencing of the diegesis.

In both respects the film offers a clear awareness of position (either through shot composition or in terms of linguistic/cultural competence) and alerts to the specificity and the limitations of the place from where spectators can make sense of and enjoy the film.

More importantly for our present concerns, the film offers an interesting dramatisation of the position of the spectator of a subtitled text. In *Black Cat, White Cat*, Grga Pitić, the wealthy gypsy patriarch who helps his friend Zarije (Zabit Memedov) to stop the arranged wedding between Matko's son Zare (Florijan Ajdani) and Dadan's sister Afrodita (Salija Ibraimova), watches in two different scenes the finale of *Casablanca*. Furthermore, in the concluding scene of *Black Cat, White Cat*, he delivers in heavily accented English the final lines of *Casablanca*: 'Louis, I think this is the beginning of a beautiful friendship.' Apart from possibly expressing Kusturica's typically European cinéphilia, this intertextual reference demonstrates the dynamics involved in the positioning of the spectator of a foreign film. As the line delivered by Grga Pitić is not included in the English subtitles it is in clear opposition to the two scenes where Serbo-Croat subtitles accompany the same line in *Casablanca* as is delivered by Rick (Humphrey Bogart) and watched by Grga Pitić. In this way the positions of linguistic and cultural familiarity/strangeness in relation to *Casablanca*, which is the foreign film for Grga Pitić, and to *Black Cat, White Cat*, which is the foreign film for us, become reversible, foregrounding the relational and limited character of both.

In his engagement with *Casablanca*, Grga Pitić, exemplifies a position that recognises difference but is also motivated by a desire to overcome it, as his rewinding and replaying of the scene on his video suggests. *Casablanca* as a 'foreign' text offers a linguistic message (interestingly, in Serbo-Croat subtitles not necessarily understood by Grga Pitić)[36] and a narrative situation: the ending of the film with the budding relationship between Rick and Louis (Claude Rains). By delivering the final line in *Black Cat, White Cat* (which is also the final line of *Casablanca*) Grga Pitić (who occupies the double position of active agent in one film and spectator of another) demonstrates an astute albeit mischievous understanding of narrative structure and in that way metaphorically testifies to the possibility of bridging the gap between the known and the unknown, of contaminating the familiar with the foreign and of domesticating the alien. Arguably, his understanding of *Casablanca*, in linguistic terms, is imperfect and incomplete: not only is the line not delivered 'properly' but also the relationship between Dadan and Matko is not equivalent to that between Rick and Louis. Furthermore, as the line is delivered to his friend Zarije, in a language that the latter, as his facial expression demonstrates, clearly does not understand, the film registers imperfection and incompleteness not as a cause of anxiety and fear but as a source for comedic celebration. It also produces an ending in which Grga, Zarije, Dadan and Matko meet Rick and Louis and *Black Cat, White Cat* converges with *Casablanca* in an incomplete yet interactive relationship that stretches across spatial and temporal boundaries and borders.

I would like to conclude *Cinematic Journeys* by proposing that Grga Pitić's position, in its playfulness, incompletion, misunderstanding, passion and humour, is emblematic of that of 'the foreign spectator' and of the essentially transnational experience of 'world cinema'. From such a position the relationship between spectator and foreign text is hard work but desirable and possible, imperfect but explosive, understanding its own limitations but not inhibited by them. Grga Pitić, perpetually in motion in the spectacular assortment of gadgetry that compensates for his physical immobility and because of his Romany nomadism, is a traveller who thrives in the interstices, in the gaps between different cultures, nations and structures of power. His travelling skills and experiences make him an ideal spectator in encounters with foreign films. Neither a victim of 'corrupt' practices nor an interpellated subject awakened to the fact of difference through 'abusive' translation, this trickster and forger has no respect for originality and fidelity. He gains his living in the illegal but highly profitable production of fake whisky and when challenged to tell the copy from the real he instantly recognises his own product by its superior taste. For him the movement between cultures is not a weakness, translation is not an act of 'deception',[37] the engagement with the foreign is not painful but an opportunity for inventiveness and celebration.

NOTES

1. For example, Elizabeth Ezra and Terry Rowden (eds), *Transnational Cinema: The Film Reader* (New York and Abingdon: Routledge, 2006); Laura U. Marks, *The Skin of the Film: Intercultural Cinema, Embodiment, and the Senses* (Durham, NC, and London: Duke University Press, 2000); Hamid Naficy, *An Accented Cinema: Exilic and Diasporic Filmaking* (Princeton, NJ, Oxford: Princeton University Press, 2001); Linda Badly, R. Barton Palmer and Steven Jay Schneider (eds), *Traditions in World Cinema* (Edinburgh: Edinburgh University Press, 2005).

2. See, for example, the series 'Traditions in World Cinema', part of Edinburgh University Press's *Film, Media and Cultural Studies* catologue; the various 'national or regional' cinematic traditions are presented within a shared framework.

3. Clearly, a multiplicity of 'world cinemas' can exist depending on the national/cultural formation within which different spectators operate and their position in the international traffic of films. A Greek version of 'world cinema', for example, can be radically different from a British one, despite significant overlaps, probably around Hollywood films or European 'art' movies; and both would be different from a Korean or Indian variant of 'world cinema'.

4. On another level, exercising the choice of watching films with subtitles can offer cultural 'distinction'. B. Ruby Rich offers an eloquent (and very honest) example of that: 'Subtitled films were the sign of hipness when I was coming of age . . . Subtitled films from other countries were our stock in trade. It's what people couldn't find elsewhere', 'To read or

not to read: subtitles, trailers, and monolinguism', in Atom Egoyan and Ian Balfour (eds), *Subtitles: On the Foreignness of Film* (Cambridge, MA, London: The MIT Press, 2004), pp. 153–69, at pp. 154–5.

5. 'Every film is a foreign film, foreign to some audience somewhere'. (Atom Egoyan and Ian Balfour, 'Introduction', in Egoyan and Balfour [eds]), *Subtitles*, pp. 21–31, at p. 21.

6. Slavoj Žižek discusses a 'foreign gaze' in his 'The foreign gaze which sees too much', in Egoyan and Balfour (eds), *Subtitles*, pp. 285–306. Such gaze (usually resulting from 'shocking encounters' [p. 289] is praised: 'the penetrating power of the perplexed foreign gaze', [p. 292]).

7. In clear contrast to the approach taken by the most comprehensive study in the field, that by Abé Mark Nornes, in *Cinema Babel: Translating Global Cinema* (Minneapolis and London: University of Minnesota Press, 2007).

8. It is important, however, to note that subtitles signal linguistic difference between source and target language that cannot be unproblematically equated to national difference.

9. Jean-Louis Baudry, 'Ideological effects of the basic cinematographic apparatus', in Leo Braudy and Marshall Cohen (eds), *Film Theory and Criticism: Introductory Readings* (New York and Oxford: Oxford University Press, 1999), pp. 345–62, p. 354.

10. Fotios Karamitroglou, 'A proposed set of subtitling standards in Europe', *Translation Journal*, 2.2 (April 1998), <http://accurapid.com/Journal/04stndrd.htm>, visited 22 June 2009.

11. Ibid.

12. Mary Carroll and Jan Ivarsson, 'Code of Good Subtitling Practice', <http://www.transedit.se/code.htm>, visited 22 June 2009.

13. Nornes, *Cinema Babel*, p. 155.

14. Baudry, 'Ideological effects of the basic cinematographic apparatus', pp. 348–50.

15. See Stephen Heath, 'On suture', *Questions of Cinema* (London and Basingstoke: Macmillan, 1981), pp. 76–112.

16. See Christian Metz, 'Story/discourse: notes on two kinds of voyeurism', *Psychoanalysis and Cinema: The Imaginary Signifier* (London and Basingstoke: Macmillan, 1983), pp. 91–8.

17. See Robert C. Allen, 'From exhibition to reception: reflections on the audience in film history', *Screen*, 34.1 (1990), pp. 347–56.

18. Ian Balfour concludes his brief reading of Godard's *Le Mépris* (France/Italy, 1963) as translation by asserting: 'Subtitles are the marks of difference, the written words that visibly render the voice of another language, and in such a way as to render the original foreign from the very start' ('Afterword: filmic translation (the most exemplary film)', in Egoyan and Balfour [eds], *Subtitles*, pp. 530–2, p. 532.)

19. Metz, 'Story/discourse', p. 97.

20. Ella Shohat and Robert Stam, 'The cinema after Babel: language, difference, power', *Screen*, 26.3–4 (1985), pp. 35–58, p. 41.

21. Ibid. p. 48.

22. Susanna Jaskanen, 'On the inside track to Loserville, USA: strategies used in translating humour in two Finnish versions of *Reality Bites*', Pro gradu thesis, Department of English, University of Helsinki, 1999, p. 9.

23. Importantly, 'symbolic' here refers to two different orders: language as a symbolic system which in the subtitled film surfaces in its disembodied materiality and the symbolic order of the cinematic apparatus.

24. Nornes, *Cinema Babel*, p. 1.

25. Ibid. p. 243.

26. Marks, *Skin of the Film*, pp. 162–3.
27. Ibid. p. 193.
28. Ibid. pp. 192–3.
29. Metz, 'Story/discourse: notes on two kinds of voyeurism', p. 91.
30. For an overview of the debate, see Dimitris Eleftheriotis, 'Cross-cultural criticism and Chinese cinema', in Dimitris Eleftheriotis and Gary Needham (eds), *Asian Cinemas: A Reader and Guide* (Edinburgh: Edinburgh University Press, 2006), pp. 148–55.
31. E. Ann Kaplan, 'Problematising cross-cultural analysis: the case of women in the recent Chinese cinema', in Eleftheriotis and Needham (eds), *Asian Cinemas*, pp. 156–67, p. 157.
32. Echoed by Amresh Sinha, 'The use and abuse of subtitles', in Egoyan and Balfour (eds), *Subtitles*, pp. 171–90.
33. Nornes, *Cinema Babel*, pp. 175–6.
34. Interestingly the title of the film never appears as a written text in the credits – instead it is represented by a drawing of a black and a white cat.
35. 'Interview: momentum and emotion, Emir Kusturica's *Black Cat, White Cat*', for <www.indiewire.com>, 9 September 1999, visited 22 June 2009.
36. In the same interview Kusturica reveals that many of his actors could not even read and had to learn their lines through tape recordings. Kusturica also confesses that he understood very little of Romany. Ibid.
37. See Jorge Luis Borges, 'Borges night at the movies', in Egoyan and Balfour (eds), *Subtitles*, pp. 111–20.

Select Bibliography

Abadzi, Helen, and Emmanuel Tasoulas, *Indoprepon Apokalypsi* (Athens: Atrapos, 1998).

Abel, Richard (ed.), *Encyclopedia of Early Cinema* (Abingdon, Oxon, and New York: Routledge, 2005).

Acland, Charles R., *Screen Traffic: Movies, Multiplexes, and Global Culture* (Durham, NC, and London: Duke Univesity Press, 2003).

Allen, Robert C., 'From exhibition to reception: reflections on the audience in film history', *Screen*, 34.1 (1990), pp. 347–56.

Altman, Rick, 'From lecturer's prop to industrial product: the early history of travel films', in Jeffrey Ruoff (ed.), *Virtual Voyages: Cinema and Travel* (Durham, NC, and London: Duke University Press, 2006), pp. 61–76.

Alvaray, Luisela, 'National, regional and global: new waves of Latin American cinema', *Cinema Journal*, 47.3 (2008), pp. 48–65.

Amad, Paula, 'Between the "familiar text" and the "book of the world": touring the ambivalent contexts of travel films', in Jeffrey Ruoff (ed.), *Virtual Voyages: Cinema and Travel* (Durham, NC, and London: Duke University Press, 2006), pp. 99–116.

Arnheim, Rudolf, *Film as Art* (London: Faber & Faber, 1958).

Arragon, Louis, *Paris Peasant* (London: Cape, 1971).

Asendorf, Christoph, *Batteries of Life: On the History of Things and Their Perception in Modernity* (Berkeley, CA, and London: University of California Press, 1993).

Atkinson, Michael, 'Crossing the frontiers', *Sight and Sound*, 4.1 (1994), pp. 14–17.

Badley, Linda, R. Barton Palmer and Steven Jay Schneider (eds), *Traditions in World Cinema* (Edinburgh: Edinburgh University Press, 2005).

Balázs, Béla, *Theory of the Film: Character and Growth of a New Art* (London: Dobson, 1952).

Balfour, Ian, 'Afterword: filmic translation (the most exemplary film)', in Atom Egoyan and Ian Balfour (eds), *Subtitles: On the Foreignness of Film* (Cambridge, MA, London: The MIT Press, 2004), pp. 530–2.

Bammer, Angelika (ed.), *Displacements: Cultural Identities in Question* (Bloomington and Indianapolis: Indiana University Press).

Barber, X. Theodore, 'The roots of travel cinema: John L. Stoddard, E. Burton Holmes and the nineteenth-century illustrated travel lecture', *Film History*, 5.1 (1993), pp. 69–84.

Baudelaire, Charles, *The Painter of Modern Life and Other Essays* (London: Phaidon, 1964).

Baudry, Jean-Louis, 'Ideological effects of the basic cinematographic apparatus', in Leo

Braudy and Marshall Cohen (eds), *Film Theory and Criticism: Introductory Readings* (New York and Oxford: Oxford University Press, 1999), pp. 345–55.

Bazin, André, *What Is Cinema?* (Berkeley, CA, and London: University of California Press, 1967).

Bellour, Raymond, *The Analysis of Film* (Bloomington and Indianapolis: Indiana University Press, 2000).

Benjamin, Walter, *The Arcades Project* (Cambridge, MA, and London: Harvard University Press, 2002).

Benjamin, Walter, *Charles Baudelaire: A Lyric Poet in the Era of High Capitalism* (London and New York: Verso, 1992).

Bennett, Tony, *The Birth of the Museum: History, Theory, Politics* (London and New York: Routledge, 2005).

Bíro, Yvette, *Turbulence and Flow in Film: The Rhythmic Design* (Bloomington and Indianapolis: Indiana University Press, 2008).

Bonitzer, Pascal, 'Here: the notion of the shot and subject in the cinema', *Film Reader 4* (Evanston, IL: Film Division, Northwestern University, 1979), pp. 108–19.

Bordwell, David, 'Camera movement and cinematic space', in Ron Burnett (ed.), *Explorations in Film Theory: Selected Essays from* Ciné-Tracts ([Bloomington and Indianapolis: Indiana University Press, 1996], pp. 229–36; first published in *Ciné-Tracts*, in 1977).

Bordwell, David, 'Modernism, minimalism, melancholy: Angelopoulos and visual style', in Horton (ed.), *Last Modernist The Films of Theo Angelopoulos* (Trowbridge: Flicks Books, 1997), pp. 11–26.

Bordwell, David, *Narration in the Fiction Film* (London: Routledge, 1990).

Bordwell, David, Janet Staiger and Kristin Thompson, *The Classical Hollywood Cinema: Film Style & Mode of Production to 1960* (London: Routledge, 1994).

Bordwell, David, and Kristin Thompson, *Film Art* (London: Addison-Wesley, 1980).

Borges, Jorge Luis, 'Borges night at the movies', in Egoyan and Balfour (eds), *Subtitles*, pp. 111–20.

Bradshaw, Peter, '*Hukkle*', *The Guardian* (26 November 2004).

Braidotti, Rosi, *Nomadic Subjects: Embodiment and Sexual Difference in Contemporary Feminist Theory* (New York: Columbia University Press, 1994).

Branigan, Edward, *Narrative Comprehension and Film* (London and New York: Routledge, 1992).

Brooke, Michael, '*Hukkle*', *Sight & Sound*, 15.1 (January 2005).

Bruno, Giuliana, *Atlas of Emotion: Journeys in Art, Architecture, and Film* (London and New York: Verso, 2002).

Burke, Edmund, *A philosophical Enquiry into the Origin of Our Ideas of the Sublime and the Beautiful* [1757] London: Routledge, 1958.

Burns, Rob, 'Towards a cinema of hybridity: Turkish-German filmmakers and the representation of alterity', *Debatte*, 15.1 (2007), pp. 3–24.

Caldwell, Genoa (ed.), *Burton Holmes: The Man Who Photographed the World, 1892–1938*, (New York: Abrams, 1977).

Carroll, Mary and Jan Ivarsson, 'Code of good subtitling practice', <http://www.transedit.se/code.htm>, visited 22 June 2009.

Caruth, Cathy, 'Unclaimed experience: trauma and the possibility of History', *Yale French Studies*, 79 (1991), pp. 181–92.

Casetti, Franco, *Inside the Gaze: The Fiction Film and Its Spectator* (Bloomington and Indianapolis: Indiana University Press, 1998).

Charney, Leo, and Vanessa R. Schwartz (eds), *Cinema and the Invention of Modern Life* (Berkeley, CA, and London: University of California Press, 1995), pp. 15–45.

Chaudhuri, Sahini, and Howard Finn, 'The open image: poetic realism and the New Iranian Cinema', *Screen*, 44.1 (2003), pp. 38–57.

Christie, Ian, 'Landscape and "location": reading filmic space historically', *Rethinking History*, 4.2 (2000), pp. 165–74.

Cohan, Steven, and Ina Rae Hark (eds), *The Road Movie Book* (London and New York: Routledge, 1997).

Crary, Jonathan, *Techniques of the Observer: On Vision and Modernity in the Nineteenth Century* (Cambridge, MA, and London, MIT Press, 1991).

Cubitt, Sean, 'Distribution and media flows', *Cultural Politics*, 1.2 (2005), pp. 193–214.

Dabashi, Hamid, *Close Up: Iranian Cinema Past, Present and Future* (London and New York: Verso, 2001).

Dalle Vacche, Angela (ed.), *The Visual Turn: Classical Film Theory and Art History* (New Brunswick, NJ, and London: Rutgers University Press, 2003).

Dargis, Manohla, 'Roads to freedom', *Sight and Sound*, 1.3 (1991), pp. 15–18.

Darwin, Charles, *The Voyage of HMS Beagle* (London: John Murray, 1890).

Dayan, Daniel, 'The tutor-code of classical cinema', in Leo Braudy and Marshall Cohen (eds), *Film Theory and Criticism: Introductory Readings* (New York and Oxford: Oxford University Press, 1999), pp. 118–29.

Deleuze, Gilles, *Cinema 1: The Movement-Image* (London and New York: Continuum, 2005).

Deleuze, Gilles, *Cinema 2: The Time-Image* (Minneapolis: University of Minnesota Press, 1989).

Deleuze, Gilles, *Foucault* (London: Athlone Press, 1989).

Dissanayake, Wimal, and Rob Wilson (eds), *Local/Global* (Durham, NC: Duke University Press, 1996).

Dyer, Richard, 'Entertainment and Utopia', in Rick Altman (ed.), *Genre: The Musical* ([London: Routledge & Kegan Paul, 1981], pp. 175–89; first published in *Movie*, 24 [Spring 1977], pp. 2–13).

Egoyan, Atom, and Ian Balfour, 'Introduction', in Egoyan and Balfour (eds), *Subtitles*, pp. 21–31

Egoyan, Atom, and Ian Balfour (eds), *Subtitles: On the Foreignness of Film* (Cambridge, MA, London: MIT Press, 2004).

Eleftheriotis, Dimitris, 'Cross-cultural criticism and Chinese cinema', in Dimitris Eleftheriotis and Gary Needham (eds), *Asian Cinemas: A Reader and Guide* (Edinburgh: Edinburgh University Press, 2006), pp. 148–55.

Eleftheriotis, Dimitris, 'Early cinema as child: historical metaphor and European cinephilia in *Lumière & Company*, *Screen*, 46.3 (2005), pp. 315–28.

Eleftheriotis, Dimitris, *Popular Cinemas of Europe: Studies of Texts, Contexts and Frameworks* (London and New York: Continuum, 2001).

Eleftheriotis, Dimitris, 'Questioning totalities: constructions of masculinity in the popular Greek cinema of the 1960s', *Screen*, 36.3 (1995), pp. 239–40.

Eleftheriotis, Dimitris, and Dina Iordanova (eds), 'Indian cinema abroad: historiography of transnational cinematic exchanges', *South Asian Popular Culture*, 4.2 (2006), pp. 79–82.

Engels, Frederick, and Karl Marx, *Manifesto of the Communist Party, Selected Works* (London: Lawrence & Wishart, 1980), pp. 31–63.

Ezra, Elizabeth, and Terry Rowden (eds), *Transnational Cinema: The Film Reader* (New York and Abingdon: Routledge, 2006).

Fischer, Michael M. J., *Mute Dreams, Blind Owls, and Dispersed Knowledges: Persian Poesis in the Transnational Circuitry* (Durham, NC, London: Duke University Press, 2004).

Forbes, Jill, 'Jean-Luc Godard: 2 into 3', *Sight and Sound*, 50.1 (1981), pp. 40–5.

Foucault, Michel, *The Birth of the Clinic* (London: Tavistock, 1973).

Foucault, Michel, *Discipline and Punish* (London: Alan Lane, 1977).

Foucault, Michel, *The History of Sexuality*, vol. 1, *The Will to Knowledge* (London: Penguin, 1978).

Foucault, Michel, *The Order of Things* (London and New York: Routledge, 1989).

Friedberg, Anne, *Window Shopping: Cinema and the Postmodern* (Berkeley, CA, and London: University of California Press, 1993).

Gall, Adam, and Fiona Probyn-Rapsey, 'Ivan Sen and the art of the road', *Screen*, 47.4 (2006), pp. 425–39.

Ganti, Tejaswini, *Bollywood: A Guidebook to Popular Hindi Cinema* (New York and London: Routledge, 2004)

Gocić, Goran, *The Cinema of Emir Kusturica: Notes from the Underground* (New York and London: Wallflower Press, 2001).

Godard, Jean-Luc, '*Sauve Qui Peut . . .* Godard', *Framework*, 13 (1980), pp. 10–13.

Göktürk, Deniz, 'Beyond paternalism: Turkish German traffic in Cinema', in Tim Bergfelder, Erica Carter and Deniz Göktürk (eds), *The German Cinema Book* (London: BFI, 2002), pp. 248–56.

Gombrich, E. H., *The Story of Art* (London: Phaidon Press, 1955).

Gopalan, Lalitha, *Cinema of Interruptions*, (London: BFI, 2002)

Grassili, Mariagiulia, 'Migrant cinema: transnational and guerrilla practices of film production and representation', *Journal of Ethnic and Migration Studies*, 34.8 (2008), pp. 1237–55.

Griffiths, Alison, '"Journeys for those who can not travel": promenade cinema and the museum life group', *Wide Angle*, 18.3 (1996), pp. 53–76.

Guback, Thomas, *The International Film Industry: Western Europe and America since 1945* (Bloomington, IN, London: Indiana University Press, 1969).

Gunning, Tom, 'The cinema of attraction: early film, its spectator and the avant-garde', *Wide Angle*, 8.3–4 (1986).

Gunning, Tom, 'Tracing the individual body: photography, detectives and early cinema', in Leo Charney and Vanessa R. Schwartz (eds), *Cinema and the Invention of Modern Life* (Berkeley, CA, and London: University of California Press, 1995), pp. 15–45.

Gunning, Tom, 'The whole world within reach', in Jeffrey Ruoff (ed.), *Virtual Voyages: Cinema and Travel* (Durham, NC, and London: Duke University Press, 2006), pp. 25–41.

Gunning, Tom, 'The world as object lesson: cinema audiences, visual culture and the St. Louis world's fair, 1904', *Film History*, 6.4 (1994), pp. 422–44.

Hammond, Joyce D., 'Difference and the I/eye of the beholder: revisioning America through travelogues', *Visual Anthropology*, 15 (2002), pp. 17–33.

Hannam, Kevin, Mimi Sheller and John Urry, 'Editorial: mobilities, immobilities and moorings', in *Mobilities*, 1.1 (2006), pp. 1–22.

Harvey, David, *The Condition of Postmodernity: An Enquiry into the Origins of Cultural Change* (Oxford: Blackwell, 1990)

Heath, Stephen, 'Notes on suture', *Screen*, 18.4 (Winter 1977/78), pp. 48–76.

Heath, Stephen, 'On suture', *Questions of Cinema* (London and Basingstoke: Macmillan, 1981), pp. 76–112.

Heath, Stephen, *Questions of Cinema* (London and Basingstoke: Macmillan, 1981).

Heidegger, Martin, 'The origin of the work of art', *Poetry, Language, Thought* (New York: Harper and Row, 1970).

Hinxman, Margaret, 'Death in Venice', *Sight and Sound*, 39.4 (1970), pp. 199–200.

Horton, Andrew, *The Films of Theo Angelopoulos* (Princeton: Princeton University Press, 1999).

Horton, Andrew, 'Preface', in Andrew Horton (ed.), *Last Modernist*, p. vi.

Horton, Andrew (ed.), *The Last Modernist: The Films of Theo Angelopoulos* (Trowbridge: Flicks Books, 1997).

Iordanova, Dina (ed.), *The Cinema of the Balkans* (London and New York: Wallflower, 2006).

Jameson, Fredric, 'Postmodernism or the cultural logic of late capitalism', *New Left Review*, 146 (1984), pp. 53–92.

Jameson, Fredric, 'Theo Angelopoulos: the past as history, the future as form', in Horton (ed.), *Last Modernist*, pp. 78–95.

Jaskanen, Susanna, 'On the inside track to Loserville, USA: strategies used in translating humour in two Finnish versions of *Reality Bites*', Pro gradu thesis, Department of English, University of Helsinki, 1999.

Johnson, G. Allen, '*Hukkle*', *San Francisco Chronicle* (26 March 2004).

Kant, Immanuel, *Observation on the Feeling of the Sublime and the Beautiful* (1764; Berkeley, CA: University of California Press, 1960).

Kaplan, E. Ann, 'Problematising cross-cultural analysis: the case of women in the recent Chinese cinema', in Dimitris Eleftheriotis and Gary Needham (eds), *Asian Cinemas: A Reader and Guide* (Edinburgh: Edinburgh University Press, 2006), pp. 156–67.

Karakitsou-Dougé, Niki, 'To Elliniko melodrama: i aisthitiki tis ekplixis' ('Greek melodrama: the aesthetic of surprise', my translation), *Optikoakoustiki Koultoura*, 1 (2002), pp. 37–52.

Karamitroglou, Fotios, 'A proposed set of subtitling standards in Europe', *Translation Journal*, 2.2 (April 1998), <http://accurapid.com/Journal/04stndrd.htm>, visited 22 June 2009.

Kartalou, Athina, 'Protasi gia ena Plaisio Anagnosis ton eidon ston Elliniko Kinimatografo' ('Proposing a framework for the reading of genre in Greek cinema', my translation), *Optikoakoustiki Koultoura*, 1 (2002), pp. 25–35.

Kent, Christopher, 'Spectacular history as an ocular discipline', *Wide Angle*, 18.3 (1996), pp. 1–21.

Kirby, Lynn, *Parallel Tracks: The Railroad and Silent Cinema* (Exeter: University of Exeter Press, 1997).

Kittler, Friedrich A., *Gramophone, Film, Typewriter* (Stanford: Stanford University Press, 1999).

Kouanis, Panos, *I Kinimatografiki Agora stin Ellada, 1944–1999* ('The film market in Greece, 1944–1999', my translation) (Athens: Finatec, 2001).

Laderman, David, *Driving Visions: Exploring the Road Movie* (Austin, TX: The University of Texas Press, 2002).

Landy, Marcia, *Italian Film* (Cambridge: Cambridge University Press, 2000).

Larkin, Brian, 'Indian films and Nigerian lovers: media and the creation of parallel modernities' *Africa*, 67.3 (Summer 1997), pp. 406–441.

Larsen, Jonas, 'Tourism mobilities and the travel glance: experiences of being on the move', *Scandinavian Journal of Hospitality and Tourism*, 1.2 (2001), pp. 80–98.

Lisle, Debbie, *The Global Politics of Contemporary Travel Writing* (Cambridge: Cambridge University Press, 2006).

Lobato, Ramon, 'Subcinema: theorizing marginal film distribution', *Limina*, 13 (2007), pp. 113–20.

Löfgren, Orvar, *On Holiday: A History of Vacationing* (Berkely, CA, and London: University of California Press, 2002).

Lowell, Robert (ed.), *The Voyage & Other Versions of Poems by Baudelaire* (New York: Farrar, Straus and Giroux, 1968).

Lyotard, Jean-François, 'Acinema', *Wide Angle*, 2.3 (1978), pp. 52–59.

Lyotard, Jean-François, *The Postmodern Condition: A Report on Knowledge* (Manchester: Manchester University Press, 1984).

Lyotard, Jean-François, 'Presenting the unpresentable: the sublime', *Artforum*, 20.8 (April 1984), pp. 64–9.

Lyotard, Jean-François, 'The sublime and the avant-garde', *Artforum*, 22.8 (April 1982), pp. 36–43.

MacDonald, Scott, 'Voyages of life', *Wide Angle*, 18.2 (1996), pp. 101–26.

Mak, Geert, *The Bridge: A Journey between Orient and Occident* (London: Harvill Secker, 2008).

Mann, Thomas, *Death in Venice; Tristan; Tonio Kröger* (Harmondsworth: Penguin, 1975).

Marks, Laura U., *The Skin of the Film: Intercultural Cinema, Embodiment, and the Senses* (Durham, NC, and London: Duke University Press, 2000).

Marx, Karl, *Grundrisse: Foundations of the Critique of Political Economy* (London: Alan Lane, 1973).

Mazierska, Ewa, and Laura Rascaroli, *Crossing New Europe: Postmodern Travel and the European Road Movie* (London and New York: Wallflower Press, 2006).

Menne, Jeff, 'A Mexican *nouvelle vague*: the logic of new waves under globalization', *Cinema Journal*, 47.1 (2007), pp. 70–92.

Metz, Christian, 'Story/discourse: notes on two kinds of voyeurism', *Psychoanalysis and Cinema: The Imaginary Signifier* (London and Basingstoke: Macmillan, 1983), pp. 91–8.

Miller, Angela, 'The Panorama, the cinema, and the emergence of the spectacular', *Wide Angle*, 18.2 (1996), pp. 34–69.

Miller, J. Hillis, *Topographies* (Stanford: Stanford, University Press, 1995).

Miller, Jacques-Alain, 'Suture (elements of the logic of the signifier)', *Screen*, 18.4 (Winter 1977/78), pp. 24–34.

Miller, Nancy K., and Jason Tougaw (eds), *Extremities: Trauma, Testimony and Community* (Urbana and Chicago: University of Illinois Press, 2002).

Mills, Sara, *Discourses of Difference: An Analysis of Women's Travel Writing and Colonialism* (London and New York: Routledge, 1993).

Mottahedeh, Negar, *Displaced Allegories: Post-Revolutionary Iranian Cinema* (Durham, NC, and London: Duke University Press, 2008).

Mulvey, Laura, 'Visual pleasure and narrative cinema', *Screen*, 16.3 (1975), pp. 6–18.

Musser, Charles, *The Emergence of Cinema: The American Screen to 1907* (New York: Macmillan, 1990).

Naficy, Hamid, *An Accented Cinema: Exilic and Diasporic Filmaking* (Princeton, NJ, and Oxford: Princeton University Press, 2001).

Naficy, Hamid, 'Phobic spaces and liminal panics: independent transnational film genre', in Dissanayake and Wilson (eds), *Local/Global*, pp. 119–44.

Naficy, Hamid, 'Theorizing "Third-World" film spectatorship', *Wide Angle*, 18.4 (1996), pp. 3–26.

Nava, Mica, *Visceral Cosmopolitanism: Gender, Culture and the Normalisation of Difference* (Oxford and New York: Berg, 2007).

Nead, Lynda, 'Strip: moving bodies in the 1890s', *Early Popular Visual Culture*, 3.2 (2005), pp. 135–50

Neale, Steve, 'Masculinity as spectacle', *Screen*, 24.6 (1983), pp. 2–16.

Nooteboom, Cees, *Nomad's Hotel: Travels in Time and Space* (London: Vintage, 2007).

Nornes, Abé Mark, *Cinema Babel: Translating Global Cinema* (Minneapolis and London: University of Minnesota Press, 2007).

Nornes, Abé Mark, 'For an abusive subtitling', *Film Quarterly* (Spring 1999), pp. 17–34.

Okoye, Ikem Stanley, 'Rending the "nomad": film and architecture reading Fulani', *Interventions*, 6.2 (2004), pp. 180–200.

Oudart, Jean-Pierre, 'Cinema and suture', *Screen*, 18.4 (Winter 1977/78), pp. 35–47.

Pamuk, Orhan, *Istanbul: Memories of a City* (London: Faber & Faber, 2005).

Papadakis, Giorgios, 'Indika . . . ki agirista', *Difonon*, 54 (1999), pp. 48–51.

Paschalidis, Grigoris, 'Elliniki tileorasi' ('Greek television', my translation), in Vernicos et al. (eds), *Politistikes Viomihanies*, pp. 173–200.

Perkins, V. F., *Film as Film: Understanding and Judging Movies* (Harmondsworth: Penguin, 1978).

Pidduck, Julianne, 'Of windows and country walks: frames of space and movement in 1990s Austen adaptations', *Screen*, 39.4 (1998), pp. 381–400.

Pinkerton, Nick, '*The Edge of Heaven* can wait: storylines and cultures crash – and isn't it arty?', *Village Voice* (20 May 2008).

Pratt, Mary Louise, *Imperial Eyes: Travel Writing and Transculturation* (New York and London: Routledge, 1992).

Pudeh, Reza J., and M. Reza Shirvani, 'Issues and paradoxes in the development of Iranian national cinema: an overview', *Iranian Studies*, 43.1 (2008), pp. 323–41.

Rabinovitz, Lauren, 'From *Hale's Tours* to *Star Tours*: virtual voyages, travel ride films, and the delirium of the hyper-real', in Jeffrey Ruoff (ed.), *Virtual Voyages: Cinema and Travel* (Durham, NC, and London: Duke University Press, 2006), pp. 42–60.

Rahimieh, Nasrin, 'Divorce seen through women's cinematic lens', *Iranian Studies*, 42.1 (2009), pp. 97–112.

Rajagopalan, Sudha, 'Emblematic of the thaw: early Indian films in Soviet cinemas', *South Asian Popular Culture*, 4.2, (2006), pp. 83–100.

Ranvaud, Don, 'Jean-Luc Godard . . . For himself: an interview', *Framework*, 13 (1980), pp. 8–9.

Ravetto, Kriss, 'Mytho-poetic cinema', *Third Text*, 12.43 (1998), pp. 43–57.

Rich, Ruby B., 'To read or not to read: subtitles, trailers, and monolinguism', in Egoyan and Balfour (eds), *Subtitles*, pp. 153–69.

Rimbaud, Arthur, *Rimbaud Complete Works, Selected Letters* (Chicago and London: University of Chicago Press, 1966).

Ruoff, Jeffrey, 'Around the world in eighty minutes: the travel lecture film', *Visual Anthropology*, 15 (2002), pp. 91–114.

Ruoff, Jeffrey, 'Show and tell: the 16mm travel lecture film', in Ruoff (ed.), *Virtual Voyages*, pp. 217–235.

Ruoff, Jeffrey (ed.), *Virtual Voyages: Cinema and Travel* (Durham, NC, and London: Duke University Press, 2006).

Rutherford, Ann, 'Precarious boundaries: affect, *mise-en-scène* and the senses in Angelopoulos's Balkan epic', *Senses of Cinema*, 31 (2004), <http://archive.sensesofcinema.com/contents/04/31/angelopoulos_balkan_epic.html>, visited on 2 June 2009.

Sadr, Hamid Reza, *Iranian Cinema: A Political History* (London and New York: I. B. Tauris, 2006).

Said, S. F., 'New cinema from the Islamic world', *Wasafiri*, 19.43 (2004), pp. 19–22.

Sallis, John, *Topographies* (Bloomington: Indiana University Press, 2006).

Salt, Barry, *Film Style and Technology: History and Analysis* (London: Starword, 1983).

Sargeant, Jack, and Stephanie Watson, *Lost Highways: An Illustrated History of Road Movies* (London: Creation Books, 1999).

Saxton, Libby, *Haunted Images: Film, Ethics and the Holocaust* (London: Wallflower, 2008).

Schaber, Bennet, '"Hitler can't keep 'em that long:" the road, the people', in Cohan and Hark (eds), *Road Movie Book*, pp. 17–44.

Scharf, Aaron, *Art and Photography* (Harmondsworth: Penguin, 1975).

Schivelbusch, Wolfgang, *The Railway Journey: Trains and Travel in the 19th Century* (Oxford: Blackwell, 1980).

Schneider, Alexandra, '*Autosonntag* (Switzerland, 1930) – a film safari in the Swiss Alps', *Visual Anthropology*, 15 (2002), pp. 115–28.

Schwartz, Vanessa R., *Spectacular Realities: Early Mass Culture in Fin-de-Siècle Paris* (Berkeley, CA, and London: University of California Press, 1998).

Scott, A. O., 'Tying knots that bind lives despite the divisions of generation and nationality', *New York Times* (11 August 2008).

Seltzer, Mark, *Bodies and Machines* (New York and London: Routledge, 1992).

Shohat, Ella, *Taboo Memories, Diasporic Voices* (Durham, NC: Duke University Press, 2006).

Shohat, Ella, and Robert Stam, 'The cinema after Babel: language, difference, power', *Screen*, 26.3–4 (1985), pp. 35–58.

Sinha, Amresh, 'The use and abuse of subtitles', in Egoyan and Balfour (eds), *Subtitles*, pp. 171–90.

Skantze, P. A., *Stillness in Motion in the Seventeenth-century Theatre* (London and New York: Routledge, 2003).

Soldatos, Yannis, *Enas anthropos pantos kairou* ('An All-weather Man', my translation) (Athens: Aigokeros, 2000).

Soldatos, Yannis, *Istoria tou Ellinikou kinimatografou* ('History of Greek Cinema', my translation), vol. 2 (Athens: Aigokeros, 1989).

Soldatos, Yannis, *Istoria tou Ellinikou Kinimatografou* ('History of Greek Cinema', my translation), vol. 3 (Athens: Aigokeros, 1990).

Sorlin, Pierre, *Italian National Cinema: 1896–1996* (London and New York: Routledge, 1996).

Stephens, Sonya, 'Paris and panoramic vision: *Lieux de mémoire, lieux communs*', *Modern & Contemporary France*, 14.2 (2006), pp. 173–187.

Staples, Amy J., 'The last of the great (foot-slogging) explorers: Lewis Cotlow and the ethnographic imaginary in popular travel film', *Visual Anthropology*, 15 (2002), pp. 35–64.

Staples, Amy J., 'Safari adventures: forgotten cinematic journeys in Africa', *Film History*, 18.4 (2006), pp. 392–411.

Strain, Ellen, 'Exotic bodies, distant landscapes: touristic viewing and popularized anthropology in the nineteenth century', *Wide Angle*, 18.2 (1996), pp. 70–100.

Strick, Philip, 'Death in Venice', *Sight and Sound*, 40.2 (1971), pp. 103–4.

Suner, Asuman, 'Dark Passion', *Sight & Sound*, 15.3 (March 2005), pp. 18–21.

Suner, Asuman, 'Outside in: "accented cinema" at large', *Inter-Asia Cultural Studies*, 7.3 (2006), pp. 363–82

Thomas, Rosie, 'Indian cinema – pleasures and popularity', *Screen*, 26.3–4 (1985), pp. 116–31.

Thompson, Kenneth, 'Border crossing and diasporic identities: media use and leisure practices of an ethnic minority', *Qualitative Sociology*, 25.3 (2002), pp. 409–18.

Tomai-Konstantopoulou, Fotini (ed.), *I Metanasteusi ston Kinimatografo* ('Emigration in Cinema', my translation) (Athens: Papazisi, 2004).

Urry, John, *The Tourist Gaze* (London: Sage, 1990).

Vasudevan, Ravi, 'Addressing the spectator of a "third world" national cinema: the Bombay "social" film of the 1940s and 1950s', *Screen*, 36.4 (1995), pp. 305–324.

Vernicos, Nicolas, Sofia Daskalopoulou, Filimon Bantiramoudis, Nicos Boubaris and Dimitris Papageorgiou (eds), *Politistikes Viomihanies: Diadikasies, Ipirisies, Agatha* ('The Culture Industries: Processes, Services, Products', my translation) (Athens: Kritiki, 2004), pp. 173–200.

Vincent, Sally, 'Beyond words', (interview with Samira Makhmalbaf), *The Guardian* (3 April 2004).

Viswanath, K., and Kavita Karan, 'India', in Shelton. A. Gunaratne (ed.), *Handbook of the Media in Asia* (New Delhi and London: Sage, 2000), pp. 84–117.

Wagstaff, Chris, 'A forkful of westerns', in Richard Dyer and Ginette Vincendeau (eds), *Popular European Cinema*, (London: Routledge, 1992), pp. 245–61.

Wagstaff, Chris, 'Italian genre films in the world market', in Geoffrey Nowell-Smith and Steven Ricci (eds), *Hollywood & Europe: Economics, Culture, National Identity 1945–95* (London: BFI, 1998), pp. 74–85.

Willis, Sharon, 'Hardware and hardbodies: what do women want? A reading of *Thelma and Louise*', in Jim Collins, Hilary Radner and Ava Preacher Collins (eds), *Film Theory Goes to the Movies* (New York: Routledge, 1993), pp. 120–8.

Wolff, Janet, *Feminine Sentences* (Berkeley, CA, and London: University of California Press, 1990).

Wood, Jason, *The Faber Book of Mexican Cinema* (London: Faber & Faber, 2006).

Wright, Terence, 'Moving images: the media representations of refugees', *Visual Studies*, 17.1 (2002), pp. 53–66.

Žižek, Slavoj, 'The foreign gaze which sees too much', in Egoyan and Balfour (eds), *Subtitles*, pp. 285–306.

Index